A Call to Arms

A Call to Arms

Propaganda, Public Opinion, and Newspapers in the Great War

EDITED BY TROY R. E. PADDOCK

Perspectives on the Twentieth Century
Edward R. Beauchamp, Series Adviser

PRAEGER

Westport, Connecticut
London

Library of Congress Cataloging-in-Publication Data

A call to arms : propaganda, public opinion, and newspapers in the Great War / edited by Troy R. E. Paddock.

p. cm. (Perspectives on the twentieth century, ISSN 1538–9626)
Includes bibliographical references and index.
ISBN 0–275–97383–2 (alk. paper)
1. World War, 1914–1918—Propaganda. 2. World War, 1914–1918—Public opinion. 3. Press and propaganda. 4. War—Press coverage. I. Paddock, Troy R. E. II. Series.
D639.P6C35   2004
940.4′88—dc22   2004023026

British Library Cataloguing in Publication Data is available.

Library of Congress Catalog Card Number: 2004023026
ISBN: 0–275–97383–2
ISSN: 1538–9626

First published in 2004

Praeger Publishers, 88 Post Road West, Westport, CT 06881
An imprint of Greenwood Publishing Group, Inc.
www.praeger.com

Printed in the United States of America

The paper used in this book complies with the Permanent Paper Standard issued by the National Information Standards Organization (Z39.48–1984).

10 9 8 7 6 5 4 3 2

Contents

Acknowledgments

First of all, I would like to thank Adrian Gregory, Eric Lohr, Michael Nolan, and Andrea Orzoff for their participation in this project. Series editor Edward Beauchamp and Heather Staines, the editor at Greenwood Press, have been supportive and patient throughout this extended process and have my deepest appreciation. I would also like to thank the staff at the Institut für Zeitungsforschung in Dortmund, Germany, for their assistance, and the Council on European Studies at Yale University for providing access to the Sterling Memorial Library. My colleagues at Southern Connecticut State University—Stephen Amerman, Polly Beals, David Bello, Nikos Chrissidis, Steven Judd, Bruce Kalk, and Michele Thompson—offered constructive criticism at various stages of the project and have my thanks. I would also like to thank Southern Connecticut State University for providing funding for summer research and Dean Donna-Jean Fredeen for granting me release time to work on this project. Most important of all, I want to thank my wife, Mary, for her support, encouragement, and help in transforming my German translations into readable English, and my son, Mack, for not caring about any of this and reminding me that there are some things more important than a missed deadline.

Series Foreword

Whoever first coined the phrase, "When the siècle hit the fin," described the twentieth century perfectly! The past century was arguably a century of intellectual, physical, and emotional violence unparalleled in world history. As Haynes Johnson of the *Washington Post* has pointed out in his *The Best of Times* (2001), "since the first century, 149 million people have died in major wars; 111 million of those deaths occurred in the twentieth century. War deaths per population soared from 3.2 deaths per 1,000 in the sixteenth century to 44.4 per 1,000 in the twentieth.[1] Giving parameters to the twentieth century, however, is no easy task. Did it begin in 1900 or 1901? Was it, as in historian Eric Hobsbawm's words, a "short twentieth century," that did not begin until 1917 and end in 1991?[2] Or was it more accurately the "long twentieth century," as Giovanni Arrighi argued in *The Long Twentieth Century: Money, Power, and the Origins of Our Times?*[3] Strong cases can be made for all of these constructs and it is each reader's prerogative to come to his or her own conclusion.

Whatever the conclusion, however, there is a short list of people, events, and intellectual currents found in the period between the nineteenth and twenty-first centuries that is, indeed, impressive in scope. There is little doubt that the hopes represented by the Paris Exhibition of 1900 represented the mood of the time—a time of optimism, even utopian expectations, in much of the so-called civilized world (which was the only world that counted in those days). Many saw the fruits of the Industrial Revolution, the application of science and technology to everyday life, as having the potential to greatly enhance life, at least in the West.

In addition to the theme of progress, the power of nationalism in conflicts—not only over territory, but also economic advantage and intellectual dominance—came to characterize the last century. It was truly a century of war, from the "little" wars of the Balkans and colonial conflicts of the early 1900s to the "Great" War of 1914–1918 that resulted in unprecedented conflict over the remainder of the century.

Every century has its "great" as well as "infamous" individuals, most often men, although that too would begin to change as the century drew to a close. Great political figures such as Lenin, Trotsky, Stalin, Hitler, Mussolini, Churchill, the two Roosevelts, de Gaulle, Adenauer, Mahatma Gandhi, Mao Tse-tung, Ho Chi Minh, and others were joined in the last part of the century by tough competent women like Golda Meir, Indira Gandhi, Margaret Thatcher, and scores of others who took the reigns of power for the first time.

A quick listing of some major events of the century includes World War I, the Russian Revolution, the Rise of Fascism, the Great Depression of the 1930s, the abdication of Edward VIII, Pearl Harbor and World War II, the unleashing of atomic bombs on Hiroshima and Nagasaki, the long Indochina War, the Cold War, the rise of nationalism (with an increase in nation states from about fifty to almost two hundred), the establishment of Israel, the triumph of the free market, an increasingly strident battle between religious fanaticism and secular preferences, and on and on. At the same time that these events occurred, there was a great creative flourishing of mass entertainment (especially television and the Internet), not to mention important literary, dramatic, cinematic, and musical contributions of all kinds.

These elements incorporate some of the subject matter of this new series focusing on "Perspectives on the Twentieth Century," which strives to illuminate the last century. The editor actively seeks out manuscripts that deal with virtually any subject and with any part of our planet, bringing a better understanding of the twentieth century to readers. He is especially interested in subjects on "small" as well as "large" events and trends, including the role of sports in various societies, the impact of popular music on the social fabric, the contribution of film studies to our understanding of the twentieth century, and so on. The success of this series is largely dependent on the creativity and imagination of its authors.

Edward R. Beauchamp

NOTES

1. Haynes Johnson, *The Best of Times: The Boom and Bust Years of America Before and After Everything Changed* (New York: A James H. Silberman Book, Harcourt, Inc., 2001), p. 3.

2. Eric Hobsbawm, *The Age of Extremes: A History of the World, 1917–1991* (New York: Pantheon, 1994).

3. Giovanni Arrighi, *The Long Twentieth Century: Money, Power, and the Origins of Our Times* (London: Verso, 1994).

Introduction: Newspapers, Public Opinion, and Propaganda

And in England they understood one more thing: that this spiritual weapon can succeed only if it is applied on a tremendous scale, but that success amply covers all costs. There, propaganda was regarded as a weapon of the first order, while in our country it was the last resort of unemployed politicians and a comfortable haven for slackers.

Adolf Hitler, Mein Kampf

The bourgeois' hat flies off his pointy head,
The air shrieks with a thousand screams.
Shinglers plunge off roofs and break in two
And the tide is rising all along the coasts (we read).
The storm is here, a wild ocean has jumped
On land, the swollen dams have burst.
Most everyone has a cold.
Locomotives drop everywhere off bridges.

Jakob van Hoddis, "Weltende"

During his time in prison, Adolf Hitler joined the crowd of people commenting on the importance of propaganda during the First World War. He, along with others, maintained that Germany's failure to mold public opinion both at home and abroad played a key role in its demise.[1] Almost as soon as the war was over, retired diplomats, government leaders, and military officials offered observations about the events leading up to the war and the conduct of the various belligerent nations during the opening days and weeks of the war.[2] Perhaps as a result of the First World War, a conflict that truly involved every facet of society, the 1920s saw the birth of "public opinion" as a source of scholarly research.[3] It should not come as a surprise that the Great War was an early object of study in this new field. From the beginning, a number of these studies focused on the importance of propaganda in influencing public opinion.[4] The focus quickly turned to the number of falsehoods that were, knowingly and unknowingly, passed on as facts. The most prominent of these, which as a result garnered the lion's share of the early attention, were the so-called atrocity stories in which every side partook, and which were often later exposed as false.[5] The exposé of these "wartime lies" had a twofold effect. Within Germany, many embraced the evidence of the Allied fabrications as proof of Allied perfidy; it also proved, at least in the minds of some, that undercutting German morale was the main reason for Germany's failure, rather than defeat on the battlefield.[6] More unfortunately, the sometimes reckless exaggerations of the First World War contributed to public skepticism about atrocities committed during the Second World War, when Hitler's Reich was able to surpass in reality the most vivid of imaginations of Great War propagandists.[7] In his pioneering 1927 study on propaganda technique, Harold Lasswell wrote,

These people probe the mysteries of propaganda with that compound of admiration and chagrin with which the victims of a new gambling trick demand to have the thing explained.... Some of those who trusted so much and hated so passionately have put their hands to the killing of a man, they have mutilated others and perhaps been mutilated in return, they have encouraged others to draw the sword, and they have derided and besmirched those who refused to rage as they did. Fooled by propaganda? If so, they writhe in the knowledge that they were blind pawns in plans which they did not incubate, and which they neither devised nor comprehended nor approved.[8]

From relatively early on, the importance of public opinion was recognized as an area that merited the historian's attention. However, a problem immediately confronts the historian. In 1931, E. Malcolm Carroll, the first historian to address the role of public opinion and foreign affairs as it related to World War I, put the problem in the following terms:

Public opinion is one of those vague terms which elude precise definition. In its common usage, it refers to the composite reactions of the general public; but as a rule, the only tangible evidence of these tendencies is to be found in the opinions of the more influential leaders. It is therefore often impossible in practice to draw a clear distinction between the leaders and the rank and file; it will be the task here to discover those leaders who were most effective in shaping and expressing the opinions, prejudices and aspirations of the general public.[9]

The more than 80 years that separate us from the Great War have not diminished the problem to any degree. Time has, however, helped us realize that the problem is even more complicated than Carroll indicated. For there is no guarantee that influential leaders, whether they are politicians or press magnates, are reflecting or shaping the opinions of the masses, in spite of repeated claims of being "one of the people" or having their finger on the proverbial pulse of the nation. Put more succinctly, there is a difference between "published opinion" and "public opinion."[10] This problem is magnified in less democratic societies such as imperial Germany, where *lèse majesté* (insulting the kaiser) was a criminal offense that could put even public figures such as the playwright and occasional cabaret performer Frank Wedekind in jail. The problem becomes even more acute during wartime when government censors, civilian or military, try to control the flow of information about the war.

In spite of these considerations, the views regarding the masses and public opinion during the Great War have changed remarkably little since the first decade after the war. The general picture can be described as follows: On all sides there was an initial burst of enthusiasm that has been called the "Spirit of 1914." Class and political divisions were overcome as citizens became brothers in arms in an effort to defend their nation and its ideals. What happened to this "Spirit" often depended on how the nation fared during the course of the war.[11]

This conventional wisdom extended to the role of propaganda in World War I to the point that propaganda and public opinion have become virtually inseparable. Moreover, the consequences of war propaganda have affected how both propaganda and public opinion are viewed. The English were the masters of propaganda who almost single-handedly undermined German morale. The success of English propaganda was one of the few things that both belligerent sides could agree on, of course for vastly different reasons. It served the English press well to note its achievements and its cooperation with the government in launching successful propaganda campaigns. That was their contribution to the war effort.

Conversely, Germans could concentrate on English successes in order to ignore their own failures and elevate themselves to a certain extent. Germans could point to the fact that they were not as good at propaganda (dirty tricks) as the English, and that this had contributed to their defeat. So, ironically, the Germans were defeated militarily, but maintained the moral superiority by generating less effective propaganda. Rather than demonize their enemy, Germans tried to explain the justness of their own cause. This type of reasoning is not only false on a factual level—Russia was demonized from early on in the war—but also reflects what can fairly be described as a German response to the question of defeat by tying the material and spiritual worlds together in an effort to explain Germany's demise.[12] In a recent challenge to this view, David Welch has shown that German claims to weakness on the propaganda front were little more than propaganda itself. In fact, Welch claims that Germany's domestic propaganda was better than Britain's.[13]

The question of Russian propaganda and public opinion has been influenced, understandably, by the subsequent Bolshevik revolution. As a result, the questions surrounding Russian public opinion and 1914 have been overshadowed by, and often discussed in terms of, the events of February and October 1917. Josh Sanborn has aptly summarized the standard view of Russian public opinion. Russia began the war with a burst of patriotic enthusiasm "that masked fatal flaws of class division in the cities and rural ignorance in the countryside."[14] Sanborn observes that virtually every account of the war in Russia has focused on urban enthusiasm and rural capitulation to explain the initial support for the war. Implicit in this view is an urban bias that assumes that the Russian peasants were provincial and thus incapable of understanding the events surrounding the war.[15] In no small part due to considerations surrounding the Bolshevik revolution, Sanborn has shown that the received historiographical tradition on Russian public opinion and mobilization is problematic at best and in desperate need of reassessment.

Historical works that address public opinion and propaganda in France and the Austro-Hungarian Empire are also surprisingly thin. French propaganda and public opinion has not been ignored, but the focus has been on the role of intellectuals and their contributions to the war effort with both pen and sword.[16] Even accounts of German atrocities and their influence on French public opinion are largely confined to French intellectuals.[17] As Mark Cornwall has noted, Austria-Hungary has been more often viewed as a victim of propaganda rather than a producer of such. As a result, one of the most effective propaganda fronts has been largely ignored in the West.[18] Cornwall's work is the first work in English to discuss propaganda in the Habsburg Empire. On the whole, the discussion of propaganda in World War I focuses on Britain's success and Germany's failure.

In addition to looking at the role of propaganda in nations where it was minimized if not ignored before, the role of propaganda in the Great War must be reassessed even further. A distinction must be made between propaganda produced and disseminated by the government and that which comes from newspapers, which are a private enterprise. Although certain individual newspapers did have a clear and close working relationship with their respective governments and would print or reiterate the "official" versions of information, not all newspapers had such relationships. Consequently, newspapers are an important source to examine in order to understand how the war was presented to the general population.

Newspapers provide a unique venue for exploring the boundaries between *public opinion* and *published opinion*. The three decades before the

First World War mark the peak of their influence. One scholar of newspapers claims that between 1880 and 1918, "the British press [was] at the height of its power and prestige."[19] The media historian Kurt Koszyk makes a similar claim about the centrality of the press in imperial Germany.[20] Newspapers truly were, as one scholar has noted, "the unrecognized cultural power."[21] The rise in influence (and numbers) of newspapers coincides with the achievement of near universal literacy in the advanced nations in Europe.[22] Certainly in urban areas virtually the entire population had access to, could read, and did read newspapers. Even in more remote rural areas, by the start of the war, a majority of the residents under the age of 40 would have achieved a basic level of literacy, meaning that they could read and comprehend the local newspaper. The rare household that had no one who possessed such skills would almost certainly know someone who did. For the overwhelming majority of citizens, newspapers were the major (and for many, the only) source of information about events that were beyond their everyday lives or direct realm of experience.

From the government's perspective, the rise of newspapers also reflected the mixed blessing that accompanied the rise of literacy. Newspapers could be viewed as a means of social control.[23] But the press was not as easy to control as governments had imagined. Even the strict procedures for licensing, supervising, and censoring newspapers established in late *ancien régime* France proved to be too liberal for Napoleon, who abolished the old system and introduced a new, stricter procedure.[24] Similarly, the Alien and Sedition Acts of 1798 were an attempt on the part of a still fledgling American government to rein in a contentious press. The problems facing revolutionary France and the newly independent United States paled by comparison in scale to the potential problems facing governments on the eve of the First World War. A more literate and better-educated public could become better citizens; however, they could just as easily challenge the traditional order. Similarly, newspapers could frame issues in a manner that favored the government or challenged the government's position. They could even bring attention to issues that the government would prefer to leave out of the public spotlight.

Thus an extension of Jürgen Habermas's notion of the public sphere is needed. Habermas defined the public sphere as a place where private individuals could challenge public (meaning state) actions.[25] This definition is useful, but must be extended beyond the coffeehouses and salons that dominated Habermas's discussion of the late eighteenth and early nineteenth centuries. The increase in literacy and access to information opened the discussion of political actions to groups excluded from Habermas's original public sphere.[26]

During the last part of the nineteenth century and the early part of the twentieth century, newspapers were an indispensable tool for both governments and their citizens because newspapers could disseminate information more quickly, cheaply, and efficiently than the government could. More importantly, for the vast majority of people, in an age before radio, television, and the Internet, newspapers were *the only means* of acquiring information in a timely fashion about international events or affairs of state beyond the citizen's immediate surroundings. As Jakob van Hoddis parenthetically observes, in the poem that opens this chapter, we know because we read.[27]

But what exactly do people know? Peter Fritzsche, in his imaginative work *Reading Berlin 1900*, suggests that what the reader knows is the chaotic world of the headline, which has the effect of turning "event into spectacle."[28] The result of the rapid transmission of news leads to an emphasis on the immediate. Drawing from Jürgen Wilke's work, Fritzsche notes that in 1856 only 11 percent of the articles in newspapers dealt with local news. By 1906, the percentage of local news articles had increased to 95.[29] The information overload from Fritzsche's "Word City," his phrase for the image of Berlin constructed by its myriad of newspapers, had the effect of constantly pushing out the old in favor of the new. Certainly the fact that many papers offered three different daily editions (excluding extra editions) lends weight to this view. However, such a position ignores the fact that amid this (apparently continual) chaotic flux, there were some constants. The journalists and editors, as well as editorial policy, remained consistent. The fact that a story disappeared from the pages does not mean that it was forgotten. Moreover, there were also larger news-cycle patterns that extended beyond 24 hours and occurred regularly—for example, elections or debates about various domestic issues or foreign policies such as protective tariffs, workers' movements, or foreign alliances. When these events were written about in newspapers, neither the journalist nor the reader was a tabula rasa. Both drew from previous knowledge and experience, as well as from their own personal and political values. Thus it is fair to assert that newspapers do not entirely "erase everything else."[30]

The connection between the immediate and "everything else" is apparent in how newspapers discussed World War I. Newspapers addressed the immediate (e.g., the assassination of Archduke Franz Ferdinand, Russian mobilization, or the invasion of Belgium), but they drew upon views and values that had to have been imparted before these events occurred. Whether the views and values were part of a particular editorial policy of a given paper or fundamental to national policy (e.g., Great Britain's policy of ensuring a balance of power on the European continent, or the American notion of Manifest Destiny), they were not simply the product of the immediate news cycle. Rather, they helped inform how the imparted information would be received.

The importance of newspapers in the early twentieth century presents two questions: what constitutes propaganda, and how is it effective? Concerning the latter issue, it can be fairly stated that the masses have often been regarded as a passive entity. Propaganda moves them in all directions as if they have no mind or will of their own. This tendency is most clear in the literature regarding Germany. Even if one wishes to discount the discussion of propaganda in the interwar period as too politically motivated to be reliable—not an entirely unreasonable position in the German case—the post–World War II work has not abandoned this premise. In his analysis of the causes of World War I, the German historian Fritz Fischer treats public opinion as entirely malleable in the hands of the imperial government. He mentions that a press war between Germany and Russia was part of the government's plan to prepare the German public for war.[31] This position is problematic for two reasons. First, he offers no evidence that the press wars, which were real, were initiated on behalf of the government.[32] Fischer's view is still cited approvingly.[33]

The lack of evidence aside, there is a second problem: the case of the press war with Russia begs two important issues. First it assumes that propaganda is effective without offering evidence. Second, it ignores the content of propaganda by assuming that because public officials say, "Jump!" the people respond with "How high?" If propaganda is going to be effective, it needs to speak in a fashion that its audience can understand.

The question of propaganda's effectiveness leads back to the first issue: what constitutes propaganda? In his work on propaganda on the front lines, Mark Cornwall defines propaganda as "'spreading of subversive, debatable or merely novel attitudes,' with the objective of persuasion. It can be transmitted through official or unofficial bodies, the work of state organizations or of private individuals."[34] Philip M. Taylor, perhaps the most prolific English-language author on propaganda, offers a distinction between propaganda and publicity. Taylor notes that before World War I, "propaganda meant simply the means which an adherent of a political or religious doctrine employed to convince the unconverted."[35] But since the war, the term *propaganda* had taken on at least a negative, if not outright sinister, connotation. Taylor writes, "The word 'propaganda' itself implies a calculated intent on the part of one person or group of people to persuade others to think or behave in a certain way."[36] Borrowing from J. A. C. Brown, he suggests that education teaches people how to think and propaganda teaches them what to think.[37]

Taylor ultimately comes to the following definitions of publicity and propaganda. Publicity is

the supply or release of information of a factual nature which is designed to provide the public in general with an opportunity for each individual member to formulate opinions for himself and to act according to his own conscience. It is a service, designed to keep the public informed of events which may benefit an individual or section of the audience to which it is directed, but without compulsion.

Propaganda can be defined as an attempt to influence the attitudes of a specific audience, through the use of facts, fictions, argument or suggestion—often supported by the suppression of inconsistent material—with the calculated purpose of instilling in the recipient certain beliefs, values or convictions which will serve the interest of the author, usually by producing a desired line of action.[38]

This passage is worth quoting at length because it immediately illustrates the problem that confronts readers and, later, historians. In wartime, the distinction between publicity and propaganda becomes much harder to find. In all the warring nations, the military controlled the release of information about the war. The government's, especially the military's, attitude toward the press was somewhere between wary and hostile. The military expected the press's full cooperation in the reporting of the war. The press was, quite naturally, skeptical of this arrangement, but also powerless to challenge it.

Dissent was virtually impossible to find in the press once the war began. In 1914, once the fighting began, even the socialist press in the belligerent nations supported the war. Any veering from what the government found to be acceptable conduct resulted in the confiscation of the offending edition, as *Vorwärts*, the official newspaper of the Social Democratic Party of Germany(SPD), would discover. With the control of military information going through military channels, and military officials determining what was permissible to print, the line between publicity and propaganda becomes hard to define. Military officials would understandably withhold "facts" that could aid the enemy or lower morale. However, if only half of the available facts are released to the public, is it publicity or propaganda? Moreover, how the facts are introduced also presents a number of problems. Is the shifting of lines at the front the result of a "retreat," or were troops "regrouping"? What constitutes "minor losses" or "significant casualties"? Without clear and consistent definitions, which the military is unlikely to maintain, information printed in newspapers is not just publicity. But is it right to dub it propaganda?

Pursuing this line of thought even further, one could credibly ask if there is ever a clear distinction between publicity and propaganda. For even in times of peace, newspapers do not print all facts relevant to a story, nor do they print every relevant story. Editorial decisions leave many facts and some entire stories completely out of the picture. As a result, one can state, without too much exaggeration, that inasmuch as newspapers shape stories for their audience with the intent of presenting a certain view, that even publicity is a form, albeit somewhat milder, of propaganda. Britain's strategy to influence opinion in the United States during World War I is a clear illustration of this issue. As Philip Taylor notes, almost as soon as the war began, the British ship *Telconia* cut the transatlantic cables connecting Germany and the United States. Great Britain now effectively controlled the flow of information from Europe to North America. Thus, British officials selected and censored what news would be sent over to the United States. Even if all of the information was "factual" (a debatable assumption in light of atrocity stories circulated by the British), it was seldom complete and always put the British position in the best possible light. What American newspaper editors decided to do with the material was entirely their decision; however, by controlling the flow of news, the decision effectively became one of how to present Britain's view of events to the American public.[39]

Control of the flow of news makes the problem of how to use newspapers to derive public opinion all the more difficult, but not insurmountable. Newspapers are a moneymaking enterprise. If a newspaper does not make money, it does not last very long. In order to make money, a newspaper must maintain its readership. Even if a significant portion of its revenues comes from advertisements, a newspaper that cannot maintain a certain level of subscription will eventually fold. Businesses do not advertise in venues that no one sees. Therefore, newspapers run stories that will appeal to their constituencies and present news in a manner that they can understand. This means not only using language that the reader can understand, but also arguing from a perspective toward which the reader will also be sympathetic. For example, a German Catholic newspaper is not going to argue from a socialist standpoint about confessional schools and public education, nor is a Polish-language newspaper likely to be sympathetic to the policies of Russification in the western provinces of imperial Russia. Similarly, Czech, German, and Hungarian newspapers will have different assumptions and opinions about Magyarization attempts within the Hungarian part of the Austro-Hungarian empire.

With this in mind, one of the interesting—and to this point largely unexamined—issues is how various newspapers sought to present the information that they had and were permitted to print. An examination of the political press in the various belligerent nations could provide insight into how the war gained and maintained at least a certain level of popular support. It is possible to get some insight into the ever-elusive public opinion by examining how various newspapers presented their views of the war to their constituencies. By taking into consideration political, confessional, regional, and ethnic differences, this collection hopes to help address the concerns about oversimplifying the view of the masses that Josh Sanborn has discussed.

The following chapters will examine the depiction of the opening phase of the war in the five major belligerents when the war began: Great Britain, France, Germany, Austria-Hungary, and Russia. The phrase *opening phase* is intentionally vague. Each contributor has been asked to determine the length and nature of the opening phase. The idea behind this approach is that the press in each of the belligerent nations took some time to determine and define the nature of the war and how to report it. The amount of time was not necessarily uniform. Immediate government censorship made the negative aspect of reporting the war clear. No information of military significance could be found in the papers. The positive aspect of how to present the war and what was permissible to print was not immediate. It took time for the governments to work out relationships with the press, and even that did not guarantee uniform results. Therefore, the opening phase of the war becomes more interesting and crucial for a close examination of how newspapers framed the issues surrounding the war and the war itself. It provides the reader with a clearer idea of how the war was thought and talked about before governments could organize their own propaganda campaigns.

In an effort to provide a comparative basis, each author was asked to define the nature of censorship, the cause of the war according to their respective newspapers, and how the enemy was presented or defined. There have been other discussions of the press and World War I, but they have tended to be more descriptive than analytical, or have focused on the relationship between publishers and politicians. The following hopes to add to the current state of knowledge by showing how regional, political, confessional, and ethnic differences were overcome (if they were) during the opening phase of the Great War. The authors have also included translations of articles that they deemed important or representative in some fashion. This will allow students to read actual articles and get a firsthand look at various perspectives on the war. More importantly, the articles will help reveal just how important newspapers were in reporting the conflict. The vast majority of people were not on the front lines, nor were they privy to the discussions that led the various nations to take up arms. Newspapers played a key role in explaining to the people why they were at war and what was at stake.

Perhaps more than anything else, this simple fact reminds us why an independent press, and now an independent electronic media as well, is essential for any society that wishes to govern itself in a responsible manner. This collection is also a reminder that even in societies where freedom of the press is assured, government control over information can lead to the selective editing, omission, or exaggeration of information to downplay or hype potential threats to a nation. The press, which at its best serves as a watchdog on the government, can also unwittingly promote an agenda that would not have public support if all of the relevant information were presented.

NOTES

1. See chapter 6, "War and Propaganda," of Hitler's, *Mein Kampf*, trans. Ralph Manheim (New York: Houghton Mifflin, 1999).

2. For just a small sampling of the memoirs, see Sir George Buchanan, *My Mission to Russia and Other Diplomatic Memories* (New York: Cassell, 1923); Sir Alfred Knox, *With the Russian Army, 1914–1917* (New York: Dutton, 1921); Maurice Paléologue, *An Ambassador's Memoirs*, vol. 1 (New York: George H. Doran, n.d.); Raymond Poincaré, *The Memoirs of Raymond Poincaré*, trans. Sir George Arthur (London: W. Heinemann, 1926), and *The Origins of the War* (New York: Cassell, 1922); H.H. Asquith, *The Genesis of the Great War* (New York: George H. Doran, 1923); Frederick Bausman, *Let France Explain* (London: G. Allen & Unwin, 1923); Prince Karl Max von Lichnowsky, *My Mission to London, 1912–1914* (New York: George H. Doran, 1918); and General Erich von Ludendorff, *My War Memoirs 1914–1918*, 2 vols. (London: Hutchinson, 1919).

3. Walter Lippmann, *Public Opinion* (New York: Harcourt, 1922).

4. Some of the early important works include Kurt Baschwitz, *Der Massenwahn* (München: C. H. Beck, 1923); Edgar Stern-Rubarth, *Die Propaganda als politisches Instrument* (Berlin: Trowitzsch, 1921); Georges Démartial, *Le geurre de 1914: Comment on mobilisa les consciences* (Paris: Éditions des cahiers internationaux, 1922); Ferdinand Tönnies, *Kritik der öffentlichen Meinung* (Berlin: J. Springer, 1922); and Harold Lasswell, *Propaganda Technique in the World War* (1927; reprint, New York: Garland Press, 1972).

5. See Arthur Ponsonby, *Falsehood in War-Time: Containing an Assortment of Lies Circulated throughout the Nations during the Great War* (1928; reprint, New York, Garland Press, 1971).

6. Lasswell, *Propaganda Technique*, 3. Two of the most prominent German proponents of the domestic *Dolchstoss* (stab-in-the-back) legend were Hitler and General Erich von Ludendorff. See Hitler's *Mein Kampf* (especially chapters 6–8) and Ludendorff's *My War Memoirs 1914–1918* (especially vol. 1, 361–83). See also Walter Nicolai, *Nachrichtendienst, Presse und Volksstimmung im Weltkrieg* (Berlin: E.S. Mittler und [S]ohn, 1920). Nicolai condemned the *Berliner Tageblatt* and *Frankfurter Zeitung*, which he called "ausgesprochen jüdische Blätter," for helping to undermine morale with their liberal and democratic tendencies (see 71, 172).

7. For a contemporary example of skepticism that can be tied to the consequences of World War I propaganda, see Charles Clayton Morrison, "Horror Stories from Poland," *Christian Century*, 9 December 1922, 1518–19. Part of Morrison's piece is reprinted in *America Views the Holocaust 1933–1945: A Brief Documentary History*, ed. Robert H. Abzug (Boston: Bedford/St. Martin's, 1999), 136–37. For an example of the effect of World War I propaganda in World War II, see Walter Laqueur, *The Terrible Secret: Suppression of the Truth about Hitler's Final Solution* (Boston: Little, Brown, 1981). See also Philip Taylor, *Munitions of the Mind: A History of Propaganda from the Ancient World to the Present Era* (New York: St. Martin's, 1995), 197.

8. Lasswell, *Propaganda Technique*, 2–3.

9. E. Malcolm Carroll, *French Public Opinion and Foreign Affairs 1870–1914* (1931; reprint, Hamden, Conn.: Archon Books, 1964), 4–5.

10. In 1937, *Public Opinion Quarterly* was founded. It is worth noting that propaganda in World War I has received scant attention in this journal. This can, perhaps, be attributed to when it was founded, a time when Nazi Germany, Fascist Italy, and the Soviet Union provided more immediate concerns as well as interesting objects of study.

11. Jeffrey Verhey argues that the "Spirit of 1914" is, at least in the German context, more myth than reality. See Jeffrey T. Verhey, *The Spirit of 1914: Militarism, Myth, and Mobilization in Germany* (New York: Cambridge University Press, 2000).

12. For an example of this approach, see Ludwig Dehio, "Thoughts on Germany's Mission, 1900–1918," in *Germany and World Politics in the Twentieth Century*, trans. Dieter Pevsner (New York: W. W. Norton, 1959), 72–108. The essay was originally published in *Historische Zeitschrift* 174:2 (1952), 479–502.

13. David Welch, *Germany, Propaganda, and Total War, 1914–1918* (New Brunswick, N.J.: Rutgers University Press, 2000), 24.

14. Josh Sanborn, "The Mobilization of 1914 and the Question of the Nation: A Re-examination," *Slavic Review* 59:2 (summer 2000): 268.

15. Ibid.

16. See Martha Hanna, *The Mobilization of Intellect: French Scholars and Writers during the Great War* (Cambridge: Harvard University Press, 1996); Roland Stromberg, *Redemption by War: The Intellectuals and 1914* (Lawrence, Kans.: Regents Press of Kansas, 1982); and Carroll, *French Public Opinion*. For brief discussions of the French press during World War I, see Raymond Manevy, *Histoire de la Presse 1914 á 1939* (Paris: Éditions Corrée & cie, 1945), 28–72.

17. John Horne and Alex Kramer, "German 'Atrocities' and Franco-German Opinion, 1914: The Evidence of German Soldiers' Diaries," *Journal of Modern History* 66:1 (March 1994), 1–33.

18. Mark Cornwall, *The Undermining of Austria-Hungary: The Battle for Hearts and Minds* (London: Macmillan, 2000).

19. George Boyce, "The Fourth Estate: The Reappraisal of a Concept," in *Newspaper History from the Seventeenth Century to the Present Day*, ed. George Boyce, James Curran, and Pauline Wingate (Beverly Hills, Calif.: Sage Publications, 1978), 27.

20. Kurt Koszyk, *Deutsche Presse im 19. Jahrhundert. Geschichte der deutschen Presse Teil II* (Berlin: Colloquim Verlag, 1966), 264.

21. Otto Groth, *Die unerkannte Kulturmacht. Grundlegung der Zeitungswissenschaft*, 7 vols. (Berlin: Walter de Gruyter, 1960–72).

22. See David Vincent, *The Rise of Mass Literacy: Reading and Writing in Modern Europe* (Malden, Mass.: Polity Press, 2000).

23. See James Curran, "The Press as an Agency of Social Control: An Historical Perspective," in Boyce, Curran, and Wingate, *Newspaper History*, 51–75.

24. John B. Thompson, *The Media and Modernity: A Social Theory of the Media* (Stanford, Calif.: Stanford University Press, 1995), 68–69.

25. Jürgen Habermas, *The Structural Transformation of the Public Sphere: An Inquiry into a Category of Bourgeois Society*, trans. Thomas Burger (Cambridge: MIT Press, 1989), 27; published in German as *Strukturwandel der Öffentlichkeit* (Darmstadt: Hermann Luchterhand Verlag, 1962).

26. For a fair critique of Habermas's concept of the public sphere, see Thompson, *Media and Modernity*, 69–75; and Craig Calhoun, ed., *Habermas and the Public Sphere* (Cambridge: MIT Press, 1999).

27. Although we have different views about the meaning and impact of van Hoddis's words, I am indebted to Peter Fritzsche for bringing this poem to my attention, as well as for this observation.

28. Peter Fritzsche, *Reading Berlin 1900* (Cambridge: Harvard University Press, 1996), 177.

29. Fritzsche, *Reading Berlin 1900*, 181. See also Jürgen Wilke, *Nachrichtenauswahl und Medianrealität in vier Jahrhunderten* (Berlin: W. de Gruyter, 1984).

30. Fritzsche, *Reading Berlin 1900*, 181.

31. Fritz Fischer, *War of Illusions: German Politics from 1911 to 1914*, trans. Marion Jackson (London: Chatto & Windus, 1975); published in German as *Krieg der Illusion* (Düsseldorf: Droste, 1969).

32. In fact, the most famous of these wars, the *Kölnische Zeitung* Affair, resulted in the severing of ties between the government and the Rhenish daily, which up to that point had been considered the mouthpiece for the government on foreign affairs.

33. Welch, *Germany*, 12. See also Martin Gilbert, *The First World War: A Complete History* (New York: Henry Holt, 1994), 8–9. Gilbert notes that his colleague Immanuel Geiss (a student of Fischer's) has published a document collection including a note from Admiral Müller which includes the discussion from December 1912 of the need to use newspapers to prepare German public opinion for a war with Russia. Müller's note does not, contrary to Fischer's, Geiss's, and Gilbert's opinion, constitute proof that the government organized a press war against Russia. At most, it shows that the government was interested in swaying public opinion in a certain direction. There is no evidence of a government-inspired press war against Russia as a result of this meeting, and there is no evidence within opposition newspapers in imperial Germany that the government was organizing such a campaign.

34. Cornwall, *Undermining of Austria-Hungary*, 2.

35. Philip M. Taylor, *The Projection of Britain: British Overseas Publicity and Propaganda 1919–1939* (Cambridge: Cambridge University Press, 1981), 2.

36. Taylor, *Projection of Britain*, 1.

37. Taylor, *Projection of Britain*, 2. Taylor is quoting J. A. C. Brown, *Techniques of Persuasion: From Propaganda to Brainwashing* (Baltimore: Penguin Books, 1975).

38. Taylor, *Projection of Britain*, 4–5.

39. Taylor, *Munitions of the Mind*, 177–78. This chapter on propaganda in World War I is essentially a chapter on British propaganda. The few comments about German propaganda have been superseded by Welch's work. See Taylor, *Munitions of the Mind*, 176–97.

Chapter 1

A Clash of Cultures: The British Press and the Opening of the Great War

Adrian Gregory

INTRODUCTION: THE PREWAR SCENE

In 1914 Great Britain had become a near universally functionally literate society.[1] A survey of European per-capita postal flows places Britain clearly at the top of the table, significantly ahead of other European nations and second only to the United States. The potential readership for a mass-market national press was enormous. Yet in practice, there remained significant constraints, partly economic and partly cultural. Robert Roberts, describing the reading habits in the "classic slum," shows that the working masses had neither the time, inclination, nor disposable income to become avid newspaper readers on a regular basis. Working-class readers were, in his opinion, generally uninterested in national events, "horse racing excepted."[2] Their principal periodical reading matter was the cheap Sunday newspapers; the weekly; or, less often, the daily evening editions of the local press and midweek racing sheets. Clippings collections such as *Tit Bits* and *Answers* were also longstanding favorites.

In the down-market world of mass readership, there was one publication that stood out. To describe *John Bull* as a newspaper would be to stretch the term, but this weekly periodical had found a distinct niche by 1914 as a robust populist voice, in a tradition that looked back to the mid-nineteenth-century radical weekly periodicals such as *Reynolds Weekly* and the *News of the World* and forward to the modern tabloid press. Its staples were sport and scandal combined with demagoguery. It described itself as the voice of the man in the street, although a more accurate description would be that it was the voice of the man in the public bar. *John Bull* was xenophobic, rabble-rousing, militantly antireligious, and skeptical about state interference with the "little man." It tended to sympathize with the condition of the working man, while at the same time being opposed to organized labor. The general view of politicians and the political establishment was hostile. It was very much the personal creation of its proprietor, Horatio Bottomley: failed businessman; disgraced politician; and, bluntly, one of the greatest con artists in modern British history. The precise circulation figures for *John Bull* are hard to establish, not least due to Bottomley's spectacularly cavalier approach to bookkeeping. It claimed a weekly circulation of 900,000, which would imply a readership in excess of a million.[3]

The regular readers of the national daily press began with the black-coated workers, the lower middle classes, and the true titan of the daily press in 1914 was the *Daily Mail*. The very identity of the "clerk," culturally and politically, had in important respects been formed by this newspaper, founded in 1896 by the greatest of all British press entrepreneurs, Alfred Harmsworth.[4] The initial advertising slogans of the *Daily Mail* are indicative of its readership: as "the busy man's newspaper" and "a penny paper for a halfpenny," it was designed to give value for money and to provide a reasonable grounding in national affairs in the course of a short train journey. Lord Salisbury's cruel quip that the newspaper was written by clerks for clerks was intended to be offensive, but was not far from the mark. Harmsworth once stated that his target readership was those who were earning 1,000 pounds per year, but he was well aware that his readership were generally considerably less prosperous, and quickly modified that description to those who expected to earn this amount. This aspirational aspect was key to understanding the newspaper's success. Equally important was Harmsworth's sensitivity to the importance of a female readership. He insisted that every copy of the newspaper would have material appealing to women. While newspaper purchasers would generally be men, he shrewdly recognized that women could influence the choice of newspaper. The radicalism of the *Daily Mail* could be found in the simplicity of the prose (foreign words were banned when possible) and the price, which made it accessible to many who would not have previously considered purchasing a daily newspaper. At the same time, it was in certain respects a rather conservative format; the *Daily Mail* in 1914 retained the old style of advertisements on the front page, eschewing banner headlines, and it was not heavily illustrated, although the back page was devoted to photographs. Despite the widespread perception of the newspaper as sensationalist, a reputation assiduously spread by its many critics, particularly on the political left, the tone of the *Daily Mail* was generally highly respectable, and Harmsworth was in certain respects quite prudish. In this, as in many other respects, it both shaped and reflected its readership. It was the politics of the *Daily Mail* that really stuck in the throat of the critics. From the outset, the newspaper had been an unabashed supporter of the Conservative and Unionist line, outspokenly supportive of the Boer War and other imperial adventures, supportive of tariff reform, unambiguously supportive of the union with Ireland, and from the very outset hostile to Germany.

Even before the *Daily Mail* was founded, Harmsworth had expressed his hostility to the German empire in his earlier publications. A lifelong Francophile, he developed an early and unshakeable Germanophobia. There can be little doubt that this was a genuinely held opinion, not merely a cynical ploy for the boosting of circulation. Nevertheless, this attitude did express itself in several notorious circulation-building stunts—the "Made in Germany" campaign against German consumer goods, and, infamously, the *Daily Mail* serialization of William Le Queux's scare story "The Invasion of 1910." This track record made Harmsworth, who was elevated to the peerage as Lord Northcliffe, a true hate figure to British liberals who sought an accommodation with Germany, and also to many German opinion makers.

The *Daily Mail* had emulators and competitors. The *Daily Express* had been founded in 1900 to compete in the same market and had broadly similar politics. The proprietor of the *Daily Express*, Max Aitken, was a Scots-Canadian political fixer for the Conservative party and a close personal friend of fellow countryman and party leader Bonar-Law. He had become a press proprietor for political reasons, principally to act as an advocate of tariff reform, but was already discovering a formidable talent for running newspapers that supplemented his enthusiasm for political intrigue.[5]

The conservative national popular press was rounded out by a second Harmsworth newspaper, the *Daily Mirror*, notable for its heavy use of photographic illustration. Although its regular circulation was lower than the *Daily Mail*'s, the emphasis on photographic illustration meant that occasional editions where photographic illustration was at a premium could outstrip all other daily newspapers. It seems likely that the *Daily Mirror* was the first newspaper to sell a million copies in one day, at the time of the sinking of the *Titanic*.

In direct competition with these newspapers were the mass-market liberal daily newspapers, the *Daily Chronicle* and the *Daily News*. The latter had been purchased by the Quaker Cadbury family specifically to counteract the influence of the "jingo" press. In turn it was derided by its conservative competitors as the archetype of the "cocoa press," a reference to the chocolate manufacturing interests of the pacifistic Cadburys. The circulation of these liberal newspapers was roughly two-thirds of their conservative opponents.

The new press was dominant in terms of circulation, but the old press maintained a unique degree of access to and influence with the political establishment. The London "quality" newspapers were all conservative in 1914. The *Daily Telegraph* had defected from its initial liberalism some 40 years previously and had settled into a comfortable establishment role. The *Morning Post* was already in decline and had begun to evince extreme right-wing tendencies. The *Times* remained the "newspaper of record," but having been controversially acquired by Northcliffe, was highly suspect in liberal circles, who feared that it was becoming a higher-priced version of the *Daily Mail*. The principal voice of establishment liberalism by 1914 was the *Manchester Guardian*.[6]

The *Manchester Guardian* occupied a unique position among British newspapers, although its position would have been familiar in the majority of nations that had a press less centralized in the capital city. It remained "first among equals" among the regional newspapers, and the focus on the Northwest remained important. In August 1914 it was still run from Manchester, proposals earlier in the year to reconfigure the newspaper as a joint London-Manchester enterprise having come to nothing. Nevertheless, it had developed a truly national significance as the mouthpiece of traditional liberal values of "peace retrenchment and reform" as well as cautiously endorsing some of the more radical progressivism of the new liberalism. Its editor, C.P. Scott, was a figure of real importance in the highest echelons of British liberalism. The other major regional newspapers lacked this national dimension, although the *Yorkshire Post* was an important voice for conservatism in the North. The Scottish press had a small readership in England but largely went its own way, as did its Irish and Welsh equivalents, and it is worth remembering that the "popular press" had a large readership throughout the islands.

The aggregate total readership of the local press probably matched the national newspapers. They were heavily dependent on the wire services and the London dailies for their coverage of national and international news, although some could retain a London correspondent. Most had an open political affiliation, and most cities of any size could boast both a liberal and a conservative newspaper. London and some other cities were also served by a specifically evening press.

The great absence in the spectrum was a truly effective mass-circulation socialist newspaper. To some extent this reflected the absence of a truly powerful socialist political party at the national level, although the relationship of cause and effect between these two phenomena might be questioned. The orthodoxy in British media studies has tended to blame the commercialization of the press as self-evidently marginalizing left-wing opinion, the high capital costs of entry into the market discriminating against radical opinion that might frighten away advertising revenue. But this is clearly not the whole story; the indifference of much of the potential readership to any form of politics, combined with a notable ineptitude on the part of would-be socialist proprietors, played an equally significant role. The *Daily Citizen*, the most ambitious socialist effort prior to 1914, foundered in part on undercapitalization, but was certainly not helped by a principled but suicidal refusal to carry the racing news that most appealed to its target audience.[7]

In a small-scale way, the socialist press was establishing a niche: the *Labour Leader* was a lively mouthpiece for Keir Hardie, the leader of the ILP; the *Clarion* served a similar purpose for the eccentric (pro-spiritualist, pro-conscription) Robert Blatchford; and by 1914 the *Herald*, in origins a strike sheet, was in embryonic form developing into a readable and effective populist and socialist newspaper under the editorship of George Lansbury.

To sum up, Britain entered the war with a wide range of periodicals, most of which had distinctive readerships and clear political views. It was a press that was essentially uncensored but that tended to have close informal relations with the political establishment. The editors and proprietors of the largest newspapers could expect to influence the decision-making processes in the parties that they supported. Press influence on public opinion was obviously important but also constrained by the fact that the vast majority of readers of the national press bought newspapers that reflected their existing political tendencies, tendencies that had to some extent been shaped by the press, but this process had been ongoing for a generation. The stance of most of the national press during the July Crisis and at the outbreak of the war would produce few surprises to newspaper readers in terms of the well-entrenched positions of the major newspapers.

THE OUTBREAK OF WAR

Events in Ireland dominated the British Press through the summer of 1914, and although the assassination at Sarajevo caused a flurry of concern, the realization that this was a crisis leading towards a pan-European conflict dawned slowly. It was only after the Austrian ultimatum to Serbia and the rejection of that ultimatum that the press really turned its attention away from the Irish Sea and across the channel. The big national papers divided predictably on habitual party lines, the conservative press emphasizing the obligation to stand by France (and, less enthusiastically, Russia), while the liberal newspapers firmly opposed any sort of continental commitment. The liberal proprietors were as much in ignorance of Edward Grey's informal commitments to France as the majority of his cabinet colleagues. This partisan division led to the usual partisan point scoring—for example, the *Manchester Guardian* attacked the Northcliffe press, and in his diary on July 27, the *Manchester Guardian* editor described that day's editorial in the *Times* as "monstrous."[8]

In many respects it is the response of the local and provincial press that is the most interesting. Here the partisan divisions were much less marked; the initial opinion most evident in editorials is that Britain's interests were not involved in the continental crisis, and that therefore neutrality was the only sensible course of action. The editorial in the liberal *Huddersfield Daily Examiner* commented on the nation's "fixed resolve" not to be drawn into a European conflict in any circumstances short of direct attack, but the conservative *Yorkshire Post* was equally convinced that it could "see no reason why Britain should be drawn in."[9] The *Cambridge Daily News* on July 28 believed that Britain's interests in the conflict were negligible, and the *Oxford Chronicle* concurred on July 31, claiming that the nation's duty was to localize the conflict and preserve its own neutrality.[10]

The isolationist instinct was powerfully echoed by *John Bull*. Despite the belligerence and anti-German rhetoric that had often marked Bottomley's publication, it is clear that the proprietor's first instinct about his readership was that they were entirely hostile to the idea of entering a European conflict. A cartoon published on August 1, 1914, showed Germany and Russia squaring off and was accompanied by this doggerel:

> Will Czar and Kaiser join the fray?
> Should Hague talk all be forgot,
> May "peace with honour" be our lot.[11]

Typically, Bottomley's position was resonant but essentially meaningless: "peace with honour" was the position of all sides—the question was what honor amounted to. The conservative press believed that honor demanded that Britain be prepared to indicate a readiness to defend France; the liberal press believed it demanded a resolute statement of neutrality. By the start of August, the press readership was able to make its views known, insofar as the press would print them. Letters to the press generally supported the latter position. Eleanor Rathbone wrote, to the *Liverpool Post*,

> Sir, Before this letter can appear in print the die may have been finally cast for war. But if not so....ought not those Liverpool citizens who feel strongly on the question of Britain's neutrality to take some steps....This might be done by a public meeting or better could be done more quickly by a collectively signed letter in your columns....No one imagines that manifestos of this kind are likely to exercise a preponderating influence on the deliberations of the Cabinet. All they are and all they are intended to do, is reflect the feelings of different segments of the public and so assist the Government to gauge how far they have the country behind them.[12]

Both individual letters and collective letters of the kind that Rathbone suggested did indeed make an increasing appearance in the first few days of August, collective letters overwhelmingly expressing pro-neutrality opinions. Press reporting concentrated on the various manifestations of the crisis mood. Much of the press was particularly concerned with the economic dislocation that made itself felt at the end of July, as the stock market plummeted and prices rose. On the eve of the war, a Trade Union official in Norwich "outlined a terrible picture of the consequences of war with food at famine prices and ordered government at an end."[13] The *Leicester Daily Post* commented on the same day, "Risen and rising prices for the necessities of life and the multiplying evils already constitute the stormy petrels of European conflict."[14] The *Daily Chronicle* suggested that the rapid rise in food prices had sobered opinion:

> For me there exists no dread of war
> No fear of Armageddon
> I ask not "Who is Russia for?
> Will Germany be led on
> to take a hand." I only see
> In Europe's posture poetry.
>
> But what is this? A rise in bread
> A threatened spurt in bacon
> My stocks and shares resembling lead
> My credit being shaken
> Nay then, poetic outlook hence
> Give place to sober common sense.[15]

The popular Sunday paper *News of the World* commented with succinct irony to its mostly working-class readership, "Just at the moment, Britain may be called the dear homeland, for everything is going up."[16] The *Liverpool Post* editorialized,

> The fears and apprehension of the citizens were reflected in the melancholy vigour of the business done in various marts and exchanges. There was a sensational drop in the cotton market, whilst the corn market was excited and nervous, the price of flour is going up to 1s 6d per sack. The Liverpool stock exchange is practically paralyzed.[17]

Such economic upheavals meant that even the most hawkish newspapers were unable to present the prospects of war as anything other than severe. On top of this was the sheer uncertainty as to the government's real position. On July 31 the *Daily Mail* reiterated its position:

> Germany's entrance will compel France.... When France is in peril and fighting for her very existence, Great Britain cannot stand by and see her friend stricken down...we must stand by our friends, if for no other and heroic reason, because without their aid we cannot be safe...at least we can be true to our duty today even if we have neglected it in the past.[18]

But on the following day, Northcliffe was thrown into crisis by a report that the government intended to "rat" on the French. His main editors were divided as to the proper response; Wickham Steed of *The Times* believed that they should continue to back France no matter what, but Marlowe of the *Daily Mail* believed that it would be inappropriate to attack a government in crisis.

The sense of crisis was equally profound on the liberal side. A significant segment of cabinet opinion in fact agreed with Northcliffe on the need to stand by the French, but growing liberal disquiet in the country, not least as expressed in the liberal press, was giving them pause. Over the course of the weekend the situation would clarify, because the invasion of Belgium by the Germans would give political cover to those, like Lloyd George, who had become increasingly convinced that Germany would have to be resisted. Nevertheless, the weekend saw frantic consultations with liberal press figures, trying to square them with the necessity of intervention if Belgium were to be invaded.

As it turned out, there were few profound shifts in position between July 31 and August 4; the newspapers that called for neutrality before the German army crossed the Belgian frontier on August 2 tended to continue to support neutrality after that event. The *Manchester Guardian* continued to call on the government to keep the nation out of the war up until the actual declaration. On August 5 the war was accepted as a fait accompli, and the *Manchester Guardian* pledged itself not to oppose the war, but in an editorial stated that the opinion of the editor that the war was a tragedy and an error had not altered, although it would not criticize the war effort.

A FREE PRESS?

British newspapers were subject to censorship in wartime. The postwar memoirs of the head of the Press Bureau, Sir Edward Cook, himself a newspaperman and former editor of the *Westminster Gazette*, a liberal London evening newspaper, set out the basic principles of a press censorship that would operate with a remarkably light touch. Under of the Defence of the Realm Act (DORA) there were two regulations relevant to censorship: Regulation 18 was specifically designed to prevent the leakage of militarily useful information to the enemy and was directed at censoring information about troop and shipping movements. This regulation obviously had serious implications for reporting of military and naval affairs. More catch-all was Regulation 27, which contained clauses that made it an offense to "spread false reports," spread reports likely to cause "disaffection to His Majesty" or "prejudice relations with foreign powers," "prejudice recruiting," or undermine public confidence in banks or the currency. Obviously a broad interpretation of Regulation 27 could be immensely restrictive.[19]

Censorship had three components. Military censorship was directly concerned with restricting the flow of information from the theaters of operations; there was also a postal and cable censorship. Most directly relevant to the press was the formation of the Press Bureau, under Cook's leadership, which came into being on August 7, 1914. The decision to use a newspaperman to head this bureau was indicative of how it would operate; Cook was firmly of the belief that a free press would be of significant assistance to the war effort. In his postwar memoirs he made four arguments why this was the case. In his view the press could act as a guardian of the home front, as a conveyor of information, as a critic, and as a propagandist. Most interesting is his argument in favor of the press as a critic. Although the wisdom of hindsight is apparent, it does seem to be a fairly accurate description of the operation of the British Press in wartime:

The newspapers served a useful purpose in preparing the way for further steps in the organization of the country for the stubborn work which confronted it. They were the *avant-couriers* of necessary policy. This was conspicuously the case with the gradual formation of public opinion in favor of compulsory military service and food control. The press helped both to carry the home front forward and keep it staunch.[20]

The practical operation of the Press Bureau relied heavily on the cooperation of the newspapers. In fact, until April 1916, the bureau had no formal and legislatively defined powers at all. The practical power of the bureau lay in the fact that all incoming and outgoing telegrams for the press were routed through it and were censored at that point. Obviously this provided the greatest level of control over military reporting and allowed some capacity to cut off militarily sensitive information at its source. No other material in the press was precensored in this fashion; editorial and opinion pieces could be submitted or not as a newspaper chose. The catch, of course, was that if a newspaper failed to submit an item to the censor, it could lay itself open to prosecution under DORA. In addition, the Press Bureau was the conduit for official government information, which gave it some potential leverage.[21]

Cook notes that "some newspapers and agencies submitted much, others little and a few nothing" in what was in many respects a system of self-censorship. It was not without its difficulties. The basic problem was that if a piece was submitted for censorship, it was likely to be censored; this could cause great annoyance when another newspaper chose not to submit an identical story, and it was therefore published without cuts. The newspaper that had played along with the Press Bureau would tend to become annoyed that it had been beaten to a scoop due to its own sense of responsibility, and would sometimes demand that its competitor suffer some form of sanction, even perhaps prosecution. But in practice this could prove difficult, because of a paradox pointed out by Cook. The bureau itself had no power to initiate prosecutions; it could only bring the attention of the crown prosecutor to the case, and any case brought under DORA regulations would have to be held in public, thereby spreading a confirmation of the leaked information: "Hence the anomaly that the more serious the indiscretion was, the more reason there might be for letting it go unpunished."[22]

Such considerations, of course, applied mostly to militarily sensitive information rather than to political opinion. The situation that developed was rather peculiar in that the Press Bureau tended to take a hard line on this variety of information, using a precautionary principle that anything that might possibly be of use to the enemy ought to be censored, but at the same time had little genuine control over what might be published unsubmitted. The latter was further exacerbated by a major loophole involving parliamentary privilege: anything said in Parliament could be reported freely, and politicians were frequently indiscreet about military and naval matters. As a result the system was heavily reliant on the discretion of the press itself, and the real operation of censorship tended to be much more on the level of self-censorship.

The most infamous case of the war was the sinking of the battleship *Audacious* in October 1914. The press was directed not to cover the story and on the whole obeyed the instruction, but was deeply unhappy that the sinking had been observed by American passengers on the liner *Olympic* and was quickly published in the American press. This has often been seen as a classic example of the counterproductive heavy-handedness of press censorship. But Cook provides a coherent defense of the decision. The reports in the American press were ambiguous as to whether the *Audacious* had actually been sunk or simply damaged, and at that moment the naval balance between Germany and Britain was so closely balanced that confirming the story would have been of major strategic importance. The more general principle, not well understood, was that even fairly widely known information of major strategic significance ought not be confirmed unless strictly unavoidable. The *Audacious* case was a judgment call, and a defensible one.[23]

The more wide-ranging powers implied in Regulation 27 were rarely invoked. Most notorious was a prosecution of the London evening paper the *Globe* for publishing a false report of Lord Kitchener's resignation in November 1915. Publication was suspended and machinery seized, but the newspaper was allowed to resume publication after a few days.[24] The range of political opinion permitted was reasonably wide, so DORA could be invoked against propaganda, against voluntary recruiting, and later against exhortations to avoid compulsory military service by breaking the law and attempts to encourage strikes or disaffection among workmen in munitions factories or shipyards. On the other hand, it was not invoked against opinions that the war should have been avoided or that it should be ended immediately by negotiation, or that conscription ought not have been introduced or that it should be immediately repealed.[25] Occasionally some left-wing publications were deemed to have crossed the line on the former counts, but it is striking how wide the range of permissible comment in the British press actually was, and freedom of press expression was almost certainly wider during the First World War than during the Second. At one time or another almost every element of government policy and strategy was vigorously criticized in the press. In part this level of criticism was sustainable because, at least until 1916 and arguably beyond, the major part of press criticism tended to be calling for a more vigorous prosecution of the war effort, and outright defeatist sentiment was rare. Even so, this could raise a problem that Cook was acutely aware of, which was that accusations that the war effort was not being conducted with sufficient vigor could in turn become grist to the mill of enemy propaganda. On balance, the Press Bureau took the view that strong criticism and as far as possible honest reporting was more rather than less helpful to the war effort, and at the end of the war they believed themselves vindicated.

One little-noticed but important element in the regulations related to the spreading of false information. This was the clause invoked in one of the most infamous atrocity stories of the early months of the war, when Kate Hume, a teenage girl in Dumfries, was prosecuted for spreading a false story that her sister, a nurse, had been mutilated by German soldiers. She was conspicuously prosecuted in December 1914 for inventing this story.[26] The fact that *inventing* an atrocity story could be and in fact in this case *was* treated as a criminal offense has been insufficiently considered. It is taken for granted that the press was full of such false and unverified stories, but a closer examination of the publication often seen as a prime offender in this respect, Northcliffe's *Daily Mail*, reveals a more complex and nuanced story.

REPORTING ATROCITIES

Arthur Ponsonby gave what has come to be the classic verdict on the British wartime press:

The narrowest patriotism could be made to appear noble, the foulest accusations could be represented as indignant outbursts of humanitarianism, the meanest and most vindictive aims, falsely disguised as idealism....Exposure may therefore be useful even when the struggle is over to show up the fraud, hypocrisy and humbug on which all war rests and the blatant and vulgar devices which have been used for so long to prevent poor ignorant people from realizing the true meaning of war.[27]

Much of the subsequent historiography has followed Ponsonby: "The press gave great prominence to atrocity stories. In the absence of factual information...atrocity stories gave much needed copy....These stories were sensational news. No effort was made to spare the gory details— they were indeed violent appeals to hate and the animal lust for blood."[28] Such is the received wisdom about the British press during the war. But in fact almost every premise of the above quotation is flawed. Atrocity stories rarely gained great prominence in the press, there was never an absence of factual information about the war, and the press was rarely in need of copy—frequently an effort *was* made to "spare the gory details."

Northcliffe's *Daily Mail* is worth considering in some detail, because the Harmsworth press would be the most demonized by both British and German critics of "hate propaganda." To a large extent the reputation for an unscrupulous readiness to libel the enemy was already established prior to 1914, due to the undoubted anti-German tone of the publication. There can be no denying that Northcliffe's antagonism increased with the outbreak of war. A memoir by one of his employees throws interesting light on this:

My first memory of Lord Northcliffe in the Great War is one that carries me to a mean hospital in the Belgian town of Furnes, where he sat beside the bedside of a poor old woman of eighty years of age who had been wounded by the splinter of a shell. He was greatly moved.... "What has she done", he asked me pointing to the pitiful white haired sufferer—"What has she done that War should punish her?" The question was characteristic of him.[29]

There is much evidence to suggest that Northcliffe was genuinely predisposed to blame the German government, and to a lesser extent Germans in general, for all of the horrors of the war. Another of Northcliffe's employees was more ambiguous about the result, saying, "He did nothing to lift men's minds above the poisonous fog of lies and artificial hatred...that is true," but he went on to qualify it with the odd comment that Northcliffe showed a "spiritual perception."[30]

The actual record of what the *Daily Mail* printed about atrocities requires closer inspection than it is usually given. The first point that needs making is that what would now be considered war crimes were indeed committed by the German armed forces in the first year of the war. Furthermore, certain military policies were undertaken that, through subsequent familiarity, seem unshocking today, but that in the cultural climate of 1914–15 were seen as gross violations of civilized standards. It follows that the act of reporting such real actions, however much it can be argued that such reporting was likely to inspire hatred of the enemy, was a perfectly normal and indeed responsible journalistic enterprise. To refuse to publish stories discreditable to the enemy that were believed to be true and for which there was reasonable evidence would have been utterly perverse. There is, of course, a world of difference between this and invention and exaggeration with the explicit purpose of blackening the reputation of the enemy.

In the opening week of the war, the stories of German misbehavior that were printed in the *Daily Mail* were, by modern standards, extremely bland. On August 6, 1914, there is a story on page 7 and an editorial about the destruction of a Belgian village. The story describes this act as "a monstrous violation of the laws of nations."[31] On August 8, two reports refer to the indiscriminate use of naval mines, describing this as a disloyal and cruel form of war. But it is the publication of the first Belgian report on "German Outrages" on August 10 that really sees attention focused on the issue.[32] The first full editorial on this subject occurs on August 12, entitled "German Brutality":

They are also reported in many places to have mistreated civilians on whom they have waged unprovoked war with appalling brutality. Our Special Correspondent in Belgium, Mr Jeffries says he cannot bring himself to believe these stories and hopes they will not be confirmed, but the grim account, which we reproduce today from the *Temps* proves that the Germans have shot unarmed Frenchmen for the sole crime of crying "Vive la France."[33]

It is a revealing editorial; it shows a willingness to express the skepticism of the paper's own correspondent, along with a willingness to accept the reliability of atrocity stories on other authority. The editorial continues,

In Belgium the Germans have treated the villages where any resistance has been offered to their attack with something like savagery. Peasants have been shot; houses have been wantonly burnt; hostages have been seized and maltreated, or forced to march in front of the German troops where they would have been most exposed to German fire. Such are the methods of the people who claim the privileges of culture and civilization. The wanton attack upon little Belgium has already covered the reputation of Germany with the broadest discredit. In the North Sea, the Germans have proceeded to show their system of maritime warfare is as cruel and callous as their system of war on land. By scattering mines in the highway of international traffic they have imperiled the shipping of neutral powers and brought the most terrible risks upon innocent non-combatants—women and children.[34]

This editorial encapsulates what might be fairly described as normative atrocity reporting in the *Daily Mail*. The first point, and it is crucial, is that not one word of this passage is actually untrue. By August 12, 1914, every one of the acts described had occurred, as would be made clear by postwar investigation. The second is that clear and undeniable evidence of a legal standard for most of these accusations was unobtainable at this date. Indeed, as noted above, the newspaper's man on the spot had expressed grave doubts. An editorial decision had been made that the accusations were warranted. It is impossible to know whether this represented a journalistic judgment that this was an important story that ought to be published despite the shortcomings of the evidence, or an ideological judgment that these reports "covered the reputation of Germany with the broadest discredit." In all likelihood the best explanation is a third possibility, that these stories were published because the editor and proprietor believed them and that they believed them because they were already predisposed to assume the worst of German military behavior. In this event, the judgment was correct. The third point is the rhetoric. "Cruelty" and "savagery" were already in evidence to describe German behavior; "wanton," with its implication of lack of self-control, is used twice. There is a revealing rhetorical slippage at the end, the equation of "innocent noncombatants" with "women and children"; in fact, in the context of the laying of naval mines, the innocent noncombatants at risk were almost exclusively merchant seamen: adult males. Already the equation between civilians and "women and children" was being made.

As the German invasion of Belgium rolled forward, the *Daily Mail* carried a steady drip of atrocity stories on its inner pages. But it was not until August 21 that the issue regained real prominence with an opinion piece by the journalist Hamilton Fyfe entitled "The Barbarity of German Troops—Sins against Civilization." Fyfe begins by claiming that he had begun as a skeptic: "In wartime all stories told by one side against the other must be read and listened to with caution. Therefore I have been skeptical about the tales of horror that appear in the French newspapers accusing the Germans of murder and brutality."[35] But now Fyfe claims he can no longer ignore the evidence:

Unfortunately there is no doubt any longer that the Germans have been making war in a way that is far from being civilized. To call it "savage" or "barbarous" would be doing a monstrous injustice to uncivilized races....Do not think I mean to apply it to all German soldiers or even most of them....But that a large number of them have acted not like men but like devils is now beyond dispute.[36]

Fyfe follows this with four paragraphs of atrocity stories from French sources. Interpreting Fyfe's motives depends a lot on competing plausible assumptions. The careful statement of initial doubts adds punch to his apparently measured conclusion that the German army had indeed behaved barbarically, and most traditional accounts of the unscrupulous British press would assume that this was merely a rhetorical strategy. But it is equally plausible that he is in fact telling the truth, that he was initially doubtful about "tales of horror" and had been swayed by the weight of evidence. The sheer volume of refugee testimony, unreliable as much of it must have been, was beginning to sway doubters. It is worth remembering that verifying these stories was intrinsically difficult; British journalists could not operate behind the path of the German armies, and the situation was fluid. As a result, the stories published were of variable reliability; as one reporter put it, "Daily, I hear stories of Prussian horrors that curdle the blood, and when all the substratum of exaggeration and distortion is removed there remains the yet unforgettable tale of the Limburg priest."[37]

While it is important to look at how the newspaper dealt with atrocities in these first weeks, there is also a danger of distorting the record. In fact, what is noticeable for most of August is how little of the newspaper was devoted to such stories. For the first three weeks of the war, stories of atrocities in Belgium and in France took up remarkably little space in the *Daily Mail*—just a couple of editorials and a few stories on inside pages. The fact is that the *Daily Mail* and other newspapers were too busy reporting the unfolding military operations and the impact of the war at home to give more than cursory attention to atrocities. It was not until August 26 that atrocity stories received headline treatment. This was in response to the first official Belgian Committee of Inquiry. It is in this reporting of the Belgian findings that the first of what we would recognize as the classically infamous atrocity stories make their appearance in the newspaper. The report claimed that a Mme Deglimme was carried "half naked" to a place two miles distant and then shot (she survived), and that an old man was hung upside down, mutilated, and burned alive. The report claimed, "Young girls have been violated and little children outraged" and "at Oramnel several inhabitants suffered mutilations too horrible to describe." It is in this edition that torture and rape are explicitly and prominently reported for the first time.[38]

It is worth noting that it is in recounting a published and official report that the newspaper for the first time gives emphasis to the lurid stories that are often seen as typical of atrocity propaganda. Yet these stories did not originate with the newspaper's own journalistic or editorial staff, but rather with an apparently credible agency of a foreign government.

It is around this date that the coverage of atrocities intensifies significantly. There were several reasons for this, not least the desire to stimulate recruiting during the panic after the first reports of the battle of Mons. But the strongest stimulus came from events at Louvain (Leuven). Louvain was significant for two reasons. The first was its particular cultural resonances. Whereas most of the Belgian towns and villages destroyed before this date were undistinguished industrial centers, Louvain was an undoubted cultural jewel, a perfect site for proposing a powerful thesis that the German army was a real enemy of civilization. The second was that after the German army committed its crime, the town was briefly recaptured, giving a rare opportunity to verify what had occurred. The first report on Louvain on August 29 was entitled "The War Lords Awful Vengeance; a Belgian City in Ashes,"[39] but it was on September 1 that the *Daily Mail* was able to publish an eyewitness account, "What I Saw in Louvain," which ran to 13 paragraphs, by far the longest report on German criminal behavior that had so far been published.[40] Stories about Louvain would remain prominent for the whole of the next week.

The editorial on September 8 represented a new level of invective:

They drove the women and children into the fields, perpetrating on them atrocities which cannot be detailed in cold prose. No language of condemnation can be too strong for such iniquity. But those who know the repulsive torture chambers of Nuremberg and Regensberg and the merciless treatment of animals in the Fatherland will not be surprised by these cruelties.[41]

The accusation of cruelty to animals is almost laughably English, but something important is developing; at this stage, a month into the war, a general indictment of German character as the root cause for atrocious behavior is starting to develop. The relative caution of earlier editorializing is being replaced by a certainty of German bestiality. Louvain seems to be a turning point. In terms of human casualties this is strange: 209 civilians were murdered over the course of four days, but appalling as this was, it was by no means the worst massacre perpetrated by German forces. It seems likely that it was the combination of verifiability and visual impact that made this particular town so important. The physical destruction visited on Louvain was massively emphasized during the first week of September with photographs at the back of the newspaper. Most of the description of "atrocity propaganda" has placed overwhelming emphasis on its sexual-sadistic aspects, which are, at least as measured by column inches, a comparatively tiny part of the initial reporting. What gets the most emphasis, both visually and in print, is the massive destruction of private property. This had two key advantages: it was photogenic, and it was readily verifiable. For obvious reasons no photographs of atrocities against persons could be obtained, but photographs of property damage were available. There is a suspicion that some of these photographs may have been faked—after all, a recycled photograph of ruins of the Messina earthquake would not have been difficult to pass off—but if such faking occurred, it does not appear to have been deliberate policy, but more a case of freelancers foisting such photographs on the press.

The shock value of such pictures was considerable, particularly to the readership of the lower-middle-class press. The cult of domesticity was strong in the *Daily Mail*, which was the sponsor of an "ideal home" exhibition before the war, and the deliberate destruction of homes and public buildings in a recognizably European setting could send shock waves through its readership. The deliberate destruction of property by the militant suffragettes in prewar Britain had further emphasized the transgressive nature of property destruction.

It is in this context that the initial use of the word *Hun* in the *Daily Mail* needs to be understood. Rudyard Kipling's poem "For All We Have and Are" had used the line "The Hun is at the gate," and its first use in the *Daily Mail* is a direct echo of this, immediately after the news of Louvain. But the usage of the term took on a very specific resonance. This can be seen in the headline for a story on November 18, 1914, entitled "The Heavy Hand of the Hun," which states, "The horror of Louvain is indescribable, one might think one was in Pompey [*sic*]."[42]

The use of *Hun* began to emerge in this very specific context, that of an assault on the physical manifestations of civilization. The destruction at Louvain included severe damage to the fifteenth-century church of St. Peters; the burning down of the Old Market and the fourteenth-century Cloth Hall; and, most important of all, the destruction of the eighteenth-century University Library, with the loss of a quarter of a million books, 800 incunabula, and 950 manuscripts. Although "only" 12 percent of the town was destroyed, the sense of massive destruction was heightened by the nature of the town; this was the worst act of cultural desecration in more than a century, involving a university town the equal of Oxford or Heidelburg. For this reason Louvain has been described as the Sarajevo of the European intelligentsia, leading to a widely reprinted exchange between British and German academics.

For the broader readership of the *Daily Mail*, the destruction of cultural heritage might seem a rather abstract offense, but Louvain could be presented as part of a pattern. The idea of "hunnish" behavior began to be established at this point. The precise initial usage was connected to an attack on buildings rather than people. In fact, these early usages show *Hun* being used in a sense that was indistinguishable from the modern usage of *vandal*. This became explicit in the coverage of the German shelling of Reims Cathedral, which was heavily covered in the press towards the end of September:

The record of German violence and vandalism is aggravated today by the sad news of the destruction of Rheims Cathedral by enemy shells. These apostles of "culture" more barbarous than the Huns of Atilla have not spared one of the supreme architectural glories of the world.[43]

Even more than Louvain, Reims provided excellent possibilities for illustration, and the photograph of the cathedral before its "destruction" was the first-ever full-page photograph printed by the *Daily Mail*. The illustration was extremely selective; the damage to the cathedral was exaggerated by foregrounding the ruins of destroyed houses, giving a misleading impression of the extent of the damage. The use of banner headlines increased the impact:

HOW RHEIMS CATHEDRAL WAS SHELLED: FULL STORY OF THE KAISER'S AWFULLEST CRIME

And the back page photograph was emblazoned with

"WORSE THAN LOUVAIN": GERMANS DESTROY RHEIMS CATHEDRAL.[44]

In reality, the issue of Reims was far more complicated in that the German army had good reason to believe that the cathedral was being utilized as an artillery observation post by the French army. Yet the tone of this reporting is very revealing of an emerging interpretation of German behavior. At first sight, this heavy emphasis on the destruction of property, particularly the destruction of sites of cultural significance, is odd. Surely if the intention is to damn German actions, a heavier emphasis on massacres and accusations of rape would be more powerful and emotive. But the reference to "culture" above is revealing. The *Daily Mail* had a policy of translating unfamiliar foreign terms; the use here is a clear translation of the German term *Kultur*, and the fact that it was still an unfamiliar term at this point shows that the readership was being slowly introduced to a powerful tool for interpreting German actions—the concept of *Kultur* as an enemy of civilization itself. A highly complex philosophical debate rooted in eighteenth- and nineteenth-century German thought was in the process of being simplified into a straightforward dichotomy, one that would define the purpose of the conflict.

This can be seen in a poem by Herbert Kaufman published on September 26, 1914, which brought these elements together:

> You seek excuse in "Die Kultur"
> For every stratagem and lure
> Outlaw device and deed of shame
> With which you play the soldier's game
> For Hunnish code and Mongol lust;
> For violated pledge and trust;
> For women raped and children slain;
> For Malines, Termonde, Rheims, Louvain.[45]

As this shows, it also followed that those with no respect for civilization itself could not be expected to show any respect for lawful behavior in any sphere, including respect for human life or sexual restraint. So *Huns*, initially used as synonymous with *vandals*, was quickly to encompass murder, as in the headline on November 21, 1914: "400 Peasants Shot in Cold Blood: Massacre by Huns in Belgium." This story, relating to the destruction of Dinant in August 1914, was in fact a remarkably accurate description of the worst massacre perpetrated by the German army during the invasion. The newspaper's claim that 700 of the inhabitants had been killed in the district tallies well with the postwar assessment of 612 murders in the town alone.

The Dinant case also once again illustrates the handicaps intrinsic to reporting atrocities: the biggest massacre was one of the most severely underreported. The result was that on occasion it is clear that reporting was reduced to recounting rumor. So, on September 18, 1914, while the bulk of the story is about incendiarism, the really lurid components are the claim that as well as 11 men being killed, "women were ravished," and that "a friend of mine, a responsible public official, found among the ruins of the houses, the foot of a little child hacked off at the ankle, a foot with its toes drawn up and its instep arched tightly with final agony."[46] This was accompanied by a photograph of a man holding a child's foot. It should be noted that this story, almost certainly untrue, was uniquely nasty in the newspaper's coverage in 1914. Such lurid stories undoubtedly created a response out of all proportion to their comparative rarity. But it must be reemphasized that they were not at all typical.

The last word on the *Daily Mail* coverage of atrocities in Belgium in 1914 ought perhaps be given to one of the newspapers journalists. J.M.N. Jeffries, cited earlier as a skeptic, claimed in his autobiography, published in 1935, that he and his fellow journalists working for the newspaper upheld fully their professional standards and reported as conscientiously as they could under very trying circumstances. He states that he was under no editorial pressure to seek out atrocities, but that his editor had written to him that such stories were coming to the newspaper from "many sources" and "wanted to know if there was any truth in them." Jeffries replied that he had not witnessed any atrocities personally, but that he had sent stories to the newspaper when he judged the eyewitness reports reliable. He ends by writing, "I write this in our defence, but I know that I write it in vain. Any article I shall ever read upon propaganda and war hysteria will assume that the 'popular press' gushed lies determinedly and without stint." By 1931, "the manifold critics of the press" had established the view that "tales of atrocities were lightly transmitted."[47]

Jeffries knew he was fighting a losing battle; the critics of the popular press had created the image, and it has held ever since. But despite the plaintive and defensive tone, examination of the content demonstrates Jeffries's testimony to be generally consistent with the content of the newspaper and a good deal more consistent with the real content than most of the poorly documented or undocumented accusations against the press in, for example, Arthur Ponsonby's work.

The most lurid stories printed tended to be drawn not from the newspaper's own staff but from official French and Belgian reports. There was an irony here in that in 1915 the Belgians would complain about the

British press usage of their materials, but initially, comparatively full reprints of reports that were themselves fairly lurid tended to make the most dramatic impact. Where the newspaper generated its own stories, the emphasis was overwhelmingly on crimes against property rather than persons, particularly actions that could be presented as crimes against "civilization." Finally, it should be noted that atrocity stories were not all that important as content—less than five percent of all reporting, easily outweighed by military news and, indeed, ordinary domestic news.

In the middle of December, atrocity stories for the first time gained massive prominence, both in quantity of reporting and in prominence. But these stories had nothing to do with Belgium. The German navy's bombardment of Scarborough and Hartlepool was by a considerable margin the most important atrocity story of 1914 for the British press and its readership. Ethel Bilsborough in her diary had occasionally noted stories from Belgium, but it was the East Coast bombardments that first truly aroused her indignation: "killing many civilians and several women, children and babies—which is apparently their idea of chivalry. Over 100 lives lost—or rather massacred." Bilsborough then goes on to link these actions with Belgium: "It is horrible to think that such things can take place in these enlightened days, but then the Germans are proving every day that they have no sense of right or justice, morality or honour." Bilsborough for the first time clipped two pictures from the newspaper and added her own comment to one of them: "House in Scarborough where dead babies were found after the bombardment."[48]

This provides an interesting guide to reader reaction. The stories of atrocities in Belgium had clearly provided an interpretive frame, but an atrocity on British soil aroused real passion. Not only that, but Hartlepool and Scarborough were much easier to report and were clearly verifiable in a way that Belgian stories were not. On December 17, 1914, the day after the raid, three full pages of the *Daily Mail* were dedicated to reporting it. There is also evidence that the press experienced a distinct spike in circulation; the *Evening News* noted on December 19 that the *Times* had sold out by a quarter past nine in the morning on December 17 and that news vendors were able to charge inflated prices.[49] The first *Daily Mail* headline once again emphasized property damage—"Damage to Churches, an Hotel and Private Houses"—but immediately below it was printed a list of casualties. The report stated, "Unfortunately there has been loss of life. The names of 17 dead have been issued by the police, but there are also some wounded. A considerable proportion of these are after the German's own heart—women and children."[50]

Alongside the logistic advantage of access for reporting was the symbolic importance: "Yesterday for the first time in two centuries, British towns were shelled by a foreign foe and British blood was spilt on British soil. What was the German objective in attacking unfortified coastal towns and resorts"?[51] The result was that in the space of a week this story generated more coverage than all alleged crimes in Belgium had received in two months. In terms of arousing opinion, this event was crucial. Ultimately the "message" of murder and destruction in Belgium was slightly abstract to the mass of the population, amounting to the proposition that unless Germany was defeated, this "could happen here." The East Coast towns delivered a more powerful message: "this has happened here." The coroners' inquests on dead men, women, and children were far more powerful than any secondhand testimony, and there was a copious amount of photographic evidence—there was nothing questionable about this atrocity.

Equally important was the human-interest potential of the stories; these families could be brought to life in their tragedies. In Hartlepool, a German shell hit the Dixon house; the father was serving in Kitchener's army, but his wife was maimed and three of their six children were killed. Not only could these verifiable stories be told, they could be illustrated with family photographs, and on its picture page the *Daily Mail* was able to show photographs of the children who had fallen victim.[52]

Scarborough was particularly evocative, as it was a seaside resort that was familiar to much of the urban population of northern England. So particular emphasis was placed on Scarborough, despite the Hartlepool's having suffered the bulk of the casualties. A poem by Jessie Pope caught the impact:

Young Brown's repast was growing chill.
Though he had just begun it.
He glared and said,
"The Castle Hill.... That's done it."...
But Scarborough! He loved the place.
The happy haunt of summer revels,
Bombarded! Blood rushed to his face,
"The Devils!"

Those Yorkshire Women lying dead
The news grew blurred—he tried to skim it
Then rose, "This is"; he calmly said,
"The Limit!"[53]

In the aftermath of the bombardment, Winston Churchill described the German navy as "baby killers," easily the strongest invective from a senior politician that had so far been be expressed. The press was equally indignant; on December 18, in an editorial entitled "The Mark of the Hun," the *Daily Mail* declared that the "debating habit of flinging articles of the Hague convention at the enemy" should cease.[54] Germany was revealed in its true colors, as an outlaw state. From now on, description of German atrocities in the paper would be the analysis of a pathology.

THE *DAILY MAIL:* CONSTRUCTING THE HUN

Depictions of the enemy in the pages of the *Daily Mail* were not all straightforward; as late as March 1915 it was still possible to find the newspaper reporting favorable examples of German behavior. Under the heading "Boats Towed by Obliging Pirate," the commander of U32 was praised for his treatment of the crew of the captured merchant ship *Delmira.* He is reported to have given them time to take to their boats and

offered them a bottle of wine, which they refused. He told them that he would take them in tow and said, "Where can I take you?" They asked to be towed to the English coast. "Well," he said, "I cannot go too near that, because I have to consider the risk of losing my boat. I'll tow you until I can put you aboard some ship."[55]

This story served to illustrate that the British could still apparently approve correct behavior on the part of their enemies. What was unacceptable was the reckless endangerment or, worse, the deliberate murder of maritime civilians.

The core of the dispute over right and wrong methods of naval warfare was a culture clash. As a leading maritime nation, the British had extremely stringent views about the acceptable humanitarian limits of war at sea. By contrast, the Germans, with far less maritime experience, were applying analogies from land warfare. The British decision to arm merchant vessels was taken by the Germans as a form of illegal *Franc-tireur* warfare that in turn rendered merchant vessels liable to sinking on sight, particularly as it could be assumed they were carrying military supplies. By contrast, the British held that the civilian rights of passengers and civilian crew were unaffected, that the traditional humanitarian courtesies of boarding and inspection still held, and that if a ship carrying contraband were captured, the safety of its passengers had to be guaranteed.

This in turn related to a second-order clash of perceptions. The British held that law and customary practice dictated care for the safety of civilians. The German attitude was that military necessity could override such formal codes, particularly as such "civilized" constructions represented a hypocritical system designed to protect the established interests of the established powers. It was almost inevitable that both the practicalities of warfare and the principles behind them would lead to ferocious clashes over the course of 1915.

The *Daily Mail* tried to express the problem, albeit in a heavily jaundiced fashion, in commenting on an interview that the kaiser had given to the American press:

There is, it appears, some vital but elusive difference between Kultur and Civilization. Thus according to the Kaiser, anyone who enters an English drawing room can see at once that we are a highly civilized nation. . . . But culture, in the true Teutonic sense, is denied us. It is some indwelling spirit, some attitude towards life, some set of instincts founded in "the deepest conscientiousness and the highest morality" that altogether escapes us. In fact only the Germans have it. So far as we in Great Britain are concerned they can keep it.[56]

The idea of *Kultur*, an expression of honest conscience, spirituality, and high morality opposed to the artificial forms of mere "civilization," was indeed a major element in German self-justification. But its use in propaganda efforts backfired badly. Shelling a cathedral that was being used by the enemy to save the lives of German soldiers might look to a German audience like honesty and conscience, but "mere" civilization mattered to the English-speaking world, and it became easy to present *Kultur* as simply a synonym for barbarism, a justification for lawlessness and moral anarchy. The view was further underpinned by the fact that during the first year of the war, almost all the technological innovations in war making came from the German side, and each of them seemed to represent an erosion of traditional moral boundaries. The use of free-floating naval mines, unrestricted submarine warfare, aerial bombardment, and poison gas were all justified on the German side as being manifestations of technical skill in search of a speedy, victorious conclusion to the war, and therefore justifiable. By contrast, the British interpreted each as a step on the path to an utterly indiscriminate totalization of warfare, unrestrained by traditional morality. German commentators then claimed that the British were simply crying foul because these methods undermined their traditional advantages; the British, in turn, saw these German apologetics as barefaced justifications for cruel behavior. After the use of poison gas at Ypres in April 1915, G. Valentine Williams unleashed his own version of poisonous vapor in the *Daily Mail* under the title "The Mind of the Hun":

His methods of warfare do not bear comparison with those of even a savage but high minded people such as the Zulus....His savagery is not of the assegai and shield variety. It is the cold blooded employment of every device of modern science, asphyxiating bombs, incendiary discs and the like, irrespective of the wars of civilized warfare....The bewildering blend of primitive barbarity, low cunning and highly trained intellect which composes the word "Kultur."[57]

By this stage there was no need to apologize for an unfamiliar term; frequent repetition of *Kultur* in a negative context had rendered it perfectly familiar.

These clashes of perception led directly to the greatest single atrocity of the war in British eyes, the sinking of the *Lusitania*. The story is too well known to require detailed repetition. It is nevertheless worth pointing to a few points that have been rather overshadowed in the never-ending arguments about the ship.[58] The first is that, however important the *Lusitania* was in shaping American attitudes, the vast majority of those who died on the ship were British. The second is that the *Lusitania* was a real case of "baby killing": 94 of the victims were children, and 35 of the 39 babies on board were drowned. Even today the photograph (genuine?), apparently from the Queenstown morgue, published in the *Daily Mail* still has the power to shock. The line of Louvain–Scarborough–zeppelins–poison gas–*Lusitania* was now drawn. *Kultur* stood condemned, but it was beginning to look like insufficient explanation. At the very start of 1915 the *Daily Mail* had reprinted a Will Dyson cartoon on its back page, of two Pickelhaube-wearing apes in an airplane dropping bombs on civilians.[59] The *Daily Mail* did not carry many cartoons, but this image of technologically advanced but underevolved "sub-humans" opened the possibility of a worse explanation than a cultural one—that the Germans as a people were intrinsically flawed, probably depraved, and possibly evil. This ape image attained classic form in the *Passing Show* in the week after the *Lusitania* sinking, with a cartoon that showed Germans worshipping a graven image of a fanged ape carrying away a child.[60]

The net result of a year's escalation towards total war was a growing belief in the "racial" depravity of the German people, a rhetoric of dehumanization. An article in the *Daily Mail* on July 7, 1915, by an American journalist, Frederick William Wile, was entitled "The German Murder Instinct." Starting with an anecdote about a Chicago butcher, August Becker, who was hanged for murdering his wife and boiling her remains in a sausage machine, Wile then detailed three more particularly gruesome murder cases from Germany. These were described as "absolutely typical and quite common place stories of German crime." Therefore, "Louvain, asphyxiating gas, and the *Lusitania* are logical expressions of the brutality and callousness of modern German nature." He then cites statistics for rape, illegitimacy, and murder in Germany and England, much to England's advantage, and then repeats that "Louvain, poison gas, and the *Lusitania* are no longer mysteries."[61] This view was reflected throughout the "yellow" press. In the *Passing Show*, William Le Queux went as far as to suggest that blaming "Prussian Militarism" was the action of "Pro-German apologists." The "most shameful and brutal deeds of the German Army...are cordially approved by the mass of that degenerate nation."[62] It is possible to take the view that the escalating racism of the *Daily Mail* was a response to pressure from weekly journals further to the right. Northcliffe had come under pressure in May for "unpatriotic" criticism of Kitchener. In the end, it is doubtful that it was such an instrumental decision. Press and public ratcheted up the hatred together. The most poisonously racist weekly, *John Bull*, saw its circulation climb by 300,000 in early 1915, proving that there was a good audience for exterminatory rhetoric. The implication and conclusion were clear: no more distinctions between good and bad Germans in the way that the earliest newspaper reports had suggested, and no more restraint and fair play. The correct response was retaliation: poison gas was to be met by poison gas and "retaliatory" bombing of German cities. In short, kill them all and let God sort them out.[63]

ENEMIES WITHIN: PROFITEERS

The moral universe of the wartime press was not simply concerned with the external enemy; the internal moral order was also important. Shirkers, strikers, enemy aliens, and profiteers were all considered appropriate targets for criticism. Profiteering in particular became a potent populist critique.

The concept of profiteering originated in the prewar socialist press, and from the very start of the war the *Daily Herald* hammered home the idea that the war would bring. On July 31, 1914, the paper stated that the war would bring "gore for the worker and gold for the shirker,"[64] and the next day published a cartoon with the caption "Every war cloud has a silver lining for the profiteer."[65] On August 12, 1914, the newspaper reported that

in Staffordshire a man has been fined...and another sent to prison for smashing windows of shops where the prices of provisions have been raised. From no part of the country do we hear of the prosecutions of those who are trying to grow rich by squeezing the poor. They do not offend against class law—only the moral law.[66]

This rhetoric spread very quickly in the first inflationary month of the war. In an ironic cartoon on August 14, the *Daily Herald* showed a fat "John Bull" carrying a banner inscribed, "To seek private profit at public expense is today a crime against the nation." The moral was supposedly, "All England is socialist today."[67]

"John Bull," in the shape of Horatio Bottomley's weekly, *John Bull,* was soon waving exactly the banner that the *Daily Herald* claimed as its own. In early January 1915 it referred to the "War Prices Swindle," claiming, "The noble British pirate is at his game again. One after another essential commodities have risen in price." The blame was placed on "shipping rings."[68] A cartoon of "The New Deity" showed a fat "capitalist" being beseeched by a ragged woman and her children. On his waistcoat was the legend "Wheat and shipping rings," and he clutched a fat bag marked "war profits."[69] Editorially, the paper commented on the "brigands who are robbing the widows and orphans of our soldiers and sailors...our own kin fatten off our own lean bodies...they pray and philander whilst they plunder the gallant men who are being maimed and killed."[70] Criticisms of war profiteering were more than a little bizarre when voiced by Bottomley. His body was anything but lean, and he was a swindler of epic proportions, indeed not averse to preying on widows and orphans while voicing pieties. The resemblance between the "New Deity" profiteer and the regular portrayal of "John Bull" himself leads the reader to suspect the cartoonist, Frank Holland, might have been engaged in a private joke at Bottomley's expense.

This rhetoric sharpened in intensity and frequency in 1917. In January the paper remarked, "This is undoubtedly a lovely war for some people, the official estimate of excess profits to April was £86,000,000."[71] In April, A. G. Hales blamed the "profit pirates" for jeopardizing victory.[72] According to the paper, bread was dear, not because of shortage of supply, but because of the dirty practices of cartels; a baker who had tried to sell cheap in Abertillery was forced to make more profits when threatened by a boycott from the mills at the behest of the local Master Bakers Association.[73] Potatoes were being kept off the market deliberately to increase prices. An internal memorandum from Sainsbury's showed them withholding tea and sugar until prices increased.[74] The weekly published the "Song of the Profiteer": "Some people declaim on the blessings of peace, but not many tradesmen, I'll warrant." The profiteer is immune to public censure:

> By some profiteering is reckoned a crime,
> Like murder though rather less gory,
> Such persons are rather too moral for words.
> They sheltered behind the fighting man,
> Kept safe by the lads who are fighting abroad
> …And dying in thousands, I'm told,
> The profiteer gloats on the growth of his hoard.

The profiteer positively revels in others' misfortune: "Here's to the war that is making us rich, while it takes the last copper from others."[75] Indicative of a leftward shift in the tone of *John Bull* in 1917, this representation climaxed with a cartoon by Frank Holland showing a worker assailed by leeches in top hats labeled "profiteers." The profiteer was now not only battening on the soldier, but also upon the working man.[76]

This shift was apparent earlier in the *Passing Show* that published a poem entitled "Socialists, Forward" that suggested that the nation should become "Socialists, pro-tem." From a publication that had usually tended to side with small business, this was remarkable, but rising prices were forcing the issue, "now in wartime when one hears, / complaints of grasping profiteers." The state should commandeer food supplies, "to squelch the domestic foes who bleed. / Our people in their time of need."[77] In a 1917 cartoon an exasperated customer is shown saying to a pork butcher, "I said how much is a pound of chops, not what is the daily cost of the war."[78] Images of profiteers now regularly appeared on the cover, such as one of a pig in a top hat marked "profiteer" surrounded by money bags.[79]

These attacks on profiteering saw the press operating as an outlet for widespread popular sentiment and as a means of shaping that sentiment.

In doing so it helped create a mood attuned to concepts of equity of sacrifice, but at the same time created an expectation that was almost impossible to fulfill. Here was the paradox identified by Cook in operation: the value of the press as critic was enormous in helping to concentrate public and political attention on domestic problems, but by identifying these problems there was a real danger of undermining public confidence in the direction of the war.

CONCLUSIONS

The wartime press in Britain has been much maligned. There is no doubt that terrible excesses were committed. For example, *John Bull* certainly played a role in creating a persecutory mood towards Germans within the United Kingdom. But it is arguable that the demonization of the Northcliffe press in particular was begun by critics, both British and German, with a specific agenda and is in many respects misleading. The press certainly did not produce a united voice urging the nation to war, and while there can be no doubt that Northcliffe's newspapers promulgated a hatred of the German regime, the extent to which he violated normal journalistic practices in doing so has been grossly overstated. Certainly by 1915 this had become a more generalized (and indeed racial) hatred of the German people, but in this respect the press reflected as much as it shaped the popular mood, and was in many respects reacting to the escalation of the war itself. On the home front a lively spirit of criticism was maintained, one that was largely untrammeled by censorship. In certain areas the war even saw an escalation of social radicalism as the critique of profiteering spread from the margins of the left-wing press into more mainstream usage. In important respects the British press was perhaps too successful for its own good. The role of the major proprietors in the political crises of 1915, 1916, and 1918 created an enormous suspicion of over-mighty subjects among the political classes, even among the conservative beneficiaries of these upheavals. In the postwar period there was a real desire to cut the mass-circulation press back down to size. But although a product of the war, that is another story.

SELECTED READINGS FROM THE BRITISH PRESS

Two Editorials from the *Herald*

The first typifies a particular rhetorical strategy of this socialist newspaper, comparing the higher moral ideals of the war with the inadequacies of peacetime capitalism and calling on the war as an example of a new moral spirit that should be channeled towards a socialist future. It remains critical of the war itself, in itself a good indication of how opinion on this issue could be freely expressed during the course of the war in the pages of the press.

Herald, **October 31, 1914, p. 7**

"In What Spirit?"

There is something infinitely moving and inspiring in the simple unselfishness
with which thousands of the poor and downtrodden have rallied to the cry of
national liberty, and shown themselves prepared to give their all to a country
which in the past has given so little to them. Inspiring, too, is the readiness of the
well to do, who in peace time have taken their ease at the expense of others, to risk
the loss of lives which have been so full of comfort and happiness, and to embrace
with ardour the agonies of war. For the soldiers, rich and poor alike, there is no
question of diplomacy or finance, they believe that the principle of freedom is in
danger and they would die rather than acquiesce in the loss of freedom. It is not
for us to discuss their political judgement; it is for us to acknowledge and reverence their selfless courage.

The bitter pity of it all is that one tithe of the same spirit shown in peace could
make England a happy and healthy nation. Every day of the year there are, on
average, more than five hundred casualties in mine, factory and workshop. Who
knows or cares?

Far vaster than that number and far vaster than the casualty list of any war, is
the tale of deaths injuries and diseases spread through the community by over-
crowding and underpaying, by long hours and bad food, by destitution and prostitution. We live in a world where youth is robbed of its promise and maidenhood
of its joy. Who cares? Who enlists in the longest war of all, the war of social justice?
Who takes up arms for liberty at home?

One thing is certain. If the spirit which the European war has roused is allowed
to run to waste, or is turned in the direction of national insolence and aggrandize-
ment, all the suffering it entails will remain a mere blot on our history and our
heroes will have died in vain. If we do not resolve to go forward in the spirit of
equality and liberty and democracy, all of us soldiers who will not rest until we
have conquered, all of us refusing to take for ourselves, whether as individuals or
as a nation, that which is not equally shared by others, if we fail to show the same
spirit as our brothers in the trenches, their blood will cry out against us and we
shall find no word to reply.

The second editorial is the response of the newspaper to the sinking of
the *Lusitania*. It is a good example of the high literary tone of the *Herald*,
which is striking in its assumption about the literacy of its predominantly
working-class audience. The sermonesque form is also revealing. George
Lansbury, the editor, was not only a prominent socialist leader, but also an
active lay preacher in the Church of England. Many of the themes of this
leader broadly resemble the general tone of commentary in the early years
of the war throughout the British press, in particular the insistence that in
the course of the war civilization itself was at stake. But, consistent with its
advocacy of a just negotiated peace, the *Herald* makes this an issue less to
do with the threat that Germany poses to civilized values than the threat
to these values posed by the continuation of the war. Nevertheless, the

unfeigned outrage at the sinking of the *Lusitania*, notable even in the leading dissenting newspaper of the time, provides valuable context for the opinions expressed in the conservative and liberal press.

Herald, **May 15, 1915, p. 7**

We need not say that we share in full the general indignation of the latest developments of German warfare. To the innumerable expressions of condemnation we have nothing further to add. That such a thing as the sudden destruction of innocent life should exist at all is the world's oldest and most insoluble problem. Storm, earthquake, disease, baffle the imagination and shake the faith of mankind. But that such things should be deliberately inflicted by human beings upon their fellows under the excuse of war—this is a horror before which speech fails and thought itself seems dazed into insanity. "It makes a goblin of the sun". It is useless to emphasize the horror with epithets and embroider it with adjectives. To do so may temporarily relieve our own feelings, but there is no other purpose it can serve. The question we have to ask is this: "How will these ever more hideous outrages affect the future of warfare and the world?"...

That is the question we have to face. For our own part we have no great belief that war has *ever* been waged chivalrously. War is murder and you cannot civilize or refine murder. Moreover, history teaches that, in all wars, mere continuance causes greater and greater bitterness. When nations are in the death grapple, each nation carefully taught to believe that the life and honour of its own women and children are at stake, no one is going to stop and ask himself if he is hitting above or below the belt. To expect this is to play childishly with the facts. As the contest gets more feverish, the pressure tighter, the fear greater, more and more will safeguards and reservations go by the board. The German Government claims the Lusitania was carrying ammunition. We neither know nor care whether it was or not, nor whether, if it was, that "justifies" or does not "justify" sinking it under international law. Murder is murder, whether there are precedents or authorities for it or whether there are not. The world is on a downward spiral. Evil persons are getting control of us. Vile expedients are being resorted to on the one side and at any rate advanced on the other. So it has always been in wars. But this war is the biggest of all and its consequences may be the worst—if it goes on. "How long, O lord, how long?" If there is no appeal to reason or right that Germany would yet hear before darkness closes. Sin gave birth to Death, and Death incestuously wedded with Sin begot a brood of indescribable calamities. It is not this or that concession or privilege or even this or that nation that is at stake. It is civilization, it is the good faith of humanity, it is the religion of Christ, it is the hope of the world.

Three Editorials from the *Manchester Guardian*

Prior to the outbreak of war, the *Manchester Guardian* was a leading advocate of Britain's neutrality. As a supporter of the Liberal government, the newspaper argued that the progressive achievements of that government would be jeopardized by war.

Manchester Guardian, **July 31, 1914, p. 6**

"The Nation's Danger"

We tried to argue yesterday from the interests of this country. It will be said that we have not only interests but duties, and that honour may sometimes bid us to do things which are against our interests. We agree. It was argued, for example, that at the time of the Agadir dispute that, though we were under no contractual obligation to assist France by force of arms, we were morally bound because we had got her into trouble by concluding with her a treaty regarding Morocco. We did not agree with the argument, but we respected it. No such argument applies now. The origin of the dispute is one with which neither we nor France have any concern whatever. It is not remotely contemplated in any of our treaties with France. We have, moreover, been specifically assured that there is no contract between us and France which impairs our freedom of choice in the event of a war. We have a completely white sheet before us on which we are free to write anything or nothing so far as our contracts with European powers are concerned. But the Government is not free as regards its own people. It is the trustee of the nation and bound above all to consider the interests of the masses of the community on whom the burden of all war really falls. It boasts, with justice, that it has tried to increase the people's sum of happiness. If it goes to war, it takes away everything that it has given and leaves them poorer than before. It is trying to relieve suffering and to diminish disease. War is the most prolific breeder of both. It came in on the country's confidence that it would protect the food of the people. There is no Protectionist tax that could be devised that is capable of raising the price of food to the extent that a fortnight of serious war will do. We are free to choose, said Sir EDWARD GREY and the PRIME MINISTER. We are free as regards Europe. We are not free as regards England. Honour is not involved abroad. It is irretrievably involved at home.

The British declaration of war presented the liberal press with a dilemma. The government was in the hands of the Liberal party, but they had opposed the policy up to the declaration of war. While some of the liberal press used the invasion of Belgium to justify the volte-face, the *Manchester Guardian* made clear that serious doubts remained even in a call for patriotic resolution.

Manchester Guardian, **August 5, 1914, p. 6**

England declared war upon Germany at eleven o'clock last night. All controversy therefore is now at an end. Our front is united. A little more knowledge, a little more time on this side, more patience and a sounder political principle on the other side would have saved us from the greatest calamity that anyone living has known. It will be a war in which we risk almost everything of which we are proud and in which we stand to gain nothing. Even those who have worked for war will enter upon it without enthusiasm and amongst the majority of our countrymen the thought of it has aroused the gravest misgivings and the most poignant regret. Some day we shall all regret it. We ourselves have contended to the utmost of our power and with a deep conviction that we were doing a patriotic duty. The memory of those efforts will not weaken our resolution now, but rather strengthen it. Some time the responsibility for one of the greatest errors in our history will have to be fixed, but that time is not now. Now there is nothing for Englishmen to do but to stand together and help by every means in their power to the attainment of our common object—an early and decisive victory over Germany.

The editorial of the *Manchester Guardian* on the sinking of the *Lusitania* shows subtle differences with that of the *Herald* to the left and the conservative press to the right. Unlike the *Herald,* the *Guardian* is willing to dwell on the specifics of the sinking and indulge in adjectival condemnation of German policy. But unlike the conservative press, it sets its face against retaliation and the blanket condemnation of the German people as a whole as infected by brutality, although it comes close to this in its comments about public reaction. The width of the *Manchester Guardian*'s readership, from strong liberal supporters of an intensive war effort to those in favor of peace through negotiations, resolves itself in the final plea for a peace of collective security.

Manchester Guardian, **May 10, 1915, p. 6**

"The Spirit of Ruthlessness"

The sinking of the Lusitania proves to have been one of the greatest crimes, as well as one of the most ghastly episodes of a war abounding in criminality and ghastliness. The facts were slow in coming through, and up to a late hour on Friday night—long after most newspapers had gone to press—it was still possible to hope that the ship only had been lost and that all on board might be safe. How far such hopes are from having been fulfilled too soon appeared. The death-roll is probably now complete and it amounts to the terrible total of 1,500 souls, more than two-thirds of the 2,160, including women, children and babies in arms, who are known to have been on board at the time that the vessel went down. Taking simply the toll of lives, it may be said that it amounts to no more than that of some nameless engagement such as takes place almost weekly in this bloodiest of wars. In the same way it may be said that the foulest murder, after all, involves only the sacrifice of a single life. It is not the life which is in question; it is the crime. And by the judgement of the whole civilised world outside the nation which is responsible for this latest atrocity, the sinking of the Lusitania without warning and without attempt at rescue, will go down in history as one of the great landmarks in the degradation of war and in the lowering of the whole standard of humanity and civilisation...

What shall we say now? That indeed, is a deep and terrible question to which the answer cannot be at once and completely apparent. For here it is plain that we have to deal with the emergence in its full development and power a new spirit in the world—the spirit of ruthlessness—a spirit which if successful and unchecked, must of necessity, change the relations of all states to one another and the whole temper of morality and civilisation. It is nothing less than that for which the sinking of the Lusitania stands, and it is that great event—an event far greater in its moment for the world than any battle—which the poor drowned corpses of the women and children and the old men and the young men proclaim to us in a silent and appalling testimony. What is the lesson for us? ...Whatever happens Germany will not be destroyed, and it is only too likely that her spirit also will remain, and our task will be to guard against its infection. Ruthlessness will not be driven from the world by ruthlessness. The only result of such a competition would be to give us a world not worth fighting for. But brutality can be disarmed and a common danger can be met by the co-operation of all against whom it is directed.

NOTES

1. D. Vincent, *The Rise of Mass Literacy* (Cambridge: Polity Press, 2000), 19–20.

2. R. Roberts, *The Classic Slum* (London: Penguin, 1971), 161–62.

3. See J. Symons, *Horatio Bottomley* (London: Cresset, 1955).

4. For some sketches of Harmsworth and the *Daily Mail*, see S.J. Taylor, *The Great Outsiders: Northcliffe, Rothermere, and the Daily Mail* (London: Phoenix, 1996); R. Bourne, *The Lords of Fleet Street: The Harmsworth Dynasty* (London: Unwin, 1990); L. Andrews and H. A. Taylor, *Lords and Laborers of the Press* (Carbondale: Southern Illinois University Press, 1970), 45–63; and J. Lee Thompson, *Politicians, Propaganda, and the Press: Lord Northcliffe and the Great War* (Kent, Ohio: Kent State University Press, 1999), 1–22.

5. The essential work on Max Aitken, Lord Beaverbrook is A. Chisolm and M. Davie, *Beaverbrook: A Life* (London: Hutchinson, 1993), which clearly supersedes A.J.P. Taylor's rather hagiographical account.

6. See J.L. Hammond, *C.P. Scott of the Manchester Guardian* (London: G. Bell, 1934).

7. The view that left-leaning newspapers failed for commercial reasons is expounded in J. Curran and J. Seaton, *Power without Responsibility: The Press and Broadcasting in Britain*, 4th ed. (London: Routledge, 1991).

8. T. Wilson, ed., *The Political Diaries of C.P. Scott* (London: Collins, 1970), 90.

9. C. Pearce, *Comrades in Conscience: The Story of an English Community's Opposition to the Great War* (London: Boutle, 2001), 229; P. Esposito, "Public Opinion and the Outbreak of the First World War: The Newspapers of Northern England" (master's thesis, Oxford University, 1996), 17.

10. *Cambridge Daily News*, 28 July 1914, p. 5; *Oxford Chronicle*, 31 July 1914, p. 6.

11.Cartoon, *John Bull*, 1 August 1914.

12. E. Rathbone, letter to the editor, *Liverpool Post*, 4 August 1914, p. 7.

13. *Eastern Daily Press*, 3 August 1914, p. 6.

14. *Leicester Daily Post*, 3 August 1914, p. 5.

15. *Daily Chronicle*, 1 August 1914, p. 3.

16. *News of the World*, 2 August 1914, p. 10.

17. *Liverpool Post*, 30 July 1914, p. 6.

18. *Daily Mail*, 31 July 1914, p. 6.

19. E. Cook, *The Press in Wartime* (London: Macmillan, 1920), 24–25.

20. Ibid., 5.

21. Ibid., 36–44.

22. Ibid., 85–86.

23. Ibid., 148–49.

24. Ibid., 112–13.

25. Ibid., 118.

26. See N. Gullace, *"The Blood of our Sons": Men, Women, and the Renegotiation of Citizenship* (New York: Palgrave, 2002), 18–19. Gullace gives a good account of the Hume case, but I would differ from some of her general conclusions about the press and propaganda.

27. A. Ponsonby, *Falsehood in Wartime* (London: E. P. Dutton, 1926), 25–26.

28. C. Haste, *Keep the Home Fires Burning* (London: Allen Lane/Penguin, 1977), 83–84.

29. M. Pemberton, *Lord Northcliffe: A Memoir* (London: Hoddar & Stoughton, n.d.), 148.

30. H. Fyfe, *Lord Northcliffe: An Intimate Biography* (London: Macmillan, 1930), 172.

31. *Daily Mail*, 7 August 1914, p. 6.

32. *Daily Mail*, 10 August 1914, p. 3.

33. "German Brutality," *Daily Mail*, 12 August 1914, p. 6.

34. Ibid.

35. H. Fyfe, "The Barbarity of German Troops—Sins against Civilization," *Daily Mail*, 21 August 1914, p. 6.

36. Ibid.

37. *Daily Mail*, 24 August 1914, p. 5.

38. *Daily Mail*, 26 August 1914, p. 3.

39. "The War Lords Awful Vengeance; a Belgian City in Ashes," *Daily Mail*, 29 August 1914, p. 6.

40. "What I Saw in Louvain," *Daily Mail*, 1 September 1914, pp. 3–4.

41. *Daily Mail*, 8 September 1914, p. 6.

42. "The Heavy Hand of the Hun," *Daily Mail*, 18 November 1914, p. 4.

43. *Daily Mail*, 21 September 1914, p. 6.

44. Both the headline and back page are from the *Daily Mail*, 21 August 1914.

45. Herbert Kaufman, *Daily Mail*, 26 September 1914, p. 6.

46. *Daily Mail*, 18 September 1914, p. 4.

47. J. M. N. Jeffries, *Front Everywhere* (London: Hutchinson, 1935), 124–25.

48. Ethel Bilsborough, diary, Imperial War Museum, London, entry for 19 December 1914 (but probably written up later).

49. *Evening News*, 19 December 1914, p. 4.

50. *Daily Mail*, 17 December 1914, p. 3.

51. *Daily Mail*, 17 December 1914, p. 6.

52. F. Miller, *The Hartlepools during the Great War* (Hartlepool: Charles Sage, 1920), 88.

53. J. Pope, "And the Consequence Was," *Daily Mail*, December 1914; a modified version of the poem appears in J. Pope, *More War Poems* (London: Grant Richards, 1915), 19.

54. *Daily Mail*, 18 December 1914, p. 6.

55. "Boats Towed by Obliging Pirate," *Daily Mail*, 27 March 1915, p. 5.

56. *Daily Mail*, 5 February 1915, p. 6.

57. G. V. Williams, "The Mind of the Hun," *Daily Mail*, 26 April 1915, p. 3.

58. The most famous book about the *Lusitania* is C. Simpson, *The Lusitania* (London: Little, Brown, 1972). Underwater archaeology has to some extent extended our understanding. The liner clearly split apart and sank very quickly. Was this a boiler-room explosion (as many believed at the time, including the U-boat commander) or a secondary explosion of an additional secret load of munitions (as Simpson argues)? Attention has tended to focus on this issue, which in my view is a red herring (see below). See also T. A. Bailey and P. B. Ryan, *The Lusitania Disaster* (New York: Free Press, 1975).

59. W. Dyson, "The Wonders of Science," cartoon, *Daily Mail*, 1 January 1915, back page—perhaps the most "classic" propaganda image that the paper ever printed. P. M. Yearsley refers to it as the *Daily Mail*'s finest cartoon, and says that "the only adverse comment I heard upon it was that it was unduly harsh on the chimpanzee" ("The Home Front," 50). Yearsley, writing up his account in the 1930s, was still a firm believer in "Hun atrocities" despite "Germanophiles who have denied them."

It is worth noting that the most famous ape image of all, a Pickelhaube-wearing gorilla carrying away a distressed maiden (a scaled-down Teutonic King Kong prototype) was not a British image of 1914 (as is sometimes erroneously suggested), but an American one of 1917. American propaganda became very nasty, very fast.

60. *Passing Show*, 15 May 1915, p. 13.

61. F. W. Wile, "The German Murder Instinct," *Daily Mail*, 7 July 1915. His figures: Germany (1897–1907), 350 murders, 9,381 rapes, 178,115 illegitimate children; England (1900–1910), 97 murders, 218 rapes, 37,041 illegitimate children. Although not total nonsense, the figures are seriously decontextualized. Ironically, one of the major long-running stories in the paper at the time was the coverage of the trial of the notorious English serial killer George Joseph Smith, of "brides in the bath" fame (e.g., *Daily Mail*, 2 July 1915, p. 2). Is an acid bath intrinsically less shocking than a sausage machine?

62. W. Le Queux, *Passing Show*, 15 May 1915, pp. 10–11.

63. In a search for ironies, the diminution of atrocity stories in significance from the summer of 1915 should be noted. It was precisely at this time that the worst single atrocity of the war was being committed by the Central Powers: the Armenian genocide undertaken by the Turkish government. The result of a year of demonizing Germany was that this event was underplayed and fundamentally misunderstood. It was presented as a German-instigated (or inspired) atrocity, which it wasn't. The British government did encourage an official inquiry, which for all its propaganda use is still a fundamental document of the genocide, and the Armenian events were noted in passing. But the shock value of systematic extermination was clearly lessened by earlier atrocity stories.

64. *Daily Herald*, 31 July 1914, p. 1.

65. Cartoon, *Daily Herald*, 1 August 1914, p. 11.

66. *Daily Herald*, 12 August 1914, p. 5.

67. Cartoon, *Daily Herald*, 14 August 1914, p. 7.

68. *John Bull*, 30 January 1915, p. 2.

69. Cartoon, *John Bull*, p. 17.

70. *John Bull*, 6 February 1915, p. 5.

71. *John Bull*, 27 January 1917, p. 5.

72. A.G. Hales, *John Bull,* 7 April 1917, p. 6.
73. *John Bull,* 28 April 1917, p. 12.
74. *John Bull,* 19 May 1917, p. 6.
75. "Song of the Profiteer," *John Bull,* 9 June 1917, pp. 12, 15.
76. F. Holland, cartoon, *John Bull,* 23 June 1917, p. 12.
77. "Socialists, Forward," *Passing Show,* 13 November 1915, p. 5.
78. Cartoon, *Passing Show,* 17 June 1917, p. 6.
79. *Passing Show,* 7 July 1917, cover.

Chapter 2

"The Eagle Soars over the Nightingale": Press and Propaganda in France in the Opening Months of the Great War

Michael Nolan

INTRODUCTION: THE PRESS IN WARTIME

The role of the press in time of war is a subject that is fraught with controversy. Wartime conditions often call into question fundamental assumptions about the purpose of the press in modern society. Is its ultimate aim to educate its readers (or, in our own day, listeners and watchers) concerning the events of the day to the best of its ability, and to maintain a free exchange of information at all times? Or under certain circumstances should it be subject to the strictures of a "national interest," the parameters of which may be dictated by the necessities of military secrecy and reasons of state decided on by military authorities and government officials? Many argue that states of emergency may sometimes require that restrictions be placed on the normal functioning of civil society, but questions inevitably arise of when and for how long. Decisions concerning the temporary suspension of civil liberties, the establishment of censorship, and the control of access to information are often made at the spur of the moment, with little regard for the long-term consequences.

The press is often faced with the problem, even in times of peace, of shaping chaotic events into a coherent narrative, and the abstract and sometimes simplistic notions this requires may obscure the infinite complexity of reality. This is never more the case than in time of war. The needs of propaganda take primacy over "getting to the truth of the matter," insofar as the latter is the ordinary state of affairs. There is always a danger that in the heat of the moment the coverage the press provides will part company with reality altogether, while insisting that what it purveys is an accurate representation of events. Much of the French press crossed this line in the late summer and autumn of 1914, but this phenomenon was hardly confined to France.

Many newspapers today lay claim to some degree of objectivity, whatever that might mean, when it comes to interpreting events. European newspapers in 1914, by contrast, were far more open about expressing their political leanings. Newspaper editors and journalists were fully caught up in the often ferocious political conflicts of the day and did not hesitate to lambaste their opponents in print. Nevertheless, there was a desire for independence among many in the newspaper business, and a certain integrity received more than mere lip service. The outbreak of war wrought far-reaching transformations. The press was not immune to the call of the nation, and to begin with there was broad agreement that the chief role of newspapers was to encourage the national war effort. Unfortunately, patriotic motives often outweighed the independent judgment of journalists, as they have done in so many subsequent conflicts.

More troubling still is the role of propaganda in the wartime press. Propaganda was, and remains, the use (and abuse) of the informative function of the press and other media to reinforce the resolve of one's own cause and to vilify that of the enemy. There were various ways of producing the desired effects. The press could focus on the successes, advantages, and strengths of the French side while neglecting to report on those aspects of the war that might show France's efforts in a negative light. By contrast, journalists could demonstrate that the Germans were evil, cowardly, and lacking in resolve. Thus propaganda could be both positive and negative, with one's own side or the enemy as the focus of attention. The danger of propaganda arose (and continues to arise) from its tendency to mislead the home front as to the true nature of the struggle it seeks to further, chiefly by hiding bad news from the public or reducing the complex circumstances of international conflict to a Manichaean confrontation between good and evil. This chapter examines recurrent themes in the presentation of propaganda in the French press during the early months of the First World War and presents some typical examples of the misleading stories and editorials newspaper readers encountered.

France in 1914 was a nation that was emerging from a decades-long struggle over the nature of French identity. The Third Republic in France, born in the inauspicious circumstances of a lost war and marked by a struggle for survival against monarchist forces in its early years, witnessed an ongoing debate concerning the essence of the French nation. Episodes of dramatic intensity punctuated and illuminated the competition for the soul of France. The Boulanger Affair of the late 1880s pitted an authoritarian general against the forces of the republic, while the Dreyfus Affair a decade later sharply divided the nation between nationalist forces bitterly opposed to the republic, many of whom dreamed of a return of the monarchy, and those who celebrated the legacy of the revolutions of 1789 and 1848. The anticlerical struggles of the early 1900s created a chasm between Catholics and nonbelievers. Divisions existed that were based on religion, class, region, town, and country, and between workers and peasants. Political struggles often spilled over into the cultural sphere, but in spite of the passionate intensity of these confrontations, political parties were relatively weak, fragmented, and loosely organized in France. Parliamentary blocs formed and dissolved with bewildering rapidity, and it was not uncommon for individuals to migrate from one side of the political spectrum to the other during the course of their careers.

The French press mirrored the complexity of the political scene. The years before the First World War were a golden age for the press in France. Literacy was virtually universal, and the newspaper-reading public was expanding rapidly. The array of newspapers from which one could choose was astonishing, especially in Paris. The *quatre grands* (big four), *Le Journal*, *Le Petit Journal*, *Le Petit Parisien*, and *Le Matin*, accounted for as much as 40 percent of newspaper circulation in France. These mass-market dailies, each having a circulation of at least half a million, were all more or less on the political right, and tended toward a reflexive nationalism. Newspapers like *Le Temps* and *Le Figaro* were more highbrow, and they also tended toward a conservative stance. The Far Right was represented by newspapers like *Action Française*, and especially *L'Echo de Paris*, which was rabidly antisocialist and criticized the shortcomings of parliamentary government. The prewar years also saw the last flourishing of relatively small-circulation papers like *Le Radical*, the official paper of the Radical-Socialists, and the irascible Georges Clemenceau's *L'Homme Libre*. There were also newspapers representing the radical Left, in particular *Le Bonnet Rouge* and *La Guerre Sociale*, the latter edited by the popular Parisian ultraradical Gustave Hervé. Provincial papers like *La Dépêche* of Toulouse and *L'Echo du Nord* had a wide readership, but they depended on Paris and the reports written by the correspondents of the major Parisian dailies for coverage of foreign affairs, and in particular the Agence Havas, the major French press agency.

THE OUTBREAK OF WAR AND THE FORMATION OF THE *UNION SACRÉE*

War came to France suddenly in 1914, like a late summer storm arriving without warning out of blue skies. There had been escalating tensions between France and Germany for the previous several years, with the Moroccan crisis of 1911 and the Balkan Wars of 1912–13 appearing to bring both countries to the brink of war. The summer of 1914, by contrast, was long remembered as peaceful and idyllic. Subsequent recollections of the "beautiful summer" of 1914 were commonplace, and in spite of the penchant of those who recorded their impressions of it years later to embellish their memories of the last months of the *belle époque*, the weather does seem to have been unusually pleasant. International crisis was far from the minds of most French citizens in June and July. The assassination of the Austrian archduke Franz Ferdinand in Sarajevo received relatively little coverage in the French press. Other stories were far more likely to draw the attention of the reading public during July. The popular Alsatian caricaturist Hansi was sentenced for the crime of *lèse majesté* by the correctional court in Leipzig. The French middleweight champion Marc Charpentier defeated the challenge of the American boxer Ed "Gunboat" Smith. The attempted assassination of a Russian monk who was a confidant of the tsar and tsarina made much of the French public aware for the first time of the name of Rasputin. However, the story that dominated headlines for much of the summer was the trial of Madame Caillaux, wife of the former prime minister, who had shot Gaston Calmette, the editor of *Le Figaro*, for publishing the intimate letters Joseph Caillaux had written to her while he was in the process of divorcing his first wife. The trial virtually monopolized news coverage until the end of July, and it was only in its closing days that the French people fully began to realize that war threatened Europe, as Austria-Hungary declared war on Serbia and the great powers prepared to mobilize.

Germany's declaration of war against France's ally Russia on August 1 and its demand for a guaranteed state of French neutrality brought home to many with shocking suddenness the looming menace that faced France. Reports of German units crossing the frontier began to occur even before the German declaration of war against France on August 3. The necessity of defending French soil united France in ways that few would have anticipated in the years of acrimonious political division before the war. Even the Socialists, whom many had feared would carry out their threat of a general strike in the event of war, rallied to the defense of *la patrie*. The assassination of the Socialist leader Jean Jaurès by a right-wing fanatic on the night of August 1 caused universal revulsion, and even his erstwhile political foes paid him homage. On August 2 President Raymond Poincaré made an emotional speech to a joint gathering of the National Assembly and the Senate calling for national unity. The response was the formation of an *Union Sacrée*, a patriotic alliance of parties along the entire political spectrum under the slogan "La France quand-même!" (France above all!) The national emergency that called the *Union Sacrée* into existence probably prolonged its life further than similar truces in the political spheres of the other great powers. However, the inevitable abuse of the ideal by those in power to advance partisan interests undoubtedly led to the gradual dissolution of a cease-fire agreement based largely on the expectation of an early French victory. While the *Union Sacrée* initially arose as a spontaneous demonstration of patriotic enthusiasm, French authorities quickly realized it could be a useful weapon to cast aspersions on the patriotism of those who challenged official policies. Thus they could wield the threat of dire consequences for disrupting the *Union Sacrée* to stifle the objections of critics. The government made effective, though relatively sparing, use of this form of chastisement until 1915, when numerous setbacks in the war effort brought increasing attacks on the army and government. In the meantime, those who criticized the policies of the government or the General Staff could find themselves accused of wishing to breach the sacred unity of the nation.

Meanwhile, the mobilization of the French army proceeded apace. As Jean-Jacques Becker demonstrated convincingly in his classic book on the entry of France into war in 1914, while patriotic demonstrations took place in many French cities and towns, the dominant mood was one of quiet determination rather than high-spirited enthusiasm.[1] It was difficult for journalists who actually covered the departure of troops for the front and the farewells of their loved ones to engage in the same kind of patriotic excess that was the specialty of their more illustrious colleagues in the editorial offices. What they did choose to emphasize was the sense of national community that appeared to be so widespread in France in the early days of August. The solidarity of the crowds that filled the trains and the stations, the orderly pace of mobilization, and the crowds along the tracks who cheered the passing trains gave many observers a sense of social cohesion that few ever again felt so strongly. *Le Temps* published a typical account of mobilized Parisians bidding farewell to their loved ones at the Gare de l'Est:

These young men nevertheless had to struggle at the moment of departure, even more than with their own feelings, with the tears of the mothers and wives who accompanied them to the station platforms. The women standing immobile before the railway carriages, awaiting the departing whistle, made for a moving spectacle. Their reddened eyes never looked away from the husband or son who was leaving to perform the supreme duty. And young mothers raised up to their men innocent little laughing children in their outstretched arms.... Around us we saw many eyes fill with tears; only those who were departing did not cry. They yelled out: "But we'll be back. It'll be over quickly!"[2]

In spite of the apparent devotion to duty of the French press in the first weeks of the war, all was not well between journalists and soldiers in France. There was a legacy of bitterness between military circles and the press in France dating back to the Dreyfus Affair at the turn of the century and prewar antimilitary campaigns by left-wing governments. Nevertheless, the French General Staff had long recognized the importance of the press in waging a successful war.[3] French law granted the military authorities power to take measures against publications that might incite or encourage disorder in the event of the declaration of a state of siege. The General Staff was also concerned about the protection of military secrets, such as the disposition of troops and the concentration of supplies and artillery. Thus, from the very beginning of the war, censorship became an important tool for the control of news. The Ministry of War set up the Press Bureau to regulate the censorship of publications and to control the flow of information from the front. All press items of a military nature had to be submitted to the Press Bureau for approval. In addition, the authorities encouraged the newspapers to engage in self-censorship and refrain from publishing what might be considered sensitive information. The Press Bureau worked in tandem with a commission of representatives of the various French press agencies, chaired by Jean Dupuy, the editor of the largest French daily, *Le Petit Parisien.*[4] The other large-circulation dailies, such as *Le Matin* and *Le Petit Journal*, were also well represented and tended to adhere closely to the official line. In addition, the right-wing, militant Catholic *L'Echo de Paris* was a sort of semiofficial organ of the General Staff.[5] Thus the French military authorities offered the carrot of cooperation in the formulation of wartime press policy to select papers while wielding the stick of censorship against more recalcitrant papers.

The General Staff could control the information coming from the front in two ways. It could rely on the cumbersome system of censorship that was in the early stages of organization at the beginning of August. Or it could control the flow of news at its source by issuing terse, carefully worded, and often deliberately misleading communiqués. It chose to follow the latter policy for much of the first month of hostilities. The consequences of this decision are startlingly clear to anyone who reads the press reports from the first weeks of the war. There was a considerable, and gradually widening, gap between the reality of the unfolding events and the information the public received. The German plan of operations in the West called for a strike through neutral Belgium and into northeastern France. However, outside of those areas immediately threatened with invasion, few of the French public were fully aware of the danger posed by the invading armies. The official communiqués tended to focus on localized "successes" in Alsace and Lorraine, though even these ephemeral victories occurred at the cost of massive casualties. The Germans fully expected and prepared for these attacks, and counted on large numbers of French troops being engaged against the German frontier as German troops carried out a vast flanking movement through Belgium and ultimately advanced on Paris. It was only in the second half of August that serious doubts concerning the military's version of events began to appear in newspaper accounts of the fighting, the result of uncertainty in the army dispatches and the inevitable questions concerning alarming developments. Why were there so many refugees from the northeastern provinces on the roads? How was it that there were reports of German troops on the Somme and in the Oise valley? Why did General Galliéni, the military governor of Paris, order the evacuation of some of the outlying towns of the northern suburbs of the capital? The answer only became fully clear at the very end of August.

The vacuum created by the reticence of France's military leaders created a serious problem for journalists hungry for news. As a result of the paucity of information from official sources, French newspapers had to rely on other methods to fill their columns. In the first days, there were glowing descriptions of patriotic demonstrations, and reporters went to the railway stations to cover the departure of the troops for the front. There was a great deal of praise for the apparently imperturbable demeanor of the people of Paris. The Belgian resistance to the German invaders was much celebrated, particularly the defense of the citadel at Liège. The first French advances into Alsace, culminating in the temporary capture of Mulhouse, brought forth stories the tone of which bordered on the ecstatic. What the public did not know was that those reporting on these events were forced to embellish their stories for want of hard information. Many of the details on which reporters chose to dwell, or which they fabricated completely, served to confirm in the minds of readers that this war, though on a larger scale, was no different from those that had preceded it. The French plan for war against Germany called for aggressive advances across the Alsatian frontier from the commencement of hostilities, and the public was fully conditioned to expect a grand offensive. There was clearly a yearning for the familiar traits of a glorious war: acts of courage under fire, humor in the face of battle, selfless devotion to duty, attacks with the bayonet, cavalry charges, and the capture of enemy standards. On the terrifying conditions of actual combat and the horrendous casualties caused to French troops by massed artillery and machine gun fire there was virtually nothing. The very use of the term *battle* to describe chaotic encounters lasting days or weeks that were little more than mass slaughters was a prime example of the use of language to draw an almost impenetrable veil between the public and the realities of modern warfare. The troops themselves never had the illusion that the savage encounters in which they participated over minute pieces of ground were battles in the normal sense of the term. Only armchair generals at a safe distance from the front had the luxury of a strategic overview.[6]

There was another trend in the French press and its reporting on the war that served to widen the gulf between the home front and the soldiers in the field. A certain patriotic excess, perhaps inevitable under the circumstances, produced the phenomenon known as *bourrage de crâne* (literally "skull stuffing"; figuratively "bullshit"). This was the term the soldiers in the front line applied to the patriotic fluff and heroic posturing of journalists safely ensconced well out of the range of German fire. The troops quickly came to despise and ridicule its most zealous and prolific practitioners, such as the nationalist Maurice Barrès, whose articles appeared in *L'Echo de Paris*. The soldiers were starved for news in the first months of the war, and eagerly seized any newspaper that came their way. However, when they began receiving papers on a regular basis in the fall, the tone of the coverage and the obvious fabrications provoked ridicule and contempt. Few bothered to read the *Bulletin des Armées de la République*, which was the official army paper and hence contained a great deal of drivel and little, if any, news. It should come as no surprise that they preferred their own trench newspapers that began to appear in the autumn, or the Swiss paper *Le Journal de Genève* if they could get it.[7]

PROPAGANDA AND COUNTERPROPAGANDA

The reading public realized by late August that initial reports of French victories were greatly exaggerated. More effective in their immediate impact and longer lasting in terms of their ultimate consequences were the images of the German cultivated by the French press from the first days of the conflict. The press in France could draw on a wide range of stereotypes of the German prevalent before the war. However, the commencement of hostilities tended to raise such rhetoric to a fever pitch. The *boche*,[8] as he was now widely known, quickly became the personification of evil, cowardice, and perfidy. The summary execution of Belgian and French civilians suspected of offering armed resistance to the invaders revived memories of the brutal treatment meted out to the *Franc-tireurs*, or irregular troops, of the war of 1870, and reinforced the image of the Germans as ruthless barbarians. There were widespread reports of these and other atrocities, real and imagined, such as widespread rape, the burning of villages, the shooting of prisoners, and the bayoneting of small children, from the war's earliest days. There were even "eyewitness" accounts of the massacre of French citizens traveling in Germany at the outbreak of hostilities. As time went on, atrocity rumors took on a life of their own, becoming increasingly strident and detailed, and ever more improbable stories found their way into print. On September 20, *Le Matin* outdid itself (and the competition) when it ran a story on two captured German soldiers allegedly found to have the severed hands of a woman and a child in their pockets. Accounts of atrocities, whether true, partially true, or wholly fabricated, contributed to a hardening of hatred toward an enemy whom many already considered as less than human. French soldiers, by contrast, usually appeared as paragons of military virtue and humane mercy, incapable of acts of cruelty other than those carried out in outraged response to the murderous deeds of the *boches*.[9]

The atrocity stories became part of a larger trend in the representation of the conflict between France and Germany, which now took on hues of a war to the death between two "races," one civilized and the other barbarous. Here too French journalists could draw on prewar images of a German *Kultur* firmly rooted in the desire for conquest and domination, an obsession with materialism, a methodical and inhuman scientific worldview, and the cult of Nietzsche and Wagner. As many French observers saw it, Prussia in particular, with its militarized *Junker* class and its slavish devotion to the army, set the tone for modern Germany. Many commentators believed that Germany had planned the war years in advance with the intention of extending Germanic dominance over all of Europe. The German people as a whole, prodded by sinister associations like the Army League, the Navy League, and the Pan-German League, desired war from the very depths of their being, above all against a France in the last stages of decadence. The French, by contrast, were fighting not for revenge for the war of 1870 or the recovery of Alsace-Lorraine, but to deliver humanity from the specter of a new dark age. There could be no talk of negotiation with an enemy who was the very negation of all human values, and as long as France maintained the struggle, French chivalry would win out over German barbarism and inhumanity. The conviction that this was a war between light and darkness extended across much of the political spectrum in the opening months of the war.

The deeds of the German military that proved to be most damaging to Germany's reputation, however, were the seemingly random acts of destruction of various towns and national monuments. One of the earliest and most dramatic episodes was the destruction of much of the Belgian city of Louvain, including the medieval town hall and the university with its historic library.[10] No one in France knew that the action was an ill-considered consequence of panic on the part of German troops who feared an ambush, and the French press expressed horror and revulsion at German savagery. French newspapers likewise treated the bombardment of the ports of Bône and Philippeville in French Algeria by the German cruisers *Goeben* and *Breslau*, in which a number of civilians were killed, as crimes against the laws of war. The most infamous case, however, was the bombardment of Reims Cathedral on September 20 by the Germans, who suspected that the French were using the cathedral spire for artillery observation. Reims Cathedral had for centuries been the site of the coronation of France's kings, and its ruins quickly came to represent the scar that war inflicted on the national psyche. French papers trumpeted the arrival of a new age of barbarian invasions, with the Vandals of the modern era using the high-tech weaponry of the twentieth century to increase the magnitude of their destruction. French reports also made much of the fact that 130 German wounded had to be evacuated from the cathedral as it was being shelled.[11] It was difficult not to conclude that Reims was an act of spite on the part of the Germans, who were in retreat after the battle of the Marne. Similarly, the bombing of Paris by German *Taube* monoplanes, beginning in mid-September, confirmed in the minds of the capital's inhabitants that the Germans were bent on the destruction of France's cultural patrimony.[12] The bombardment of other towns in the north of France, such as Arras, Ypres, and Senlis, served little if any military purpose for the Germans, but joined a long list of real and alleged acts of murder, pillage, rapine, and destruction that proved to be a boon to the French propaganda effort.

The chief malefactor of all the Germans from the French point of view was, as one might expect, Kaiser Wilhelm II. Wilhelm's popular image in France had already reached a nadir before 1914. His habits of making bombastic speeches and of engaging in inopportune saber rattling had by turns amused and alarmed observers in France. While theoretically the authoritarian monarch of imperial Germany, Wilhelm was becoming increasingly irrelevant to the day-to-day workings of the German government and military. However, few of the French public doubted that he was the real mastermind behind a war planned years in advance. Newspaper accounts also tended to portray him as a barbarian chieftain, and the authors of such fare had no difficulty finding numerous quotes from his previous speeches to demonstrate his bloodthirstiness. *La Dépêche* of Toulouse used Wilhelm's past behavior to indict him for present crimes:

Supreme leader of the barbarians, he is the author responsible for all the crimes perpetrated by individuals who no longer have any of the attributes of the soldier except a uniform. What is more, the past speeches of this mystical and grandiloquent emperor, a savage with a spiked helmet, have long familiarized us with his boundless ferocity. Did he not once say, in a moment of sincerity, that "when you make war, you must do it with all necessary means?" Today he passes from words to deeds, and all of the innocent blood already spilled falls on his sinister face. As with Macbeth, the spot will not be rubbed out. There is an eternal stigma on the forehead of this Hohenzollern, and his name, when one now utters it, provokes disgust among all civilized people, and perhaps even among the last cannibals of darkest Africa.[13]

The French government and military authorities, with the assistance of newspaper editors, made skillful use of such propaganda in appealing for sympathy to neutral "civilized" peoples, particularly the United States. However, they were also very well informed about German news reports and propaganda campaigns and worked assiduously to counter them. One focus of their efforts was the Wolff Agency, the Berlin-based press bureau that sent dispatches on the war to newspapers in neutral countries. Time and again during August, the dispatches of the Wolff Agency were held up to ridicule in the columns of French newspapers as "false news": the fortress of Liège had not fallen to the Germans; the French cavalry were in fact pursuing the German cavalry across Belgium; the Germans had not crossed the Belgian frontier into France; the French had not suffered heavy casualties during their advance into Alsace; and so on. It was not until late August that some French journalists began to suspect that the German reports were not all completely fabricated, and that they had to treat their own army's communiqués with a healthy degree of skepticism. However, the French were generally more successful in playing the propaganda game in neutral countries, in spite of the fact that the Germans constructed an elaborate network for the dissemination of favorable propaganda in the United States and elsewhere.[14]

French artists and intellectuals mobilized for war just as other social groups did, and they frequently played a useful role in parrying German propaganda. Prominent figures in literature, the arts, the scientific world, and academia added their voices and pens to the war effort. Many members of the *Académie Française* took part in the propaganda effort, bringing the authority of this symbol of the French intellectual establishment into the fray. These prominent members of the intelligentsia represented every conceivable political line, for the *Union Sacrée* temporarily united many of them (albeit uneasily) just as it did other disparate sectors of French society. The composer Camille Saint-Saëns railed against the influence of Wagner in the French music world, and welcomed back into the patriotic fold those French composers who renounced their former infatuation with the evil genius of Bayreuth. The actress Sarah Bernhardt, asked her opinion on the outbreak of war, proclaimed that it was a war of deliverance that would bring an end to all war:

It's a holy war, the most holy of all wars that men have ever suffered. It's not for a flag that the soldiers are falling, but for all of humanity; it's for the end of all wars, for universal peace.

When I learned that our tricolor was flying on Alsatian soil, my joy and my emotions were so great that I fainted.

Ah! I regret that I am not a man, that I might take part in the great task: to fight against the barbarians who for all too long have been the scourge of the entire world.[15]

Anatole France, the doyen of French letters, became the model of the patriotic *littérateur engagé*, while the radical nationalist from Lorraine, Maurice Barrès, contributed an inexhaustible flow of articles on every conceivable theme of the war to *L'Echo de Paris*. Barrès foresaw a rebirth of vitality in French culture emerging from the war, and encouraged young Frenchmen fighting at the front to surpass their petty prewar dreams and ambitions, just as the eagle soars over the nightingale. The historian Ernest Lavisse, well known to a generation of French school children who had used his textbook of French history, published an article in the *Bulletin des Armées de la République*, reproduced in other papers, in which he envisioned the young soldiers recounting the glorious battles of their youth to their grandchildren from the vantage point of a distant old age. These were just a few of the leading lights in French thought to contribute their talents to the war effort.

French intellectuals and their allies in the press engaged in polemical attacks against Germany, and occasionally crossed swords in a war of words with their German counterparts. In early October, in a bid to gain sympathy for the German cause in neutral nations, a group of 93 leading German scientists, professors, and men of letters released a so-called "Appeal to the Cultured World," often referred to in the French press of the time as the "Manifesto of the German Intellectuals." The French response was predictably savage. German professors were already great figures of fun for French humorists before the war, and they were a favorite target of the immensely popular Alsatian caricaturist Hansi. The familiar image of the heavy, pedantic, bearded German academic was now pressed into service for the attack on the Manifesto. The focus tended to be on ad hominem attacks rather than on the document itself, which most French commentators considered beneath contempt, as the account published in *Le Temps* demonstrates:

In honor of the Kaiser, a bloody fetish, these gentlemen clad with weighty erudition, full of bookish self-importance, puffed up with vain doctrine and ponderously proud of their bombastic titles, invoke their *Wissenschaft* [scientific knowledge] like a kind of savage divinity, with gestures that would be ludicrous if they were not so macabre.

The instinctive reaction of the barbarian caught *in flagrante* is to deny the acts for which he is reproached and which are evident for all to see. The Kaiser, in violating the neutrality of Luxemburg and Belgium in defiance of the treaties that his distinguished chancellor Bethmann-Hollweg considered as "scraps of paper," repudiated his own signature; he violated the formal engagements of his own government. It is a fact known to all—a fact that has scandalized all civilized nations, all human societies where respect for word given is maintained, where the cult of honor survives. Do you know how the representatives of German *Kultur* respond? They deny everything, just as do vulgar delinquents when questioned by judges. "It is not true," they say. *Es ist nicht wahr.*

Now among the authors of this unlikely document, one notices an entire team of history professors! From the manner in which these Teutonic academics relate the events of the present time, one can judge the fashion in which they teach their students the history of past centuries. We should beware of the big books of formidable erudition in which they amass supposed proofs that are impossible to verify.[16]

THE MARNE AND AFTER

At the end of August, the French General Staff found itself on the horns of a peculiar dilemma. The bulk of the German army had advanced through Belgium, pushing units of the Belgian, French, and British armies before it. Five German armies crossed the Franco-Belgian frontier and advanced on Paris like a juggernaut. The main French offensives into Alsace and Lorraine had suffered heavy casualties and were bogged down on the frontier, well to the east of the capital. Worst of all, the General Staff had failed to inform the French public of the reverses suffered in the first weeks of battle. In a misguided attempt to preserve civilian morale, military authorities had concealed the extent of the setbacks the French army had suffered in the first month of the war. However, they were unable to quell the rising uneasiness of press reports that mirrored the uncertainty of army communiqués and the frightening rumors pouring into Paris. The formation of a government of national unity on August 26 brought matters to a head. On the 29th, at the instigation of the new minister of war, Alexandre Millerand, the General Staff revealed offhandedly in a communiqué that the German offensive had been halted on the Somme, a few dozen miles from Paris.

The initial reaction in the French press was one of surprise and consternation, but the panic that the General Staff had feared failed to materialize, at least in the columns of the newspapers. Whatever their private anxieties, many French journalists wrote that it was better to know the truth and face up to it than to proceed with a blind optimism. By way of consolation, there was a great deal of comparison with the situation of France during the dark days of 1870, when Napoleon III had surrendered with one French army at Sedan while another was surrounded at Metz, and Paris came under siege by German forces. In 1914, by contrast, the French and their British allies had withdrawn in good order to the east of Paris, and the capital itself was surrounded by a ring of powerful fortresses that were sure to break any invading force. There was much focus on the vaunted stoic determination of Parisians, though little reporting on the streams of refugees leaving the capital. The decision of the government to move to Bordeaux, announced on September 3, brought home the full seriousness of the situation. Some of the Parisian newspapers chose to follow the government south, but others decided to stay in the capital and follow events. When the German armies turned to the east of Paris to face the combined French and British forces along the banks of the river Marne, it appeared that the decisive battle was at hand.

Even as Paris was threatened by the German advance, the French press continued to place great confidence in France's ally Russia. The alliance with the tsarist empire had presented a number of awkward difficulties for the French republic since the 1890s. Russia was an authoritarian monarchy that oppressed its national and religious minorities and tried to stifle most political dissent. Such policies made even the moderate Left and much of the political center in France uncomfortable with the Russian alliance. Russian industry, while it had recently experienced phenomenal growth, lagged behind that of the other European great powers and depended on French capital for expansion. Russian railways were not up to the enormous tasks of transporting the troops to the front and supplying them with provisions once they got there. The Russian army, though it could draw on an enormous number of peasant soldiers, was poorly trained and woefully underequipped. In spite of this, the Germans feared the potential of a Russian invasion, and France's Russian alliance appeared to be a valuable insurance for victory in the event of war.

The German declaration of war against Russia on August 1 caused a certain degree of consternation in France, where some feared that the French nation would be drawn into a Russo-German conflict that had no bearing on French interests. However, it soon became clear that France was the primary target of German invasion, and the German declaration of war on August 3 removed many doubts about the Russian alliance, at least temporarily. Nevertheless, some uncertainties remained on the propaganda front. It was difficult for France to maintain that it was fighting for the cause of civilization against barbarism when its main ally was the autocratic empire of the tsars. For this reason, the French press greeted with enthusiasm the decrees of the Russian government concerning the postwar establishment of an autonomous Polish state and the liberalization of policies toward the Jews. Even the militant socialist Gustave Hervé could write an article stating that such reforms should allay the fears of those who found an alliance with the "empire of the knout" repugnant.[17] While some journalists may have confided privately that these were cynical attempts to win over public opinion, the response of the French press was apparently positive.

In any event, the invasion of East Prussia in late August by two Russian army corps proved to be to France's benefit, though not quite in the way many had envisioned it. The headlines of French newspapers hailed the progress of their ally's armies even as fears rose of the unclear situation on the western front. It was widely believed that the Germans were fleeing westward across the Vistula, that Königsberg was under siege, and that the Russians were marching on Berlin. *Le Matin*, ever prone to hyperbole, carried a headline on September 5 claiming that the Cossacks were only five days' ride from the German capital. At about the same time, it was reported (correctly, as it turned out) that the German commander von Moltke had detached significant forces from the main German offensive outside embattled Paris to send as reinforcements to the east. However, the finale proved to be anticlimactic for those expecting a decisive Russian triumph. The crushing German victory over the Russians at Tannenberg received scant mention in the French press, which treated it as a localized success having no great long-term consequence.[18] French newspaper accounts now even transformed Russia's inadequate railroad system into a strategic asset, claiming it posed an insuperable obstacle to German invasion. The French press could at least take solace in the much greater successes of the Russian army against the Austrians in Galicia.

Events closer to home attracted much greater attention from the French press. The collision of opposing forces that occurred to the east of Paris from approximately September 6th to the 12th, 1914, is usually misleadingly referred to as the "battle" of the Marne. In reality it was an enormous bloodbath, with small detachments of the hostile armies encountering each other over minuscule pieces of territory and doing their best to exterminate each other. One recruit, writing in the immediate aftermath of the battle, described in unnerving detail the carnage inflicted on the Germans:

There are German bodies, here by the side of the road, there in the ravines and in the fields; blackened and greenish decomposing corpses around which buzz swarms of flies under the September sun; bodies of men who retain their strange poses, knees folded in the air or the arm leaning on the edge of the trench; bodies of horses, even more distressing than the bodies of men, with their entrails spilled out on the ground; bodies that one covers with lime or straw, with earth or sand, and that one burns or buries. A frightful odor, the smell of a slaughterhouse, arises from all this decay. It takes us by the throat, and for four hours it does not leave us. Even as I write these lines, I can still detect its faint traces around me, and it sickens my heart. Vainly the wind blowing in gusts on the plain strives to sweep away all of it; it succeeds in driving off the columns of smoke that rise from all those burning heaps, but it cannot eliminate the smell of death.[19]

The fact that French dead do not appear in this account mitigates its brutal realism, and the author quickly repudiates his momentary feelings of pity for the barbarous foe. While refusing to reveal the full extent of French casualties at the Marne, the army's communiqués reported the general outlines of the "battle" far more fully than previous encounters. A number of images came to be associated with the slaughter in the popular imagination. The proximity of Châlons, the site of a fifth-century battle pitting the Romans and their barbarian allies against the invading armies of Attila the Hun, suggested a useful metaphor for French journalists writing about the present encounter. The use of some Parisian taxis to transport reinforcements from the Paris garrison to the battlefield became an enduring legend and a symbol of French *élan*. Most of all, however, it was the conviction that the Marne represented the decisive battle, on which the outcome of the entire war would hinge, that impressed itself on contemporaries. Accordingly, when the German armies, threatened on their flanks, began to pull back in mid-September, many French observers believed that the war was almost won.[20] However, the pursuing French and British armies soon encountered a series of hastily constructed German field fortifications in the valley of the Aisne. Although few as yet realized it, a long and bloody war of attrition ultimately lasting four years had begun.

In spite of the revelations of initial French defeats in late August, there was continuing uncertainty among French journalists and editors concerning the proper way to address stories that might embarrass French military leaders or even damage the French war effort. By contrast, there was little reluctance in the French press, right from the beginning of the war, to read the worst possible consequences into rumors of difficulties and setbacks suffered by the German army and the often ludicrous reports of disaffection on the German home front. There were numerous stories attesting that German soldiers were short of food and other provisions, low on morale, and more fearful of their officers than of the French. Even more fantastic were the reports on the material conditions and state of morale within Germany, based as they were on the slimmest of evidence, often unconfirmed reports from the foreign press. French journalists wrote of the imminent famine that threatened German cities, the widespread fear of Russian invasion, and the specter of revolution that haunted Berlin. This kind of coverage reached its climax in the immediate aftermath of the Marne, when it was widely believed that the spirit of the German army was broken and that panic was sweeping across Germany at news of the defeat. The French press spent the rest of the war searching vigilantly for signs of Germany's impending collapse. A few enterprising journalists, bearing Swiss passports, were able to travel within Germany itself, and they returned with reports of shortages of food and fuel, as well as unflattering portraits of the enemy.

The first weeks of trench warfare proved to be something of a puzzle to those French reporters who covered the war. The Germans had picked the terrain for the advantages it offered to the defense, and given the relatively short span of time allotted to them, had prepared a formidable line of trenches and dugouts in the valley of the Aisne, now supported by machine-gun nests and artillery. Thick coils of barbed wire were placed in front of the German positions to block attacking forces. It was clear to the most casual observer that the Germans were settling in for the long term. In contrast to the German positions, the French and British lines were initially hastily prepared, temporary affairs. The expectation shared by most French observers was that the German lines would be stormed with little delay and the victorious advance would continue. Most newspaper accounts conceded that successful attacks against the German lines would require heavy casualties. In spite of this, few doubted that the halt was a temporary respite, and that the French and their British allies would soon successfully drive back the German invaders.

Nothing in the education or experience of those who wrote about the war for the French press prepared them for this new style of warfare. At first, many of them considered the trenches to be a cowardly German innovation, and they referred to the Germans as "beasts" or "moles" who burrowed into the earth and refused to show their heads. The *poilus* knew better, and doubtless were as relieved as their adversaries to seek subterranean shelter after the murderous battles in the open fields of August and September. Few journalists were allowed to visit the trenches themselves, and thus they had to rely mostly on secondhand reports. It was difficult to adapt the old ideals of glory and honor in combat into the framework of the new methods of warfare, especially when one might not be able to see the enemy at all for days or even weeks at a time, and death could arrive anonymously in the form of an artillery shell or grenade at any moment. Nevertheless, new conceptions of duty arose in the reporting on the troops in the front lines, those of patience, cheerfulness, endurance, and fortitude in the face of privation, intense physical discomfort, and fear. The belief that a major breakthrough was imminent and that the long wait would soon come to an end persisted in the press long after it had died in the trenches.

MAINTAINING MORALE: THE HOME FRONT

The French General Staff had learned the lesson from August that it was dangerous to withhold too much information on the course of the war from the civilian population. It became somewhat more liberal in offering a broad picture of developments in its communiqués. Nevertheless, much of the press became far more skeptical about the official version of events, and it never again allowed itself to be used to the extent that it had been in August. It was now clear that censorship touched not only on matters of military secrecy, but was also concerned with the maintenance of national morale, and its reach became correspondingly longer. One result of the shift of emphasis was that the Press Bureau of the Ministry of War took a much more active role in censoring articles that it considered too sensitive for publication. In the second half of September, the number of blank spaces indicating articles that had been excised by the censor began to increase, dramatically so in the case of some newspapers. There was bitter resentment at the heavy hand of censorship, and some editors, such as Clemenceau, delighted in confronting the censors in the name of a free exchange of information. (Clemenceau often mailed censored articles directly to his paper's subscribers.) Nevertheless, French authorities maintained tight control over publications, and the French censorship was far more rigorous than that in Britain or even Germany for the duration of the war.[21]

Even as trench warfare was commencing at the firing line, a major scandal concerning the treatment of wounded soldiers threatened to break on the home front. Casualties presented an almost insurmountable problem for those concerned with the official policy of controlling information about the war and putting the best possible face on events. The number of dead and wounded from the early battles was enormous, reaching at least 480,000 by November. The lists of dead published by the newspapers gave some idea of the extent of the carnage to their readers until the government asked editors to stop printing such lists. It proved to be far more difficult to conceal the wounded from the French public. Large trainloads of wounded were transported from the front to various parts of France, while numerous restrictions were placed on contact between civilians and wounded soldiers in the railway stations. Nevertheless, some prefects decided that preventing press access to the wounded entirely would ultimately be counterproductive. Hence interviews of wounded troops by reporters took place from fairly early on, though they were carefully monitored. Reporters rarely mentioned the nature of wounds, and those who were interviewed invariably seemed to be lightly wounded and in high spirits. In reading such accounts, one rarely gets any sense of the horrors the hospital transports almost invariably contained.

The first serious challenges to the government on any issue related to its handling of the war were the investigations launched independently by the socialist Gustave Hervé in *La Guerre Sociale* and by Georges Clemenceau in his paper *L'Homme Libre* of alleged deficiencies in the French army's medical service. It was widely rumored that overcrowded hospital trains faced frequent delays in transporting casualties from the front, and shortages of doctors, nurses, and essential medical supplies aggravated the plight of wounded men in transit for up to several days. (Clemenceau himself saw one of these trains in the station at Bordeaux and was shocked by the neglect he witnessed.) Government authorities found the investigations by Hervé and Clemenceau so threatening that their articles were heavily censored, and *L'Homme Libre* was even closed down completely for an entire week in early October. Clemenceau subsequently changed the name of his paper to *L'Homme Enchaîné* to protest the zealotry of the censors. The French government encouraged a countercampaign of positive propaganda to calm public fears regarding the treatment of wounded troops. The nationalist writer Albert de Mun, writing in *L'Echo de Paris*, described the efficiency and devotion of the medical corps and the courage of the troops under their care. He then excoriated the (unnamed) critics of the measures taken to care for the wounded:

Ah! During these hours spent in this beautiful atmosphere of national sacrifice, how far it is from the shabbiness, shamefulness, and abasement of politics, imagine how one feels coming home when, in the pile of letters that await, one finds some, as I have all too often in the past few days, relating the criminal misdeeds of the artisans of discord. I receive them from all parts of France. I hesitate to speak of them, but I must do it, in the name of the brave men whose hands I shake every day, in order to stigmatize those who dare, at the present time, when the children of the nation joyously shed their blood, trouble their families with their foolishness and slander.[22]

However, the government also felt compelled to undertake a series of measures to make the medical service more efficient. Hence, while most of the articles about the investigations of the medical service failed to see the light of day, they succeeded in prompting action on the part of the authorities to correct the worst abuses.[23]

The war was causing upheavals in French society that were as yet little noted by the French press. There was scant expectation in France at the beginning of the war that French women would be called upon to perform more than their "traditional" roles of keeping the home fires burning, gathering the harvest, caring for families, and perhaps nursing the wounded. The relatively limited expected duration of hostilities initially precluded any notion of a wide-ranging transformation of accepted gender roles. Nevertheless, in spite of the prevailing belief in a short war, the French government recognized that it could no longer take for granted the ability of French families to do without the father's wages in time of war. A regime of "separation allowances" from the French government to those families of mobilized soldiers most in need did a great deal to maintain morale on the home front, even if some objected to women being made, in effect, financially independent of men.[24] Newspaper accounts paid tribute to the patriotism and courage in the face of tribulation of French women, and their ability to maintain farms and households in straitened circumstances. French nurses were the object of special veneration for their efforts to ease the suffering of tens of thousands of wounded. Equally striking, however, were the accounts in which women were portrayed as victims of German atrocities, clearly meant to reinforce the national will to resist German barbarism. That these stories often contained salacious details probably contributed to their fascination for the newspaper-reading public. The transformation of gender roles, particularly among urban working-class women mobilized for work in armaments factories and elsewhere, that was already in progress was little in evidence in the columns of French newspapers during the war's first months.

In spite of all the efforts by French government and military authorities and their associates in press circles to put a rosy glow on reports of the war's progress, it was impossible to quell completely rumors of setbacks; heavy casualties; panicked retreats; and, from the beginning of October, the grinding stalemate of the opposing forces at the front lines. The French government and the General Staff considered pessimism to be the greatest threat to the war effort, and acted vigorously to nip it in the bud whenever it appeared. It was no accident that there were two points in time when articles castigating "pessimists" and spreaders of "false news" were especially likely to appear in French newspapers: in late August prior to the General Staff communiqué apprising the population of the true extent of the German advance, and in November as it became clear that the French and German armies were bogged down in a war of attrition.

On August 21, *La Dépêche* of Toulouse published an account of the military situation that was meant to calm fears caused by the announcement of the Belgian government that it was moving from Brussels to Antwerp. The account reads, in part,

The news that arrived here yesterday of the transfer of the seat of the Belgian government to Antwerp seems to have made an unfavorable impression on some people. What, however, has really changed? Has the situation suddenly become critical because the king of the Belgians and his ministers have left Brussels for a city where they can deliberate at length in greater security? Having considered the situation carefully, we do not think so. The allied troops continue to hold their ground against the Germans. It is true that the latter have crossed the Meuse in considerable numbers. It is also true that it appears they intend to occupy Brussels. But all that does not prove that they have made decisive advances into Belgian territory. On the contrary, the latest dispatches inform us that everywhere the Germans have encountered our troops they have been masterfully checked.[25]

There is no sense here of the reality of the situation on the ground in Belgium: Belgian troops, with their French and British allies, were being pushed back by overwhelming German forces, and the Belgian capital was about to fall to the enemy. During the following week, in spite of the optimistic tone of the communiqués, even more alarming rumors of defeat on *French* soil were reaching Paris. At this point the major papers, particularly those of the Right, saw fit to publish articles calling for silence from the "sowers of terror" and "useless spirits." In a typical editorial, *Le Figaro* issued stern warnings against the announcements of pessimists:

There is a category of individuals against which we must be on our guard nowadays: that of the sowers of terror. These people are certainly driven by the best intentions, but being of a pessimistic nature, and being truly distraught on account of the bad news they may receive, they nevertheless experience a certain sense of pride if they can boast of having been good prophets. Having foreseen every possible misfortune, they are somewhat delighted when one actually occurs....

The carriers of false or exaggerated news aid the enemy's design of intimidation. They should be on their guard: without meaning to do it intentionally, they act as bad Frenchmen or, which is even worse, like the best Germans.

It is our duty to hope, to have confidence, to believe in the success that sooner or later cannot fail to crown the heroic efforts of our armies.

In a time of war, optimism is absolutely necessary. It makes the happy days even more beautiful, and in the days of reverses it is the money saved for a rainy day that brings succor and sometimes salvation.[26]

When the General Staff revealed the true seriousness of the situation in its communiqué of August 29, the attacks on "pessimists" abruptly ceased. A number of those in the press were mortified by the way they had been used by the authorities for purposes of dissimulation, and were accordingly more skeptical toward the army's communiqués in the following months. Nevertheless, with the coming of trench warfare and the realization that no easy end was in sight, some papers warned of a resurgence of negative thinking that could cripple the national defense.[27] In spite of the prognosis of the debilitating effects of negative rumors on the home front, the morale of the civilian sector remained relatively stable until the grueling battles of 1915 brought home to many that the war might last for years. Grim reality had a far more serious effect on French morale than mere rumor did.

If there was one trend in attitudes toward the war other than that of the "pessimists" that the mainstream press and the extreme Right found even more repugnant, it was that of the pacifists. Pacifism was not popular current of opinion in France in the late summer and autumn of 1914. Few public figures would have dared to come out in favor of a peaceful settlement of the conflict at that time even if they favored it. Pacifist sentiment within France was largely confined to the more radical groupings of the socialists and some trade-union circles, but advocates for peace were still isolated at this stage and found little response from the general public. The most visible French critic of the war, and the one who attracted the greatest opprobrium from nationalist critics, was Romain Rolland. Rolland was best known for his epic novel *Jean Christophe*, published before the war, an admiring portrayal of modern German culture, particularly music, and he had numerous friends in Germany. Rolland was in Switzerland at the beginning of hostilities, and undertook volunteer work in Geneva on behalf of prisoners of war.

Rolland had mixed emotions about the war. He was deeply troubled by the German invasion of France, yet he was even more concerned about the threat to European civilization posed by what he considered to be a monstrous civil war. At the end of August, Rolland published an open letter to Gerhard Hauptmann in the *Journal de Genève*, calling on the German playwright to protest against the acts of destruction of the German army in Belgium and France. In mid-September, after the battle of the Marne had seemed to remove the imminent threat of a German victory, Rolland published a longer article in the same journal entitled "Above the Battle." Rolland began by praising the bravery of the men fighting on *all* sides. While he made his belief in Germany's culpability clear, he attacked the statesmen and masters of opinion of all the major European powers, a minority who used the press to serve their own selfish interests and provoked a savage war to establish their domination. Rolland countered French charges of German barbarism with attacks on the Allied use of Cossacks and troops from Africa and Asia, a policy that, in his view, further undermined European civilization. While Rolland called for a peaceful settlement to the conflict, he admitted that he did not expect his voice to be heard.[28]

Initially, this was indeed the case. The *Journal de Genève* did not have a wide circulation in France, and due to the censorship, Rolland's article was not readily available until it was published in book form in 1915. However, this did not prevent Rolland's critics from launching acerbic attacks on his declaration. Few could understand his claim to being "above the battle," decrying Rolland's principled stance as sympathy for Germany. Critics on the right accused him of having been pro-German all along and of choosing a time of great danger to France to reveal his true colors. At the same time, Rolland received little positive response from the Left. Eugène Hollande, writing in *Le Radical*, an organ of the moderate Left, delivered a scathing response to Rolland's declaration:

You wished, so you said, to console the consciences of thousands who are less courageous than you in saying out loud what they think in their hearts. So be it. What do they think in this case, these thousands of consciences, as you would have us believe? That war is an abominable scourge: Does it take so much courage to say it? Does one need your grandiloquence? No, but it takes a peculiar blindness to assert that it is the Allies, not Germany, who "shake the pillars of civilization." And why? Because they call to their aid the troops of their loyal colonies, "skins and souls of all colors," in your own elegant words. Good god, whence did this great disdain come to you, Romain Rolland? I would never have thought that the color of one's skin would trouble you so. We respect these men as the equals of the very best because they possess the most noble of all virtues, Romain Rolland: the courage to die. And as for the result, we see, in what we hope is the near future, the triumph of true civilization over the most abject barbarians, cruel savages wearing the masks of conceited pedants. The instinct of these races of which you speak with such shocking contempt has enlightened them much more effectively, Romain Rolland, than all your muddled reasoning. What is your point?[29]

Rolland's prognosis of an initially scornful reaction to his call for a negotiated settlement proved to be all too accurate. However, support for such a policy increased as the war dragged on relentlessly.

Anticipating victory after the battle of the Marne, French journalists eagerly reported on an additional weapon in France's arsenal. Late August saw the first large-scale arrivals of colonial troops in France. The French had for decades considered the so-called *force noire* as a possible counterweight to Germany's superior population and correspondingly larger pool of available recruits. They accordingly placed great hopes on soldiers from far-flung parts of the French overseas empire, such as Algeria, Senegal, and Vietnam. The initial reports were enthusiastic and sought to encourage the belief that France's confidence in its colonial army was well founded. Seemingly fearless soldiers from the colonies, such as the so-called *turcos* of North Africa and the Senegalese *tirailleurs* (sharpshooters), fought valiantly on the western front, as well as in the campaigns against the German colonies in Africa, most of which were quickly overrun by French and British forces. The British Indian army, often referred to in the French press as the "Hindus," also drew a great deal of curiosity. There was considerable self-flattery concerning the apparent willingness of France's colonial troops to help the *métropole* in its hour of need, and much description of their natural bravery and martial skill. By contrast, there was little reporting on the often appalling conditions aboard the ships that transported recruits from the colonies to France, the inadequate training and equipment provided for colonial troops, and the acute suffering that men accustomed to the tropical or desert climates of their homelands endured in the trenches of northern France with the descent of winter weather. Above all, press accounts tended to emphasize that the soldiers of France's colonies embodied simple virtues of courage, endurance, and loyalty, and that by catering to what many believed were their simple wants and needs, the authorities would assure that they would remain loyal and effective warriors for France.[30] There was even a call for a funding drive to build a mosque in Paris, so that France's Muslim troops might have a place to pray in the capital.[31]

On the surface, admiration for France's colonial troops was boundless, and their many virtues unquestioned. However, one issue the French press was reluctant to engage was that of everyday relations between colonial troops and local populations. One of the most (inadvertently) revealing press accounts skirts the issue almost entirely. The article, published in *Le Petit Parisien*, begins by describing the patriotic efforts of the citizens of Legé, a town in the Vendée. The townspeople banded together, with considerable enthusiasm, to transform an abandoned convent into a fully equipped hospital, and the medical service sent doctors, nurses, and orderlies to staff the new institution. However, when the first trainload of wounded arrives, the inhabitants receive an unexpected surprise:

They arrived on a mild September afternoon, warm with the sun, and the people of Legé will long remember the surprising appearance of the black devils. Imagine, in this peaceful village piously slumbering in the shadows of three churches, the slow march of an African horde. Because it was our Moroccan soldiers who came up from the station, and in such a sublime state of slovenliness! This was hardly like those first wounded who returned smiling from the front as if from a holiday, with flowering dahlias on their coats and miniature flags stuck in their rifles. These ones here, their bronze skin darkened with fatigue, regarded the Legéans with the ferocious and savage looks of men angered to find themselves powerless, taken away from their task and feeling useless.

From this point on, the Legéans, the original focus of the article, disappear entirely from the narrative, and the African soldiers take central stage. The haggard veterans eventually recover from their ordeal, and the narrator presents an idyllic vision of the convalescent warriors:

It's good, in fact. You need only see them now in the refectory or the courtyard of the convent. It has been necessary to double, even triple, the ration of bread given to them, and they gnaw on whatever is given to them with great haste. They cut wood for the cook and rinse out his pots in order to acquire an extra portion in addition to what the regulations provide. The gift of a few cigarettes makes this delightful stay complete, and the convent's orchard suddenly takes on the appearance of a garden in Algiers. The only things missing are the sun and the woody tendrils of the baobab trees. Seated in the Arab manner, they sing, celebrating the glories of Allah in a nasal chant, interminable and of an indescribable melancholy. They play lotto with childish exclamations, or else creep like cats amongst the corn; one can see their khaki jackets ornamented with colonial medals among the high stalks. They arrived worn out, in despair, almost hostile; now they smile at everyone, are confident, considerate with their nurses, offering their seashell bracelets, taking down addresses so that they might send some souvenirs: Prussian helmets, officers' swords, etc. And yet they never forget the little wife they left behind in a bamboo hut in Dakar.

It is difficult to escape the impression that the writer considers these soldiers as little more than cheerful and obedient pets. There is nothing here that might disturb the complacent sensibilities of the French home front. There are no reports of unpleasant encounters between the black troops and the locals. The North Africans and Senegalese, like their French-born counterparts, are separated from their wives and lovers, yet they are apparently asexual beings. The possibility that these troops might be asking for, and even engaging in, sex with the nurses or local women is, of course, a taboo subject.[32] The tense relations that often arose between the French and their colonial troops is as yet nowhere in evidence.[33]

CONCLUSION

Christmas of 1914 found the French and their British and Belgian allies locked in a murderous stalemate against the Germans from the North Sea to the Swiss frontier. The general expectation among the French public was that the offensive would resume as soon as the weather permitted. The troops freezing and dying in the front line saw the situation quite differently, and their commanders were uncertain how to proceed. Though there was little evidence of it in the French press, the army had expended most of its prewar stockpile of ammunition and now faced a severe shortage of shells. The supply of winter clothing for front-line soldiers was grossly inadequate, and many of the *poilus* were sick or suffering from frostbite. Nevertheless, reports from the front spoke of the fortitude and cheerfulness of France's troops as they awaited the order to resume their advance against the enemy.

Under such circumstances, and given the information most French citizens received from their newspapers, victory seemed to be within reach, though perhaps only after a few more months and some disagreeably heavy casualties. The enticing prospect of a successful conclusion to the war ruled out serious consideration of a negotiated peace at this early stage. The propaganda generated by the French press played an important part in hardening French opinion against the option of a peaceful settlement in late 1914. Virtually no one in France envisioned a war lasting over four years and costing millions of casualties. The popular perception of the German as a barbaric looter, rapist, and murderer, and of German *Kultur* as a soulless force bent on European domination, made any talk of negotiation seem frivolous, if not treasonous. The French press cultivated the conviction that German troops, in contrast to the French, were demoralized, hungry, and poorly supplied, while Germany itself faced famine and teetered on the brink of revolution. Little of the disturbing reality of front-line conditions appeared in the columns of French newspapers, and many dissenting voices were effectively silenced, at least temporarily. The General Staff was largely successful in its efforts at controlling the flow of information concerning the war, but now faced the daunting task of delivering the promised victory with the coming of spring.

One of the most striking qualities of the French press in the early months of the war was its apparent uniformity of opinion in the face of the events it described. The mortal danger that threatened France brought about a real, albeit temporary, truce between political parties and factions. Individuals like Clemenceau and Rolland might draw the ire of the mainstream press, but the *Union Sacrée* remained relatively stable into early 1915. Reports of German atrocities horrified both socialists and nationalists, while the destruction of Reims Cathedral outraged Catholics and anticlericals alike. Such a state of affairs could not last. The attempts to break through the German lines in 1915 failed, at the cost of massive casualties, and as the war dragged on, "politics as usual" returned.

Propaganda harmed the French press in the long run, as more and more of its readers came to realize that its version of events was a pale reflection of reality. It was impossible to prevent soldiers from informing their families and friends about the truth of conditions at the front or to halt speculation on matters such as the numbers of casualties or the progress of the war. The credibility of the press among the French public was already plummeting well before the end of the war, and the *poilus* in particular were quick to ridicule its gross inaccuracies and patriotic *bourrage de crâne*. At the same time they faced dissatisfaction from subscribers and a shrinking readership, French newspapers were confronted with continuing pressure from the government and the General Staff in the form of direct censorship and the "suggestion" of self-censorship. Moreover, wartime conditions brought about a shortage of newsprint, and government rationing and selective distribution of this precious commodity proved to be a valuable weapon in bringing newspapers into line. In any event, a number of the smaller French papers succumbed as the result of declining subscriptions and falling profits during the course of the war.

The notion that the press presented a reasonably accurate depiction of events was one of the casualties of the Great War, in France as in many other countries. The betrayal of public trust by the press fed a mounting skepticism and cynicism in France that persisted after the war's end, and fed an increasing demand for entertainment and sensationalism in post-war newspapers. Propaganda poisoned confidence in many venerable French institutions other than the press, including the army and the republican government. Although it is misleading to speak of the years before the war as a time of great public trust in the press, government, and the military in France, the years following the war saw a real decline of public faith in the traditional centers of authority in France and the beginning of a search for alternative foci of loyalty and devotion among broad segments of the population.

Writing in the middle of September, the socialist Gustave Hervé took the unusual step of composing a moving tribute to a fallen German comrade, Leopold Franck, who was killed in action at Lunéville. In paying homage to an old friend, Hervé parted company with the deluge of propaganda appearing in other, more prominent French newspapers. In reflecting on Franck's possible motives for going to war, Hervé considered the role that German propaganda may have played in Franck's decision, but also the nobler convictions of his erstwhile companion in the Socialist International:

Franck responded to the appeal of the German fatherland. Did he believe that it was a victim of aggression on our part? Did he believe the fairy tale about French planes coming to bomb Nuremberg in peacetime? Did he believe the other story about Jaurès being shot in a nationalist, authoritarian uprising that was supposed to have triumphed in Paris? Did his clear understanding allow itself to be convinced by the contemptuous lies of the official German agencies?

Or did he believe, being both a Jew and a German who detested with ferocious hatred Cossack and anti-Semitic Russia, that in allying ourselves with tsarist Russia we were committing a crime against Germany and against civilization?

Or did he simply tell himself that, even with all its faults, his country was his country all the same, and that he owed it his life?

Head of the most moderate, and the most realist, faction of the German Socialist Party, did he understand, with his lucid intelligence, that Social Democracy would be unable to profit from the revolutionary situation created by the war in order to liberate the German people if it did not start out by doing its national duty?

What we can be sure of is that if Franck consented to serve under the kaiser's flag, it was not for love of the kaiser, but for love of the German people, and because such a course seemed to be his overriding duty.

At the end of his eulogy, Hervé offered an optimistic view of future developments, promising that Franck's death will not have been in vain:

My dear Franck, do not believe that our French national passion, which you know so well, has tarnished our hearts with an imbecile hatred against the German people, which has so many solid virtues, in spite of its faults.

When the soldiers of the Republic are in Berlin—because clearly you never doubted our victory—we will remind our government, if they need to be reminded, that we are not making war against the German people, but on the band of Prussian *Junkers* and the Hohenzollerns, whom you detest as least as much as we detest them.[34]

Hervé's tribute was a message of hope and stood out at the time for its assumption of a future reconciliation between France and Germany. However, as the war progressed, Hervé grew increasingly despondent, and gradually became an ardent supporter of *jusqu'au boutisme,* or "seeing things through to the bitter end." Following the war, Hervé moved further and further to the political right, until finally in the 1930s he became a fervent partisan of Marshall Philippe Pétain as a potential savior of a France riven by political discord. Hervé's case is an extreme example of the disillusionment that set in after the war's first months and the long-term results that the cynicism bred by the war and wartime propaganda had for society and politics in France.

SELECTED READINGS FROM THE FRENCH PRESS

The first two selections highlight the notion of French unity and indicate the potential political use that the concept of *Union Sacrée* has for the conservative press. The second article, published two and a half months after the preceding one, has a more menacing tone. It targets those who have criticized the censorship, the preparedness of the medical service, the intelligence agencies, and other branches of the government and the army.

Le Figaro, **August 3, 1914, p. 1**

"The Present Hour" by Alfred Capus

Whatever course events may take from one minute to the next, even if war should suddenly break out, the French will never forget the hours through which they have lived the past two days. Nothing will wipe away the memory. They are unique in our national history, of which they are already a part, whatever might happen.

Unique by the nature and intensity of the enthusiasm, and by all that this enthusiasm has swept away in the obliteration of internal hatreds and divisions. That alone would be enough to distinguish these as being among the greatest days in the moral history of our country.

At this moment, each French citizen is a complete and total representative of the race, with all its instincts, all of its past, and all its hopes. It is impossible to make more patriotic the gestures, shouts, and demonstrations [that we have witnessed]. It is also impossible to enclose more emotion and energy within our hearts without causing them to burst.

It is in such a state that the entire nation marches out to face the aggressor. One cannot imagine better conditions for action, for a fierce devotion to country, for the sacrifice of existence itself.

Yet another feeling enlivens and exalts us, that of fighting not only for our soil, but for civilization itself. We have all come to the same conclusion, we have all seen with a blinding clarity that it is barbarism itself that is coming with the formidable Germanic horde. It is a barbarism that seeks to conquer and stifle Europe, just like the first invasions of the Roman world from the east until the day they were crushed at the Catalaunian Fields [Châlons-sur-Marne]....

And now it is the destiny of France, just as it was for our ancestors, to halt the barbarian hordes. It is a grand honor of which we shall show ourselves worthy. Let us recall that it was in the Gallic fields once before that the abyss opened beneath the feet of the "Scourge of God."

Le Petit Parisien, October 17, 1914, p. 1

"France First" (editorial)

We must return to a subject that is particularly delicate, but which must not be neglected. It is a matter of great interest, of the supreme interest of the country, and thus cannot be disdained or challenged.

When the European crisis broke, France established a truce in its divisions, its political and religious differences. By a free and tacit agreement, it decided to place first that which united its citizens: the defense of the soil; to relegate to the shadows those things which divided them into contending groups: philosophical, social, and other concepts. If those who have the mandate to write or speak on behalf of parties had not themselves renounced controversy, the nation would have been strong enough to force the necessary discretion on them. Each French citizen must focus on the primeval task at end: the driving back of the enemy and the achievement of victory. In order that we should have any discussion in the future, it is necessary first of all that the country be free.

However, in the past two or three weeks, it appears that some have forgotten this indispensable armistice. Here and there polemics arise, which can only be sterile, but more importantly appear dangerous, contrary to the vital interests that we have evoked above. Those who forget the pact must be recalled to respect for duty. No one must be allowed to take advantage of circumstances, to place events at the service of a political concept or party. Further, the party that shall most certainly merit the votes, the respect, and the loyalty of the country will be the one that most loyally sacrifices its own self interest in order to devote itself entirely to the safeguarding of the nation.

The enemy is still too close to us all for us to concern ourselves too long with this delicate and irritating issue. On the battlefields of the Marne, the Aisne, and the Somme, our soldiers have closed ranks as brothers, without asking their neighbors if they voted right, center, or extreme left. All of us who remain in civilian life and wield a pen are, however, soldiers in the same cause. We shall betray this cause if we provoke lamentable controversies and subordinate the national interest to interests of party.

Let us then also close ranks, until the hour when our soil is liberated and German aggression broken, when it will be right to discuss among ourselves the political and social conditions of a victorious and rejuvenated France.

Let us deny the enemy the desired spectacle of divisions renewed before the proper time. And, in order the better to crush him, let us first know how to triumph over ourselves.

The shelling of the Reims Cathedral was ideal material for anti-German propaganda. The following article notes how the Reims atrocity is characteristic of German barbarism.

Le Figaro, September 21, 1914, p. 1

"The Target" (editorial)

The official communique brings us incredible news. It increases our indignation, if that is possible, and at the same time it reinforces our just anger against an enemy who never loses a day in affirming his reputation as a barbarian and a coward.

Thrown back to the north of Reims by the heroic offensive of our troops, pushed back from Paris, which was their objective, and which they believed to have already had in their grasp, defeated on the Marne, hard pressed on the Aisne, the Germans, increasingly seized by rage and spite, resolved to avenge themselves at any price. As they were unable to attack the men who made them pay too dearly for their impudence, they decided to vent their rage on objects, and from the heights of the hills that overlook the capital of Champagne, the generals told their artillerymen: "Target: the cathedral." And all day yesterday the German batteries bombarded the illustrious and venerable towers, which are now no more than a pile of ruins and rubble.

One could not imagine a more horrendous crime, a more abominable act of cowardice. The destruction of Louvain is such a wonderful memory for these vandals that they dreamed of a sequel. They wanted a French Louvain. They wished to inflict on us what they believed to be a tremendous humiliation and what would be a deep and lasting wound. They wanted to crucify our art and our glory, but they forgot that Christ's most brilliant victory was on the summit of Calvary, and that his agony was followed by the resurrection, which was the victory of light over darkness.

It was natural that the thought of this inconceivably heinous crime should come to these people without faith or law, who seem to go to great lengths to demonstrate their ignominy. It was natural that they felt outraged and in some way insulted by this monument, a masterpiece of grace and power whose beauty is so supreme that it belongs not only to all the French, but to all those who are worthy to love and admire it, to the entire world, excepting *them*. It was natural that they wished to annihilate this superb dream in stone that it took men three centuries to realize, and which is a magnificent symbol of faith, of the ideal of beauty, something like the gesture of an entire country toward its god. It was natural that they would seek, through iron and fire, to strike down this nave that cleaves the heavens, these radiant chapels, these stained-glass windows in which the rose and the sun combine their blood and their light. It was natural that they would try to mutilate this gathering of statues and images, angels, martyrs, virgins, confessors.

Their abominable act will be in vain. Our cathedrals were born of miracles. They will be resurrected through miracles, and if the glorious basilica of Reims collapses, it will crush under its mountain of stones, just as did the Archangel Michael, the evil dragon of barbarism.

The next two selections are examples of leading French intellectuals lending their support and talent on behalf of the war. Note the idea that war can lead to a moral and cultural regeneration.

L'Echo de Paris, August 25, 1914, p. 1

"The Eagle Soars over the Nightingale" by Maurice Barrès

France has all of its young men in the armies, the purest and warmest blood of our race. None of us can think of anything other than the danger this treasure faces. But how can we speak of danger, when they wish to see only honor and the joy of combat? We salute our defenders as a collective, and then those we know individually. I think of the young men of my profession, my brothers in spirit, those young writers from whom I receive such noble letters each day. Their images rise up before me, dressed in greatcoats and wearing *képis*. But soon I am distracted by my surroundings, where I am not accustomed to seeing them. Then I imagine myself in a time soon to come, marked by a sublime atmosphere. I can see their glorious return, and already I discern how the rising generation in literature, emerging from the lessons of the war, will witness a new renaissance, their reward for the role they are playing in the great effort.

How beautiful France will be, regenerated after victory! It is a new world that is beginning. All manner of activities will be carried out with greater ardor. Above all, spirit will be expanded, made nobler, elevated. We shall have books that have come out of the gravest human experiences, and poems bursting with the virtues of battle. I foresee a virile high culture, intelligent and clear for all. It will be the end of whining and foolishness, and the young artists who at this minute are gathered amongst the ranks of an exulted nation will face with aplomb the extremes of fear and courage, and will no longer fail to take account of the great interests of the life of peoples or the divinity of the soul.

How can such ordeals not perfect us? How can they not make us more alive? War will call forth that which lies dormant in our deepest being and reveal it to us. From now on each of us understands that he is not by himself a complete and accomplished human being; we are no longer tempted to justify our particular points of view, our whims, our fancies; we bow and we close ranks within a much greater assemblage, the national purpose, the fatherland, all the bitter and sweet laws of life in society. Never have we felt so clearly and urgently as today that we are part of a greater whole. There is not one of us who has not seen his own selfishness, his attachment to his own person, swallowed up in a wave of awe and enthusiasm.

Events pass over us like wind over ears of grain, and full of humility, good will, and piety, we bow down and then stand straight again with the whole field in the face of the storm. But at the same time that each acquires a sense of the whole, a mutual sympathy develops. The esteem of individuals for each other is one of the consequences of war. It is with pleasure that we see a boy who wants to join up, a mother who lets him go, a poor man who does not recriminate, a rich man who joyously discovers that to brave death sharpens the sense of life....

Writers, tear up the unfinished page; poets, abandon your song, even if it should be the middle of a strophe that is the truest reflection of your soul. Bid a quick "Adieu!" to your love of yesterday. Returning from the Rhine, you will fly so high, with wings so strong, that you will surpass all your dreams, just as the eagle soars over the nightingale. Destiny calls us. The teachers have finished with their lessons, and you, with your fortunate hands, shall pick the miraculous fruit, the fruit which grew without our knowledge during the years we believed to be barren.

Le Petit Parisien, September 24, 1914, p. 1

"To Valiant Youth, a Glorious Old Age" by Ernest Lavisse

The *Bulletin des Armées de la République* has just published the following marvelous article by M. Ernest Lavisse:

Dear Children of France,

You will be old one day and, as it is with the old, you will take pleasure in remembering past times.

There will come evenings when your grandchildren, seeing you lost in thought, will say to you, "Tell us a story, grandfather," and you will tell them one.

It will be about some episode of the war, a long march, an alert, an assault with the bayonet, the exploits of a battery of "75's," a swathe of enemy dead on the field or even, in the streets of a town, the closed ranks of corpses remaining standing because there is no room for them to fall; and then the death of comrades, the frightening losses of your company and regiment, your wounds received in Belgium, in Champagne, on the banks of the Rhine, beyond the Rhine; but also the joy of victories...and triumphal entries....

On those evenings, after those children have gone to bed filled with wonder, you will open a drawer in which you have gathered precious objects, a bullet extracted from a wound, a shell fragment, a bandage stained with your blood, a cross of honor, I hope, or a military medal, at any rate a medal of the war of 1914, on the ribbons of which silver fastenings will carry the names of immortal battles.

And however your life will have turned out, happy or unhappy, you will be able to say: "I lived through great days, such as the history of man had never before seen."

And you will have reason to be proud of your youth, because you are sublime young people.

I have read your letters; I have spoken with the wounded. From you, I know what heroism is. I have heard a great deal spoken of it, being a historian by profession, but now I see it, I touch it, and what a beautiful thing is your heroism, embellished with grace, and smiling *à la française.*

Young soldiers, in one month you have fought in more battles than the armies of old fought in years of campaigning.

Young soldiers, if they gave you one stripe per battle, your sleeve would not be long enough to hold them all, because at the end of the war you would have more stripes than years of age.

Young soldiers, you are glorious old warriors!

Oh, thank you, thank you! Thank you for the beautiful end of life that you give to old men who have suffered so much from the abasement of the country for forty-four years.

The next three pieces provide an opportunity to compare France and Germany. The first two selections are typical unflattering characterizations of the Germans, both at home and on the front. It is worth comparing the characterization of German soldiers in the second piece with that of the French in the third reading. The clear superiority of French forces should inspire confidence and allay the fears of the people at home who have no knowledge of what is happening at the front.

Le Matin, **October 26, 1914, p. 1**

"In Wilhelm's Lair" by Max Aghion

Berlin, 15 October—Well, this time, I am in the tiger's lair. I am in the infernal city, in the capital of the emperor who dreams of glory and conquest and who only knows how to harvest the unanimous hatred, loathing, and revulsion of the civilized world!

I arrive in Berlin at eight o'clock in the evening. The streets are poorly lighted, but by contrast the Hotel Bristol, where I am staying, is gleaming with light. This hotel is moreover a masterpiece of poor architectural taste: stucco, marble, bronze, gold, speckled, striped, and grooved wood combine and collide in every room.

The moment I enter into the main lobby, I freeze. There in front of me, settled in a leather armchair, I see a man reading his newspaper whom I saw more than a hundred times in Paris before the war, driving through the park or being the center of attention at the party of the moment. Doubtless he was one of those thousand Germans who infested Paris three months ago and who managed to pass for good "Parizians."

What an encounter! To arrive in an enemy city, to find oneself surrounded by people one hates and despises, amongst a people whose customs, habits, language, physique, and everything else offends and revolts us—and to find there before you one who belongs to that detestable bunch and who, yesterday even, strutted and swaggered about on the boulevards! I felt a strong desire to strangle him right there, behind his newspaper in his leather armchair!

Berlin does not yet seem to have suffered much from the war, though one feels in the streets, in the squares, in the cafés, the gloomy mood that precedes great catastrophes. Berlin tries to laugh, to amuse itself; but a torpor envelops it and grips it. Revenge is there at the gates of the city, and you might say that the great mansions of marble and stone, the immense palaces of stucco and bronze already feel the proximity of the avenging wind that will destroy them.

A big electric taxi—because they are reduced, due to the lack of fuel, to using electric cars—carries me down the immense streets, laid out at right angles, of the

Prussian capital. The shops are almost all open; nevertheless the war has left its imprint here as well. In the brilliantly-lighted stores one finds only pictures of the war and idiotic postcards portraying the glories of Germany in livid colors. There are military supplies; above all, in every conceivable form, there are reproductions of the famous "420" shell. Ah, the barbarians are so proud of their instrument of long-range carnage. Think of it: a gun that kills from a range of fourteen kilometers and that strikes at everyone blindly, including women and children. They display it in every kind of material: chocolate, gold, wood, paper. The shops are full of the image of this monster vomited up by the factories of Krupp.

My car passes in front of the Königlicher Schloss, the palace of the emperor. At the base of the façade are displayed four cannon captured from the Russians. They are four small pieces of polished steel with the two-headed eagles engraved on the barrels. And the crowd of blond oafs passes in front of these meager trophies, happy and reassured.

On Unter den Linden, the principle thoroughfare of Berlin, the crowd is quite dense; people pass by, brush against each other, and continue on in a rush; groups gather and stop near the Hotel Bristol, in front of the *Berliner Zeitung*, which displays the latest news of the war on gray transparencies in it windows. Not far away is the Russian embassy, with its military guard and its triple row of windows with closed shutters.

The Café Bauer, the favorite café of Berliners, is swarming with people. Behind the windows, I see the big red snouts of Teutons seated before enormous mugs of beer.

Further down, my car passes the Brandenburg Gate. And there a wave of intense emotion comes over me while looking at this enormous and banal gateway, in a poor imitation of Greek style. It was through this gate that Napoleon entered into the capital of conquered Prussia in 1806, and it is through there as well that the allies, French, Belgians, Russians, and British, might one day soon enter into Wilhelm's lair.

There are few soldiers in the street; however, in the Tiergarten, I encounter a detachment of recruits. They are all quite young men, still beardless. They wear a variety of contrasting uniforms: some wear the grey uniform, others the dark blue jacket; some wear helmets, while other have the simple cap without a visor. Headed by fifes, drums and even a gleaming drum major, they march stiffly and rigidly, and the street kids follow them, trying to imitate their heavy, puppet-like step.

Apparently everyday life still has not changed very much. The cafés are open until two o'clock in the morning; the theaters give their usual performances and the streets are quite lively. But the economy has received a frightful blow. Gold is now unobtainable in Germany; all gold coins have been requisitioned by the government and whoever has ten- or twenty-mark coins in the bank is required to deliver them to the public treasury, under penalty of imprisonment. One finds only paper money and even notes of one or two marks.

Food can still be had at a reasonable price; but some items of great necessity, like coal, iron, and gasoline, are already almost totally lacking. Today it is still hardly more than an inconvenience for the German people; tomorrow it will be misery, dreadful and irreparable misery!

And as I pass again before the Reichstag, the Kurfürstendamm, and all the other gigantic monuments of poor taste of Berlin, I consider all the horrors and all the cruelties of which these grave, placid, weak-willed, babyish people, who march with a heavy tread on the wide sidewalks, are capable. The same people who cry over the inane sentimentality of Werther or Gretchen kill children, burn villages, and slaughter the innocent, unfortunate populations of the countryside. What more monstrous spirit is there than that of these people who juxtapose the little blue flower with a 420 mm. artillery shell!

Le Petit Journal, **September 25, 1914, p. 1**

"The Moles" by Jean Richepin

"Well, what now?" asked an old worker friend, who remains mischievous despite our age, "What now? They've had enough of pretending to be little birds with their *Taubes*. What they're playing at now, and more to their nature, is being moles (*taupes*).

Yes, that's the word for it, about this battle of the Aisne that is now in its tenth day; we are now fighting against moles.

These gluttonous beasts, who supposed that they would be in Paris in the first days of September, now find themselves opposite the Franco-British forces, dug into trenches, with dugouts, covered passages, fortified points, and parapets; and it is we who are laying siege to this Great Wall of China, where they are delaying for a short while their inevitable flight.

Every besieged fortress, goes an old military adage, is inevitably doomed to be taken, if no help can reach it from outside. And this one is besides a fortress whose front extends for hundreds of kilometers, which has its full complement of garrison troops that cannot be reinforced, which every day will lose platoon after platoon, and eventually the entire mole burrow must collapse entirely or surrender, and the moles within save themselves or perish.

Oh, doubtless it will be long and difficult. The moles are numerous, and these moles have become rabid. Their fury at the thwarting of their vaunted offensive, at having been forced to retreat, drums beating and our bayonets in their kidneys, humiliated by the loss of their standards and the decimation and defeat of the imperial guard, has now transformed them more and more into demented, savage, ferocious beasts.

Before they burrowed into the ground they attempted again to demonstrate to us that they are capable of the most heinous crimes and the most wicked deeds, and having bombarded and set fire to the cathedral of Reims, they would have fired on the Good Lord himself had he appeared before their monstrous mortars. But their final crime, which provoked horror the world over, caused no fear among our soldiers.

They have only become more zealous in their hunt for the evil beasts. Foot by foot for the last ten days, and for as many days as it will take, they are being pushed back into their holes, they will be driven back without mercy, until they are either dislodged or buried forever.

Rabid moles who have gone mad are no more than demented beasts cowering in their burrows. Go to it, our soldiers! Be bold, mole hunters!

Why did they bury themselves in this way, as if they had dug their own graves in advance, these self-proclaimed invincible men, these pretend supermen transformed into moles, why did their commanders, their plans thwarted, inflict on them this fate more pitiful than tragic? They probably do not even know, the imbeciles! We must tell them, so that in their approaching agony they will gnash their teeth as their death rattles sound.

Whether one slaughters them in this manner, in the trenches where they will have their graves, or they are made to come out from time to time in compact masses so that our "75's" can mow them down and our soldiers spear them with forks, it will all be for the gratification of the demented vanity of the degenerate who is their emperor, and to secure the rear (tactically speaking) of the bloody, sadistic, weasel-faced *kronprinz*, even more hideous than his father.

It will be necessary for the kaiser to be able to lie one last time, affirming that the troops have withdrawn from French soil after heroic resistance, so that the Wolff Agency will be able to create another counterfeit victory.

Le Matin, December 10, 1914, p. 1

"A Cry from the Front: Confidence!" (editorial)

Doctors, and common sense, recommend fresh air for convalescents.

I know that no one, either in Paris or in the provinces, has not been touched by this malady known as fear.

But if it should happen that someone contracts this illness, if only in its least malignant form, doubt, then I would recommend, free of charge, a resort where he could definitely recover. This resort, not yet overrun by tourists, or by snobs, has space for quite a few guests: it extends from the north of Belgium to the southernmost point of the Vosges mountains, and it's called the front.

There one encounters death. One never crosses paths there with melancholy—that of doubt least of all.

A visit to the front is the best of restoratives for morale. It is a tonic with a base of iron and powder—and of confidence.

Everything in our lines cries out faith in the final victory—a faith that has nothing of blindness....

It is enough to see and hear.

If you wish to go to the front, you must first cross the lines, and if this passage is relatively easy for someone coming from Paris toward the frontier, duly provided by the authorities with papers that one must constantly have at hand, one has the distinct impression that it would be an insane enterprise for the *boches* coming from the opposite direction.

Our forward trenches are, as you know, directly opposite the German trenches. The proof is that our soldiers sometimes go over to the enemy trenches, where they kill or drive out the occupants and establish themselves; this is what the communiques, in their own language, refer to as "making progress." But, if it enters into the minds of the Germans to do the same to us, it goes quite differently. They have barely sketched their plans for an offensive when, in our trenches, we are prepared to refuse hospitality to the visitors; in front of our trenches, between ours and those of the *boches*, we have observation points. These are shafts dug into the earth, veritable tunnels. A man is posted within; he arrives there by way of a cross trench, specially constructed for the purpose, a traverse trench. There he spies on the Germans, who cannot see him.

That is not all. Between our trenches and theirs, the *boches*, if they decide to come out in order to advance, would be broken on our defensive works: rolls of barbed wire, portable wire entanglements, cut-down trees, mines—have I left out anything? And if, by using a wire cutter, a saw, a hatchet, and a pick, they were able to get past these obstacles, our artillery, posted behind our trenches, hidden under the soil or beneath a haystack, or in a grove of trees, would rain down on them a generous supply of shells.

And if the spectacle of this thorough and terrible defense brings for from you the cry:

"They cannot pass! They shall not pass!"

Officers and soldiers will regard you with a pitying eye and, in spite of their equanimity, will not refrain from saying:

"But of course they won't pass! Didn't you know that already?"

And, from that point on, you will pay no more than the slightest attention to the trenches and the works of the second line, no less formidable. You will be tempted to tell yourself:

"What's the point? They'll never get that far."

And you will be right.

The last two readings provide an unintentional contrast concerning the changing role of women that occurs during the war. The first is undoubtedly written to help quell the concerns about the medical treatment of wounded soldiers. The second returns to the traditional roles of women and depicts French women as bravely waiting at home for their husbands, brothers, and sons to return from the front. The former article is written by a nurse and unintentionally reveals the transformation that is occurring in France (and other warring nations). Rather than staying home and simply waiting for their men to return, women are taking the place of men in the workforce and, in some instances, are in direct danger at the front.

Le Matin, October 4, 1914, p. 1

"How Women See the War: Notes of a Nurse"

It is for you, dear worried women, it is for you, mothers, wives, and sisters of soldiers, it is especially for you that I write today.

I know that you possess tremendous courage, but I can imagine that you cry sometimes, and I do not want my notes, which speak of the wounded and their wounds and suffering, to bring to mind your worst fears.

On the contrary, I wish to tell you: If you have learned, or are learning now, that those who are in your hearts find themselves wounded in a hospital, then you can breathe a sigh of relief.

From the moment when our soldiers arrive in our wards, they recover, believe me, at the rate of a thousand to one.

I saw an infantryman with his stomach pierced by a bullet that remained lodged in the wound. Our chief doctor, not being able to trace the path of the bullet without risk of harming vital organs, ordered his immediate transfer to the xray room and emergency surgery. I learned the following day that the bullet had been extracted from near the liver, and that the patient, recovered from the effects of the chloroform, was sleeping without fever....

I have seen chests torn open, ribs exposed to the light of day, torsos opened up by exploding shells, and so on, but do not tremble, my friends, all that is as nothing once our doctors have done their work.

In my ward, good old ward B, I have seen broken arms and legs, fractured in several places...but have no fear, they will all be repaired, healed, and made good as new by our magnificent technicians, the doctors.

I have seen mangled flesh, wounds the shredded edges of which seemed impossible to put back together...patience, they all close up, scar over, and heal.

I have seen limbs in which the bloody holes have become infected. The characteristic odor of gangrene emanated from those bandages!

Do you think that amputations were the result of this terrible complication? Not at all. It was necessary to make incisions, to clean out the wounds, to drain the blood, to apply a liberal amount of antiseptic, it was necessary, in short, to struggle against the gruesome invader, but it was beaten. And instead of a mutilated invalid, it was a hale, hearty, and whole young man who left our hospital.

I saw one patient with a head wound. A bullet had entered above the temple and traveled downward, lodging in the palate. The bullet was removed, the wound cleansed, and no complication, immediate or in the future, is expected to result.

And so, I tell you again, have confidence! It is impossible that the efforts, the devotion, the scientific training, and the steadfast perseverance of our doctors shall not be rewarded by the complete recovery of those under their care.

So if you receive a little scribbled letter saying: "I am at such and such hospital, lightly wounded," do not cry, my friends, but smile with hope! Even if the "light" wound mentioned should be somewhat serious, have no fear, all will be well.

If that little letter is written by a nurse instead of in his own hand, do not be afraid for him. I myself have written many such letters, dictated by wounded men now completely recovered; keep in mind that they may have a bruised right hand that should not be strained, or perhaps it is carefully wrapped in bandages.

Reply immediately with a nice telegram, quite calm and reassuring, and follow it up with a long and very tender letter, one of those letters that are read and reread, placed under the mattress, and read again.

And when on his rounds the doctors says brightly, "Ah! It seems you are doing much better, my friend," the nurse will reply, "Oh yes, doctor. Besides, he's so happy! He got a letter!"

Le Petit Journal, **October 28, 1914, p. 1**

"The Lamps" by Marcelle Tinayre

The rain falls, fine and cold, from the twilit sky, and the odor of autumn arises from the damp gardens. One would say that all the tumults of the world fade away before reaching this lost corner of the provinces where, in the past year, nothing has changed.

Just as one has seen this little village before, one sees it now. The gas lanterns flicker in the fog. There are few or no passers-by. A church bell sounds, quite slowly, and reverberates from the gray roofs. Behind the closed shutters and the drawn curtains, the first lamps are lit.

Dear veiled lights, delicately enclosed in unknown rooms, what do they say to those who see them from without? At other times, they told of the intimacy of families gathered for the evening meal; the spotless furniture, the glittering tableware, the babies who fall asleep during dessert and that one takes to bed, heads tilted back and hair flowing; and then the evenings of married couples around the fire, the woman with her knitting and the man with his book.

Peace, tenderness, quiet conversations, study, love, venerable and touching secrets of domestic life, security of couples and the little ones in a house that upholds laws and traditions—that is what the lamps lit on an autumn evening not long ago.

But our evenings of October 1914 recall those of last October only in their smells and colors. In the houses of villages like this one, defended by distance from the hazards of war, the lamps that are lighted now no longer speak of peaceful tenderness and repose.

Here, the light illuminates a family table. The mother is seated in her usual place, surrounded by her children. The grandmother is seated across from the grandfather. But where is the father? And where is the eldest son? The table where they are gathered has grown too large. There are one or several empty places.

There are no flowers on the tablecloth. There is no joy in the pensive faces. How the grandmother has aged! Meanwhile the grandfather has found a kind of second youth, especially when he speaks of the "other war," the one that seems so far from us now, receded into the shadows of a vanished century within the depths of history.

The little ones listen without understanding. The boy of thirteen takes in the grandfather's words, asks questions, pores over the map and the newspapers, and discusses matters with the tone and seriousness of a man. His handsome eyes burn with jealous admiration when he utters the name of his older brother. The sisters tremble, and in order not to cry mama tries to smile bravely, which is even more moving than tears.

In another house, the lamp throws light on a young woman who dreams curled up by the fire and discerns some vague premonition amongst the play of sparks. Elsewhere it is an elderly woman, quite poor, who leans her white head on her knotted hands, weary from so much toil. And somewhere else there are two mute old people sitting next to each other, two elderly souls more alone than orphans, already separated from a world in which their vanished children will not carry on their lineage.

What the evening lamp lights most often is an evening of hard work, of women sewing, knitting, and fashioning woolens for their absent loved ones. Sometimes one of these women stops work, and takes on herself the task of re-reading aloud the last letter received, a scrap of paper scribbled in haste with a bad pencil, and warmly optimistic.

Young wives who sleep alone tonight, young mothers who console themselves with the rocking of a cradle, young girls who may not yet be engaged, grey-haired women who rediscover in their tormented souls the old heartbreak of their maternal compassion, French women of every age and class, strong and determined though battered, I think of you who keep watch this evening beneath the lamp.

You do not admit what you are suffering to anyone. Each has their duty. That of men is to fight; that of women is to withstand the ordeal without crying. No one will see you shed tears that call forth the tears of others, troubling weak spirits and spreading the contagion of despair. No one will hear you express concerns that serve to spread panic. You will know how to maintain a serene face and a dignified calm in the face of sadness, which is the supreme and most sanctified modesty. You shall carry out your daily chores, the humble duties ennobled by the circumstances, you shall teach your children, care for the wounded, console your sisters in mourning, and each of your days will be an exercise in charity, patience, and silent courage.

NOTES

1. Jean-Jacques Becker, *1914: Comment les français sont entrés dan la guerre* (Paris: Presses de la Fondation Nationale des Sciences Politiques, 1977).

2. "Dans les gares," *Le Temps*, 3 August 1914, p. 3.

3. Two excellent accounts of the press in France during the First World War are Claude Bellanger et al., *Histoire générale de la presse française*, vol. 3 (Paris: PUF, 1972), 407–45; and Jean-Jacques Becker, *The Great War and the French People* (Providence, R.I.: Berg, 1985), 29–63.

4. Becker, *Great War*, 48–49.

5. Bellanger, *Histoire générale*, 431.

6. See John Horne, "Soldiers, Civilians, and the Warfare of Attrition: Representations of Combat in France, 1914–1918," in *Authority, Identity, and the Social History of the Great War*, ed. Frans Coetzee and Marilyn Shevin-Coetzee (Providence, R.I.: Berghahn Books, 1995), 223–49.

7. See Stéphane Audoin-Rouzeau, *Men at War 1914–1918: National Sentiment and Trench Journalism in France during the First World War* (Providence, R.I.: Berg, 1992), especially 92–109.

8. The origins of the term are disputed, but the most convincing etymology is the following: In 1870, the popular nickname for the Germans was *têtes carrées*, or "square heads." The term *boche* probably derives from *caboche*, a square-headed hobnail used in the making of heavy boots. It thus combines the stereotyped physical appearance of the German soldier with a certain onomatopoetic inelegance. See Wolfgang Leiner, *Das Deutschlandbild in der französischen Literatur* (Darmstadt: Wissenschaftliche Buchgesellschaft, 1989), 183ff.

9. For an excellent account of German atrocities in France and Belgium in the early months of the war and their repercussions, see John Horne and Alan Kramer, *German Atrocities, 1914: A History of Denial* (New Haven, Conn.: Yale University Press, 2001).

10. See Horne and Kramer, *German Atrocities*, 38–42.

11. See "Dans la cathédrale en flammes," *Le Radical*, 24 September 1914, p. 2.

12. See, for example, Georges Clemenceau, "Le temps d'attendre," *L'Homme Enchaîné*, 17 October 1914, p. 1.

13. "La Situation," *La Dépêche*, 21 August 1914, p. 1.

14. See "L'Echec allemand aux Etats-Unis," *Le Radical*, 6 October 1914; "Vaine Propagande," *Le Temps*, 16 October 1914; and "La Propagande allemande," *Le Temps*, 23 October 1914.

15. "Pour la guerre de délivrance: Opinions et impressions," *Le Petit Parisien*, 11 August 1914, p. 1.

16. "Un Document," *Le Temps*, 10 October 1914, p. 1; see also Georges Clemenceau, "A l'Université de Leipzig," *L'Homme Enchaîné*, 10 October 1914; H. Gomot, "Bataille de paroles," *Le Petit Journal*, 19 December 1914.

17. Gustave Hervé, "Vive le Tsar!" *La Guerre Sociale*, 12 September 1914, p. 1.

18. See, for example, "L'engagement de Tannenberg," *Le Temps*, 6 September 1914, which also misidentifies the commander-in-chief of German forces as "General von Heydenbourg." On 16 September *Le Petit Journal* even reported that the Russians were continuing to lay siege to Königsberg.

19. "Dans le charnier," *Le Matin*, 16 September 1914, p. 1.

20. See, for example, the rabid Jean Richepin, "Taiaut! Taiaut!," *Le Petit Journal*, 15 September 1914; and Camille Pelletan, "La Victoire définitive," *Le Radical*, 16 September 1914.

21. Bellanger, *Histoire générale*, 413.

22. Albert de Mun, "L'Union des Ames," *L'Echo de Paris*, 23 September 1914, p. 1.

23. For an account of Clemenceau's role in the scandal *manqué*, see David S. Newhall, *Clemenceau: A Life at War* (Lewiston: Edwin Mellen Press, 1991), 313.

24. See Becker, *Great War*, 17–21.

25. "La Situation," *La Dépêche*, 21 August 1914, p. 1.

26. "Les semeurs de terreur," *Le Figaro*, 27 August 1914, p. 1; see also Georges Lecomte, "Les âmes inutiles," *Le Matin*, 27 August 1914; and "Silence!" *Le Temps*, 28 August 1914, p. 1.

27. See "Les racontars pernicieux," *Le Temps*, 5 November 1914.

28. Rolland's article was published as part of a collection in Paris in 1915. See Romain Rolland, *Au-dessus de la mêlée* (Paris: Librairie Paul Ollendorff, 1915), 21–38; for an English translation, see *Above the Battle*, trans. C. K. Ogden (Chicago: Open Court Publishing, 1916), 37–55.

29. "Lettre ouverte à Romain Rolland," *Le Radical*, 10 December 1914, p. 1. For an account of pacifism in France at the beginning of the war and of Rolland's intervention, see Becker, *Great War*, 85–93. For contemporary responses, see Albert de Mun, "Delenda Carthago," *L'Echo de Paris*, 25 September 1914; and "Anatole France et Romain Rolland," *Le Radical*, 28 October 1914.

30. See "Nos troupes d'Afrique au feu," *L'Echo de Paris*, 28 August 1914; "Les Hindous sont arrivés," *L'Homme Enchaîné*, 9 October 1914 (originally published in *La Dépêche*); "Au camp des Indiens," *Le Petit Parisien*, 12 October 1914; "Les nègres devant la neige," *Le Matin*, 29 November 1914; and "Nos colonies et la guerre," *Le Figaro*, 7 December 1914.

31. "Une Mosquée à Paris," *Le Petit Journal*, 13 December 1914.

32. To be fair, the same was true of native-born French troops. There is no mention in the press of the houses of prostitution maintained by the army in the rest areas behind the front line.

33. "Nos troupes noirs: Dans un hôpital vendéen," *Le Petit Parisien*, 10 November 1914, p. 1.

34. Gustave Hervé, "Sur la mort d'un ami allemand," *La Guerre Sociale*, 13 September 1914, p. 1.

Chapter 3

The Russian Press and the "Internal Peace" at the Beginning of World War I

Eric Lohr

From the *Burgfrieden* in Germany to the *Union Sacrée* in France, the domestic unification of all classes, parties, and citizens behind the common war effort was the most powerful theme in the mainstream press throughout Europe during the early stages of World War I. In Russia, with few exceptions, the major papers likewise extolled the in many ways comparable slogan of the *vnutrennii mir* (internal peace).

Journalists turned to this theme with an edgy sense of urgency because it was even more critical to the war effort in Russia than in most other countries. This is because when World War I struck, Russia was in the throes of several difficult transitions, and the domestic conflicts the *vnutrennii mir* aimed to resolve were sharp and numerous. In politics, the regime was precariously suspended between autocracy and representative government. The tsar, the radical intelligentsia, and the extreme Right all refused—each in their own mutually contradictory ways—to recognize the legitimacy of the new political system. Tensions came not only from the political struggle between autocracy, constitutionalism, and socialism, but also from the wrenching process of rapid economic growth. Massive internal migration and the rapid growth of working classes and cities put strains on rudimentary institutions and limited budgets. A wave of strikes was growing in intensity in the weeks immediately preceding the declaration of war. In the countryside, already beset by overpopulation and the influx of new ideas and expectations, the regime embarked on a major attempt to replace communal land tenure with private individual ownership. This attempt to bring long-term political and social stability by creating a class of independent landowning farmers that had a stake in the existing order had clearly destabilizing short-run effects in the countryside, where the peasants who took part in the reform were deeply resented. Not least, national consciousness was rapidly growing among the various nationalities of the empire, and new iconoclastic trends challenged old orthodoxies within the cultural and intellectual elites.[1] Scholars have long argued whether revolution was inevitable even had World War I not occurred. One need not accept the inevitability argument to accept that Russia had its problems, and that revolution of one sort or another was conceivable even in peacetime.[2] Thus the outbreak of World War I has often been read as a great test. Would society use the war as many had in 1904–5 to press for reform or revolution, or would society come together to support the common war effort?

On the surface, the answer was clear and unequivocal. All newspapers published in Russia during the first months of the war fully supported the government and the common struggle against the external enemy. The sentence from the tsar's declaration of war—"in the terrible hour of trial, all internal differences will be forgotten and the union of tsar and people will be made even stronger, and Russia, rising like a single person, will boldly strike the enemy"[3]—was repeated and celebrated in newspapers of nearly all political persuasions. This moment of unification of the various classes and peoples of the empire, as in other countries, quickly became an idealized symbolic reference point that remained central in public discourse for the rest of the war.[4] This chapter explores the motives, meanings, and strategies behind the facade of the *vnutrennii mir* during the first weeks of the war, the period when the theme was at the height of its power and ubiquity. The historiography has generally been quite skeptical of the depth and staying power of the theme, and it is not a great revelation that this analysis finds many fault lines and conflicts under the umbrella of the *vnutrennii mir*—even in the enthusiastically patriotic first weeks of the war. But what has not been so widely noted is that the end of the *vnutrennii mir* is not simply a story of socialist parties and masses rejecting their temporary support for the regime. The seeds of its dissolution lay also within the ways in which the conservative, liberal, and radical Right press framed their versions of the *vnutrennii mir* from the very period when they declared support for the slogan at the start of the war. Before turning to an analysis of the legal press, the role of state censorship and subsidies in defining the general contours of expression will be explored—both to provide a grounds for comparison to the countries analyzed in other chapters and to determine the degree to which the appearance of unity on the issue of the *vnutrennii mir* was a product of state controls of the press.

THE REGIME AND THE PRESS: CENSORSHIP AND OTHER OFFICIAL INFLUENCES ON THE RANGE OF ALLOWABLE PUBLICATION

No medium was more important in framing, communicating, and reflecting public responses to the war than the newspaper. The mass-circulation press was really coming into its own in Russia in the decades prior to 1914. Although Russia lagged behind much of Europe, the government's relaxation of censorship in the 1860s following the emancipation of the serfs and the rapid spread of literacy throughout the late nineteenth and early twentieth centuries did a great deal to foster the growth of the Russian periodical press. The floodgates really opened in the wake of the 1905 revolution, when the regime was forced to make a series of constitutional concessions, including the abolition of preliminary censorship and the granting of nearly full freedom of the press.

The drama and personal investment of millions of families in the events created overnight a massive increase in the demand for news about the war, and the newspaper was the main source of news. Not only was there a large increase in the number of new publications (in 1914 alone, 431 new newspapers appeared—186 of them specifically devoted to the war),[5] but nearly all papers experienced a large increase in sales and subscriptions.[6] To cover the war, the format of most papers changed dramatically to accommodate the new story. Serialized novels and nonwar reportage were pared down or replaced to make way for more coverage of the war, and many papers became thicker, adding extra pages, special evening editions, and illustrated supplements devoted exclusively to the war. Even illiteracy was not a barrier to the influence of papers; the hunger for news was so sharp during the war that even in villages where only a couple people knew how to read, news would spread through gatherings at the post office where a literate villager would read the paper along with letters from the front to the rest of the peasants.[7]

Even after the reforms of 1905, the government retained quite broadly defined powers to impose fines or even prison sentences upon editors who overstepped certain bounds in their criticisms of the government or tsar. But in practice, publishers found ways to get around the restrictions. One popular ploy was to hire a peasant as the nominal "editor" of the paper with the understanding that his role was only to serve the three-month jail term often meted out to editors as punishment for publishing on the broader topics. Moreover, even though fines could be expensive, publishing companies learned to treat them like any other business expense, incorporating them as a planned expense in their budgets. In short, while the government retained significant nominal control over the press from 1905 to 1914, in practice its influence was actually quite limited.[8]

With the outbreak of war, the regime reasserted a substantial degree of control over the press. On July 20, the tsar issued the "temporary statute on military censorship" with a very broadly defined mandate to ban the publication, distribution, and discussion of any "information capable of harming the military interests of the state."[9] This created a new two-tiered system of military censorship in addition to the regular civilian apparatus. First, it made the military responsible for censorship in all areas of military activity, as well as within a vast area declared under military rule. This latter zone covered nearly half the population of the empire, including the capital, Finland, Poland, the Caucasus, the Baltics, Central Asia, the Far East, and most of what is now Ukraine and Belarus. Second, a special committee for military censorship was created in Petrograd that oversaw the publication of most periodicals with national distribution. This form of censorship ostensibly applied only to specifically military topics with the intent of preventing the enemy from learning about the deployment and conditions of Russian troops. But the military censors often applied broader criteria. For example, the statute on military censorship strictly banned any critical discussion of the Russian army and its actions in the press. In fact, any news that might give the enemy the impression that public opinion in Russia was not united and firmly in support of the war was often struck by the military censors.

Moreover, actual reportage from the front was very strictly limited and controlled. Only 20 war correspondents were accredited to actually go to the front (and half of these were foreign reporters). The war correspondents themselves were most often kept behind the lines, and it was relatively rare for interviews with soldiers or officers from the field to make it into the papers.[10] These structural limitations help to explain why the biggest story of the day was most often treated by the press primarily through vanilla official press releases from army headquarters that avoided mentioning any bad news, details about battles, or any discussion of Russian military strategy. The most colorful news from the front was found in the tabloid press, and it was based more on rumors and adumbration than on real interviews and reports—and even here, the censorship authorities in early August decided to crack down on all reports not based firmly on official army press releases.[11] Predictably, the result was that only dry, vague, and uncritical reports made it to the newsstand.[12] All the restrictions on access and content in reports from the front arguably missed an opportunity for the regime to garner support from the genuine interest in the course of events by the reading public. They also quickly taught the public to trust in rumors more than official reports and the press—a development that came to play a crucial role in the decline of the regime's legitimacy during the war.[13]

While the military imposed an entire new layer of censorship, the primary responsibility for broader forms of censorship continued to reside within the civilian Main Administration for Press Affairs *(Glavnoe upravlenie po delam pechati)*. These censors gained substantial new powers, primarily through the fact that all provinces in the country were declared under a state of "extraordinary safeguard," which gave local officials the power to apply extensive administrative sanctions outside the constraints of the semiconstitutional post-1905 order—including curbs on the press. However, while its powers were ostensibly broad, the Main Administration for Press Affairs was severely understaffed and clearly incapable of meticulously managing the press. In 1914, fewer than 100 censors, with a budget amounting to 0.2 percent of the Ministry of Internal Affairs budget, were supposed to oversee the publication of 32,000 books and pamphlets and 3,111 periodicals in 50 different languages.[14] Furthermore, the Main Administration spent a substantial part of its energies not censoring, but compiling reports on the contents of domestic and foreign periodicals—as a means of gauging the attitudes and concerns of non-Russian groups within the Russian empire, as well as public opinion within the Russian empire both among Russians and non-Russians. These reports, compiled by the Information Bureau *(Osvedomitel'noe biuro)*, provided the basis for summary reports sent to the minister of interior and occasionally to the Council of Ministers or the tsar.[15] Given the personnel and funds available, censorship was clearly a hit-or-miss affair, as the compilers of the Information Bureau reports themselves often noted with exasperation.

While censorship was far from omniscient, it did seriously circumscribe the range of permissible legal publication. Shortly after the war began, the censors shut down about 80 periodicals, concentrating on socialist publications that took an antiwar line and on non-Russian publications, particularly in Ukraine and the Caucasus.[16] Thus, in one fell swoop, the regime eliminated from public discourse most explicit opposition to the theme of patriotic unity. Even from the police point of view, this may have been an unnecessarily drastic policy, because, as it turned out, the socialist parties were far from unanimous on the policy of opposing the war. It is true that prior to the war's outbreak, all the socialist factions spoke strongly in favor of peace and against involvement in an "imperialist war." Moreover, at the crucial meeting of the State Duma days after the declaration of war, the leader of the Social Democrat deputies was the only faction leader to denounce the war and directly challenge the *vnutrennii mir*, claiming that "there could not be a unification with the authorities of the many peoples of Russia, who are subject to violence and live in an atmosphere of repression."[17] However, as in other countries, the major socialist factions quickly split, with majorities in the Menshevik and Social Revolutionary parties supporting a "defensist" position of support for a war without annexations against German and Austrian aggression. Only the Bolshevik faction of the Social Democratic party stood against the war, although some leaders—and more of the rank and file—of even this radical faction supported the war effort as well.[18]

By shutting down an entire range of periodicals, the regime—despite the relatively small amount of resources devoted to censorship—considerably narrowed the range of opinions that reached the newsstand. It also affected content through its relatively new program of providing subsidies. In 1906, after the abolition of preliminary censorship, the Main Administration for Press Affairs started the so-called reptile fund, a secret slush fund to subsidize and support certain private publications. The government expanded this approach shortly after the war began. In 1914 the budget for the fund was roughly 1 million rubles (four times the official budget for censorship organs)—and its budget continued to grow in the following years.[19] It subsidized 54 different periodicals, and gave a major subsidy (50,000 rubles) to the Russian Bureau of Journalists, a press agency that provided daily bulletins and complete stories to the "moderate and right press."[20] On July 13, the tsar approved the proposal of the Ministry of Interior and the Ministry of Agriculture and Land Settlement to create an additional organ, the Committee for the People's Publications, with a mandate to expand the number and quality of publications by government branches and to actively seek the cooperation of private publishing ventures aimed at the audience of the common people—primarily the peasantry. In their report to the tsar, the ministers argued that it was propitious to act, "given the recent upswing in economic activity in the countryside and the surfeit of positively harmful [socialist] publications that were trying to win the loyalty of the peasants—but had not yet succeeded."[21] Soon after the outbreak of the war, the Council of Ministers discussed the new committee and decided to add extra funding and shift its mandate toward encouraging support for the war and providing publications for the lower ranks of the army and navy.[22]

In addition to secretly subsidizing selected private papers, the regime tried to influence popular responses to the war by expanding the range of official publications funded entirely by government and army departments. For example, the Holy Synod widely distributed a new flyer, *Prikhodskii listok* (the *Parish Bulletin*) to instruct priests and Orthodox congregations how to patriotically support the war effort. Official publications of this sort were particularly important for the millions of men who served in the armed forces. The army directly controlled censorship of publications distributed at the front, and for the most part, soldiers had access to only a limited range of newspapers like the propagandistic and moralistic official army paper *Armeiskii vestnik* (the *Army Herald*).

So the state significantly influenced the general contours of discourse in the press by shutting down most of the socialist papers, encouraging "patriotic" periodicals through subsidies and indirect assistance, and finally by publishing and distributing a series of its own new periodicals.

All this should be kept in mind when considering use of the press as a gauge of public responses to the war, and it raises questions about the seemingly universal enthusiasm for the *vnutrennii mir* expressed in the legal press. However, the conclusion of the leading Soviet historian of the press during the war, that "as a result of the various government measures, supported and developed by the journalists themselves, the Russian legal press in the first days of the war was turned into a powerful and sharp weapon of the government," is too strong.[23] Neither funding, personnel, nor mandate made it possible for the censors to control the press that extensively. Moreover, a closer look at expressions of support for the *vnutrennii mir* reveals sharply conflicting interpretations of what it meant to its adherents.

THE CONSERVATIVE PRESS

The most prominent papers on the conservative side of the political spectrum were the papers of the Suvorin publishing empire—*Novoe vremia* and *Vechernee vremia* (the *New Times* and the *Evening Times*). *Novoe vremia* was the most widely read and respected paper among Russian officials, and it has been portrayed at times as a semiofficial paper. However, the paper certainly did not shy away from criticizing the government, often by advocating a more explicitly nationalist line than the government.

This was evident from the Balkan Crisis to the beginning of the war, throughout which both *Novoe vremia* and *Vechernee vremia* pushed the government very hard to take an aggressive position. On the day after the Austrian ultimatum to Serbia, *Novoe vremia* declared that "not a single one of the ten demands is fulfillable," and wrote that the "Austrian ultimatum to Serbia is aimed directly at Russia."[24] In a series of articles, the two papers used inflated rhetoric to claim that to back down would be an utter humiliation and the end of Russia as a great power.[25]

Novoe vremia welcomed the outbreak of war as a chance to unite the populace through patriotism. But it was not the civic liberal form of patriotic mobilization so much as a more ethnoculturally defined form of Russian nationalism. This built on a tradition that the founder and dominant force of the Suvorin empire, Aleksei S. Suvorin, had long seen as his role— "raising and strengthening national consciousness in the Russian people, faith in their own strength and in their great historical vocation."[26] Unlike the liberal press, neither *Novoe vremia* nor *Vechernee vremia* paid much attention to the calling of the Duma for its declaration of support for the war. While both papers supported the post-1905 semiconstitutional order (unlike the Far Right), they stressed not so much the role of the Duma and "society" in the war effort as the ways the war would "force us to feel our moral power and raise the consciousness of our national identity and [of our] great world tasks."[27]

Even before the outbreak of hostilities, *Novoe vremia* began to develop one of the most important themes in the paper during the war years, its campaign for a domestic "war on German and foreign dominance" to accompany the external struggle. The paper became obsessed with this campaign after the war began and printed more than an article per day under its rubric. The paper claimed that Germans and foreigners controlled many of the leading positions in the Russian economy, that German influence in Russian culture was excessive, and especially that immigrant settlers from Germany from the eighteenth century to the late nineteenth century had settled on some of Russia's best farmland and continued to acquire land from Russians at an intolerable rate.[28] The paper called on the government to act decisively to take away the Germans' land (even if they were Russian subjects) and give it to true Russians. More generally, it called on the government to use the war as an opportunity to make the empire more Russian by chasing out the foreigners and Germans from positions of influence.[29] Although *Novoe vremia* much less frequently attacked Jews directly, it was far from sympathetic toward Jews.[30] While it is often considered to be among the closest of all papers to the government and monarchy, the censors should perhaps have paid closer attention. For the nationalist ideas about turning the empire into a more Russian and more national entity can be seen as quite subversive ideas for a vast empire where less than half the population was Russian. In fact, from the very early days of the war, the paper often had quite sharp words of criticism for the government, which it portrayed as lacking a strong nationalist grounding. These conflicts contained early seeds of the idea that became a key driving force toward the February revolution—that the monarchy, the imperial government, and the country were not "national" enough, and in fact, to win the war, a transformation of the state and government would need to take place.[31] Even the conservative papers closest to the government promoted a vision of domestic unification and the *vnutrennii mir* that they thought the government unlikely to embrace.

THE EXTREME RIGHT

On the extreme right, the press took a somewhat surprising stance on questions of war and peace. The extreme Right papers like *Russkoe znamia*, the organ of the proto-fascist Union of Russian People, were extremely nationalistic, but they were not the most aggressive in their editorials on foreign affairs. While all the rest of the press was devoting pages to the Balkan crisis and the Austrian ultimatum, *Russkoe znamia* practically ignored the war. A lead editorial on July 20 explained why, declaring that mass demonstrations—whether organized by socialists against the war or by patriots in favor—were both inappropriate. The paper claimed that foreign policy was for sovereigns and their governments to decide, and popular pressures from "random people in the street," uninformed about the complexities of the situation, could only end up reducing the chances for a diplomatic resolution.[32] In fact, the paper ran a series of editorials on the Balkan situation that were among the most moderate of any paper across the political spectrum. That the most chauvinist and nationalist paper in the country would take such a calm and pacific stance is on the surface puzzling and certainly a sharp contrast to the jingoistic role of the Far Right in other countries in matters of foreign policy.[33]

However, while the prewar discussions of foreign policy in *Russkoe znamia* were relatively few and relatively sober—even compared to the moderate and conservative press—once the war began, the paper turned to a vehement attack on all things German. It supported the war effort, to be sure, but not the *vnutrennii mir.* It continued and even stepped up its bilious attacks on Jews, Poles, foreigners, and socialists after the outbreak of war. The only change was that the paper added Russian Germans to its list of internal enemies and scapegoats for all problems besetting the country.

By allowing *Russkoe znamia* and other papers like it to publish violent tirades against Russian-subject Germans and to continue its similarly virulent attacks on Jews, Poles, foreigners, socialists, and others, the censors were allowing the open expression of what was in many ways a quite subversive message. The articles often took a sharp antigovernmental tone through their constant complaints that the government was not "Russian" enough and was not doing enough to combat Jewish, Polish, German, and foreign influence—and that it was not cracking down hard enough on socialists. The paper's attacks on Poles not only excluded one of the largest minorities in the empire outside the core "Russian" entity at war, but also directly undermined the official diplomatic and strategic decision to try to gain Polish loyalty through the promise of an enlarged Poland with greater autonomy under the tsar.

Although there is little direct evidence, it is likely that the personal support of the tsar had something to do with the relatively lenient stand toward *Russkoe znamia* and the Union of Russian People in general—for *Russkoe znamia*'s position directly undermined a clear policy within the Ministry of Internal Affairs (MVD) to try to maintain the sense of domestic unity that came with the outbreak of the war.[34] Leading officials within the MVD intervened many times during the early stages of the war to try to defuse conflicts between nationalities, and the censors often struck out attacks by one part of the population upon the other.[35] But *Russkoe znamia* continued to push its extreme vision of an ethnically Russian core population fused ever more tightly around the tsar in a common struggle against both the enemy without and the enemy within. As if this were not enough, the paper's attacks on the intelligentsia; the ministries of industry, trade, and finance; as well as upon big business and finance—the kind of "socialism of the far right" that Hans Rogger has noted—allowed a quite revolutionary message to be printed almost without hindrance throughout the course of the war.[36] Even the Petrograd Censorship Committee was somewhat concerned, and noted in its annual report at the end of 1914 that "the paper irreconcilably and passionately attacked its political opponents and minorities, and was very sharp and unrestrained in its critical remarks about the activities of the government."[37] But far from change to a more active policy of restraining the Far Right, the government continued to provide subsidies and fined even the most intensely patriotic of the liberal papers far more often than *Russkoe znamia* and other extreme right-wing papers. The extreme Right gained dramatically in influence when the leader of the Right faction in the Duma, Aleksei Khvostov, was appointed minister of the interior in September 1915 and declared many of its themes to be central to his ministry.

THE LIBERAL PRESS

If the forms of patriotism of both the conservative Suvorin papers and the monarchist extreme right-wing papers showed serious signs of incompatibility with the old regime even in the early stages of the war, then it should not be surprising that the ideas about national unification and support for the government declared by the liberal papers upon closer inspection also appear to have been in sharp conflict with the government—even at the outbreak of the war.

Long before the war began, the major liberal party, the Constitutional Democrats (the Kadet party, after the Russian initials), had played an important role in Russian foreign policy, and an informal split within the party developed primarily over issues of Russian foreign policy. A group of relatively nationalist party members, centered around Peter Struve, the founding father of the liberal movement and the Kadet party, formed a loose group that came to be known as the Right Kadets. Struve led a major critique of the intelligentsia ethos, claiming that Russia needed to develop a stronger sense of national identity based on religion, responsible political realism at home, and support for the idea of Russia as a great power abroad.[38] Using constitutional Britain as his model, Struve argued that Russia could be both democratic and a great power at the same time. His close associate Grigorii Trubetskoi, scion of one of the oldest noble families in Russia and the acting foreign minister in Serbia during the Balkan crisis of 1914, promoted this set of views within the Foreign Ministry.[39] The Right Kadets focused much of their polemics about Russia as a great power on the Balkans, and took a leading role in supporting the ideas of neo-Slavism in the immediate prewar years.[40]

But their views did not prevail in the main liberal paper, *Rech'*, in part because its most influential editor, Pavel Miliukov, was the leading voice of the Left Kadets and held much more pacifistic views. A series of unsigned editorials, clearly written by Miliukov, argued against Russian involvement in the war in the weeks of the Balkan crisis. After the Austrian attack on Serbia, the paper continued to argue that the conflict must be localized and warned of the scale of the catastrophe to come if the conflict could not be contained. *Rech'* was nearly alone among the liberal-to-moderate papers in its initial opposition to Russian involvement in the war. In fact, *Rech'*s stand on the war provided the grist for extensive polemics between papers throughout the period of the Balkan crisis, with *Novoe vremia* and *Vechernee vremia* frequently commenting scathingly on Miliukov's stand, and even the more liberal papers like *Birzhevye vedomosti* criticizing *Rech'* as the lone voice opposed to a firm Russian stand in support of Serbia.[41]

The two largest-circulation papers in the country, *Gazeta kopeika* and *Russkoe slovo*, were liberal papers for the lower classes. Neither usually commented much on foreign affairs in general, and they did not take a great interest in the European events until Austria issued its ultimatum. Both then quickly switched to extensive coverage of the events, and maintained a fairly sober stance, but unmistakably supported the government and the war. While *Gazeta kopeika* focused on preaching against anti-Semitic and national prejudice and in favor of civic virtues of all kinds prior to the war, once hostilities commenced, the paper turned its focus to preaching the virtues of support for the war effort. This built upon and intensified a long-term goal of the editors to try to integrate their working-class readership into national society.[42]

Other papers on the conservative side of the liberal spectrum, like *Golos Moskvy*, which was closely associated with the centrist "Octobrist" party, took a much more openly aggressive tone before the war. Immediately after Austria delivered its ultimatum to Serbia, the paper ran a provocative banner headline, "On the Eve of War," and claimed that the ultimatum was "unacceptable for any sovereign government."[43] The paper went on to put serious pressure on the government to stand in defense of Serbia, calling on Russia to make absolutely clear to Austria that "Russia would in no circumstance remain disinterested if Austria attacked Serbia." The respected moderate-liberal *Birzhevye vedomosti* called on Serbia to think carefully and consider the stakes involved, but also wrote about the great changes in Russian military potential over the previous five years, and declared that "Russia can never, under any circumstances allow pretensions to Serbian territory and independence."[44] While the paper took a generally sober and rational approach to the conflict, it put its hopes in balance-of-power considerations, and promoted the idea that Russia could best avoid a conflict by unequivocally declaring support for Serbia.[45]

On July 20, with the outbreak of war, the authorities ordered *Rech'* and most socialist periodicals to stop publication. However, Miliukov, the

Kadets, and the paper's editorial board made a crucial decision to support the war. The Kadet central committee overcame arguments from a few members on the left that the party should make its support conditional upon concessions from the government. In part, this was a concession to party unity with the Right Kadets, who were much more supportive of the war. In part, it may also have been a tactical decision to regain permission to publish the paper; if so, it was a successful strategy. The government responded by allowing *Rech'* to resume publication after only two days' suspension. In its first issue, the paper declared full and unconditional support for the war and the government—although, as we shall see, liberal support for the government was in fact framed in highly conditional terms. According to his biographer, Miliukov supported the war in part because Russia's allies were democracies that, with victory, could dictate conditions that would prevent future wars.[46] But the main reason the Kadets and other liberals decided to support the war and the government was grounded in their vision of patriotism, a vision that differed sharply from the one promoted by the government.

This was a patriotism that centered not on the union of tsar and people as a union of monarch and subjects, but on the theme that the liberal press had put at the center of its agenda since 1905, namely the promotion of a form of "Russian civil nationalism," based on the idea that Russia was a "political unit awaiting suitable government."[47] All of the liberal papers stressed the calling of the Duma as the crucial symbolic moment when the entire citizenry came together to vote democratically for the war effort. Following the French revolutionary paradigm, liberals conceived of the war as a chance to forge a new citizenry—even a new civic nation.[48]

According to this conception, the historic meeting of the State Duma on July 26 to vote for war credits and to give all the various parties and nationalities of the empire a chance to voice their support for the war became the great foundational moment for the *vnutrennii mir. Rech'* and all the liberal and moderate papers published verbatim accounts of the speeches and declarations of all the various political factions and national groups with representation in the Duma, demonstratively highlighting the fact that all the minorities—Jews, Germans, Latvians, Lithuanians, Tatars, Chuvash, Chermysh, and Poles included—declared their full support for the war. *Rech'* stressed that this was to be a new kind of war, for "never before had Russia waged a war while a representative elected body existed."[49] This was to be a war of the citizens (*grazhdan'e*) of Russia, united with the republican allies of Britain and France against the conservative powers.[50] While *Rech'* and the liberals imposed no formal conditions on their support for the war, the themes they stressed made it clear that they expected the government to move toward greater consolidation of the modern principle of citizenship, toward the formal equation of rights for all citizens. The notion was strongly grounded in the model of the French revolutionary idea of the nation-in-arms, on the idea that Russia would fight best if it was fighting as a newly minted citizenry with something to really fight for.

The liberal papers not only stressed the crucial role the Duma was to play in the coming "people's war" (*narodnaia voina*), but also from the very first weeks highlighted the role society could play in mobilizing for the war. They led the way early on and throughout the war in publicizing efforts of aid associations for victims of war, the efforts of industrialists and worker organizations to cooperate to direct wartime production, and the efforts of local elected bodies to play a major role in organizing the war effort. Liberal journalists stressed how important these initiatives from society were in the great "uplifting of the national spirit" that was central to their notion of how to win a modern war. As an editorial in the Left-liberal *Den'* put it, "All must admit that in Holy Russia a great citizenship has been born. And where there is citizenship, there is a readiness to sacrifice for the general good."[51]

While on the surface the liberal papers declared full and unconditional support for the war, the stress on these themes and on the symbolic meeting of the Duma foreshadowed conflicts to come. Only a year after the war began—after the government had continued to obstruct rather than facilitate society's participation in the mobilization for the war effort; after it made clear that there was to be no new partnership between the Duma and the government; and after the army had pursued policies of mass deportation and repression of Russian citizens of Jewish, German, and other ethnic background in the front zones—the liberals and moderates moved into open opposition, forming the Progressive Bloc. The Progressive Bloc made the liberal interpretation of the *vnutrennii mir* central to its platform and used it as a powerful argument against the old regime.

While it is true that the legal press as a whole supported the war effort, what was important was the *way* in which it supported the war and the *vnutrennii mir*. For the opposition to the regime that emerged in the legal press as the war ground on was not at all rooted in opposition to the war, but rather in sharply opposing worldviews on how to best mobilize society to fight it. *Russkoe znamia* and other right-wing papers' vision of a small Russian core fused around the autocracy found some expression in official policy, but certainly not enough to satisfy these papers or their readers. The papers' attacks upon the government for not being "national" enough undermined the regime's legitimacy in the eyes of its purportedly strongest defenders. From the very first week of the war, but especially by the end of 1916, the most extreme antigovernment statements in all the legal press were to be found in *Russkoe znamia* and other right-wing papers. *Novoe* and *Vechernee vremia*'s more moderate visions nonetheless included some of these themes, and likewise undermined the sense of domestic unity. The tolerance of the government for these papers' attacks on minorities itself became a major issue that pushed the liberals and moderates toward overthrowing the old regime—for it was undermining the domestic unity needed to win the war.[52] When the tsar made clear that he did not intend to move toward the kind of civic nationalism predicated upon the liberal variant of the *vnutrennii mir*, the liberals gathered together with moderates and conservatives to abandon their support for the tsar, and eventually to take power themselves—not to withdraw from the war, but to turn it into a truly national effort.

SELECTED READINGS FROM THE RUSSIAN PRESS

The first reading is representative of the internal tensions Russia faced even before the war began.

Den', July 12/25, 1914, p. 2

Editorial

The general strike, caused by events at the Putilov factory, has taken an extremely sharp and alarming form. The events of the last three days in Petersburg appear to be completely unexpected, not only for the authorities and for the masses, but also for the conscious elements of the worker movement. News has already appeared in the press that factory meetings have accepted resolutions calling on workers to restrain themselves from any excesses. It is obvious that the sharp form of the movement can hardly be attributed to the existing "strike committee," which *Vechernee vremia* wanted arrested. But the matter concerns not only the form [of the strike movement].

For several years already, all openings and outlets for the expression of even the most moderate forms of collective activity have been sealed. From lectures in clubs on the most innocent of topics to legally-allowed economic strikes—all are looked upon as a dangerous source of rebellion. Worker organizations have died by the dozen, the worker press has been subjected to unbelievable repression, and prominent workers, who have influence among their peers, have been expelled from the capital.

Over three years, only one attempt to concede social reforms to the working class has been undertaken—the law on insurance. The law was bad. But its implementation was even worse. An instrument of social peace according to the intent of legislators, in practice it becomes a systematic irritant of the working masses.

The reaction cannot back down. But it did not want to back down from anything. And the feeling has arisen that even the most composed person may lose control. But the working masses, with all the conditions of their economic and political daily life, have not been in a calm and composed condition. The mass hysteria surrounding the poisoning at the *Treugol'nik* (Triangle) factory serves as a warning. But this warning sign did not mean anything to the guardians of peace and order. A dangerous wound in the spirit of the working masses was opened, and they began to treat it...we know how.

The Baku strike with all its deeply disturbing details, could not but cause a response from the worker region [of Petrograd]. It shook not only the foundations of industry, but also the heart of all people with feelings. And it is true, that in various forms, the workers expressed their sympathy and gave their assistance. But declarations banning collections for the strikers were published at that very time in a number of places.

The events at the Putilov factory show that the workers are forbidden not only to give material aid to their comrades, but even moral support. Genuine and undying expressions of feelings of solidarity are forbidden.

The further events are well-known. They took an extremely sharp turn. The situation intensified with the closing of worker newspapers. It is not difficult to understand, that in the days of the extreme agitation of the masses, what is dangerous is neither sharp criticisms, nor passionate articles, but the absence of principles and the absence of the corrective forces of political thought, which, precisely because it is thoughtful, cleanses the movement of the masses from slanderous thoughts, and cleanses the movement of the masses from the murkiness of contemporary passions. In these troubled days, the masses have been deprived of that substitute for a planned and organized character, which the workers' press could have given, and that circumstance wore even harder on the people's movement.

This is how the prevailing chaos was created. At the beginning of the events stand the economic demands of the workers, the urgency of which the most moderate layers of the population recognize, but at the end—an occurrence raising sharp concern.

And this incompatibility of facts cannot be traced to any kind of ill will. It is clear that the country is living in conditions that are taking on a tragic complexion, when it is daily running into insurmountable obstacles. The contradictions between the living interests not only of the working class, but also the entire population of Russia, and the conditions of their satisfaction grow with great speed, penetrating into the consciousness of the broad masses, but the mechanism directing the life of Russia stands still, crushing everything that does not correspond to its structure.

The next reading is a call for unity from the conservative *Novoe vremia* and can be read as an attempt to mask over the tensions highlighted in the previous reading. It is a call to set aside individual interests for the protection of Russia.

Novoe vremia, **July 14/27, 1914, p. 3**

"V groznyi den'" (On the Terrible Day)

The war has created a sharp moral uplift. The peaceful flow of troops passing to the front, the sight of tens of thousands of people, ready to die for their fatherland, the concentrated pressure of popular energies, the enthusiastic cheers of the crowd, the sense of having witnessed historical catastrophes—all this unwillingly forces the mass of the people to live not their personal, but incomparably greater and deeper social lives, awakens in every soul the highest instincts of patriotism and heroic self-sacrifice. The horror of bloodshed, the humane compassion for the countless victims of the international conflict dictates to us a prayer: "Let us survive the ordeal. But the very preparedness to go through it all, if the great bloody ordeal turns out to be unavoidable, forces us to feel our moral strength and to tap the ennobling consciousness of our national character and its great world tasks."

The next article proclaims the glory of an ethnically diverse but spiritually united Russia (a result of successful Russification) and attempts to contrast Russian unity with the sharp ethnic conflict that was occurring within the multiethnic Habsburg Empire.

Novoe vremia, July 18/31, 1914, p. 1

"Edinaia Rossiia" (United Russia)

Amidst the upsurge of patriotism that has seized Russian society, one highly distinctive and significant aspect catches the eye. When along the streets of Petersburg—this rather cosmopolitan city—streams of people flow by singing the national hymn and carrying national flags shaded by national flags, alien voices could be heard here and there, but if a translator was needed at that time, then he would have to convey in our language those same rapturous words, that we heard around us. These were foreign languages, but not foreign hearts: the non-Russian citizens of Russia felt themselves to be Russians. The consciousness of approaching danger united them, firmly welded them to the greater fatherland.

Just as different metals are alloyed in fire under the blows of a heavy hammer, so do diverse ethnic elements, entering into the ranks of a great Empire, meld together on their own precisely in the trying days of great national tests.

Everything that is elevated and morally alive in the soul of those adopted by Russia responds to the misfortunes of their motherland, makes them feel her sorrows and take pride in her glory. In the hearts of millions of people a secret process of cultural-civic russification is invisibly taking place. Morally they are becoming Russians of a different ethnic origin. Remaining distinct, each one of the peoples entering into the Russian family becomes a carrier of Russian culture, involuntarily and unconsciously penetrated by a passionate faith in that light of the world which is hidden in the soul of the people who gave us Pushkin, Dostoevsky, and Tolstoy.

The elements of Russian life and especially our miraculous, inexhaustibly rich language—the living expression of the limitlessly broad Russian spirit—absorbs people with foreign names in the course of a few generations, and sometimes even just a few years, [changing them] into the most fiery Russian patriots. Dal', Gil'ferding, Del'vig, Orest, Miller, Barklai-de-Tolli—and how many other names I could cite!—all will forever remain testaments to such cultural and national transformations. It is remarkable that the souls of the sons of Russia sense and accept these changes in the hearts of the transformed. It would seem that at a moment of external danger an instinctive suspicion and distrustfulness should arise toward any foreign element. But in reality the opposite scenario is observed: in the general outburst of love and concern for Russia, all enmity and alienation fade away. All are bound by one feeling!

In Paris, the Austro-Hungarian embassy was subjected to the insults of the crowd. The French government was forced to apologize to Austria and arrest the perpetrators. [The perpetrators, it turns out] were…*Austrian* subjects, Czechs. We, across our endless motherland, now passionately greet all representatives of the Russian army—our hope and pride. In Austria, regiments of Slavic composition are sent to the border of Italy; Hungarians and Germans are sent to the borders of Russia. Under one and the same uniform can be found both defenders and enemies. We could endlessly cite such parallels, but enough: there suspicion, mistrust, and hidden hostility [prevail], but here we are now one, all of our hearts beat together for Russia and her victory.

A nation, capable of eliciting such transformations, able to bring unity to diversity, having at its disposal a secret gift of spiritual amalgamation and fusion, is indisputably a great, world nation. And proud of our great motherland, which has grown stronger "in the temptations of a long punishment," we calmly stand before the future. We are not afraid of its falling curtain; let the ringing of swords be heard behind it. Above the endless Russian fields the peaceful sound of bells rang out, and the hand of the plowman leaning firmly against his peaceful plow. It is not by our doing that the tocsin of war was sounded; millions of Russian people will merely give a start at it, but will not tremble, and will take up arms just as firmly as they did the plow, and will step out into the bloody fields.

Powerful currents have flown into the sea of the people, but, whatever the names of those currents, they flowed together through a love for Russia, a strong belief in her, great love of God and truth! Yes, [while] the heavy hammer shatters glass, [it also] forges a sword—and as the others became weak, the northern giant grew and gained strength. United, indestructible, tempered by ordeals, Russia rose to look forward, loyal to her friends, terrible to her enemies, intercessor of the weak, defender of truth.

The next three articles reveal to different kinds of support for the tsar and the war. The first article, representing the monarchical extreme Right, supports the tsar and his traditional role as autocrat unconditionally. The second and third articles, representing leftist views, also support the tsar, but suggest that for the war to be successful, more power must be given to the Duma and the people.

Russkoe znamia, July 20/August 2, 1914, p. 1

Lead editorial

It is disgraceful that these gentlemen, these modern Tushintsy,[53] at a time when all of Russia is merging with its unlimited autocratic Tsar, when Russia is living through one of the greatest moments in its history, maybe even at the beginning of a new epoch in the life of humanity, that these "constitutionally" oriented gentlemen cannot find anything better than to declare their "constitutional" nonsense, such shameful utterances as we read today in an article that was plunged in the depths of time from "Russia" and you have touched the surface of the plague-infested puddle of *Golos Rus'*, of Mr. Syromiatnikov. "Russia is not that," with a difficult scratch of his pen, he distantly grumbled, with the much diluted nasty stroke of the pen, "which it was before the Japanese war, and it is obligated to accept a bloody baptism, her citizens should show themselves worthy of those rights (??) which they received and those new rights which give victory not only over the external enemy, but also over internal dissension and differences of opinion.... "

This absurd and empty tirade cannot better show that Mr. Syromiatnikov has no comprehension of the Russian popular soul, Russian mind, or the Russian heart. The Russian people are not thinking about your laws, that is, as you understand laws—the usurpation of the prerogatives of the Highest Authority—nor about your awkward Tauride [parliamentary] talking shop—it's all a horrible Masonic scum on the healthy Russian body. Is all that has passed before your eyes not enough to bring you to your senses? Does that which the people are declaring before all in their demonstrations really mean nothing for you? The Russian, with heart and soul, along with the call to "citizens to show their worthily received rights, would say that in the next, perhaps fatal struggle, the Russian people will show itself fully worthy of its great predecessors, and those great victories, which covered them with glory.

Of course, from the Tushino camp we can expect only Tushino speeches, but in every Russian heart these Tushino speeches will call forth great indignation.

Rech', July 22/August 4, 1914, p. 1

Editorial

The publishers of the closed newspaper *Rech'* consider it their patriotic duty in the difficult moment all Russia is living through to use the printed word to help bring about the unification of all Russian society without regard for [political] orientation, to join in the general feeling of selfless preparation to defend the motherland and protect its honor. [The publishers therefore] turned to His Imperial Majesty the Supreme Commander with a petition to allow the publication of this newspaper to continue.

His Imperial Majesty, in the firm conviction, that all organs of the Russian press without exception will fulfill in these historic days their duty before Sovereign and Russia, granted approval to this petition. (O.B.)

S.-Petersburg, 22 July/4 August

> "In the threatening hour of trial, all internal differences will be forgotten; and the union of Tsar with His people will become still tighter, and Russia, rising like one person, will repulse the audacious attack of the enemy."

These remarkable words of the Royal manifesto precisely point to the fundamental task of the current moment. The pressure of the enemy demands a unified response, and all of us, one way or another, should participate in this general resistance. Not one bit of the popular will should be wasted; all this force, no matter how it is expressed, should be organized and concentrated around the general goal, simple, undeniable, understood by all, and felt by all, as the personal goal of each.

But among the millions of the population there are individuals, by law called to express their thoughts and will. For the first time war finds Russia under the conditions of the existence of a peoples' government. And it is natural that the thoughts of the monarch first of all turned to the legislative institutions, as the closest means to enter into unity with the people. "In view of the trials which fate has placed before our fatherland, wishing to be in full union with the people, We call the State Council and State Duma." So speaks the Royal decree in the name of the tsar to the ruling senate.

Clearly, the legislative institutions gather this time not for legislation and even not for voting necessary credits. Our law arms the government with enough means, to give it the possibility, in the absence of people's representatives, to satisfy all urgent needs through extraordinary measures. The calling of the State Duma has in this way particular moral significance. This significance is fully clear from the words of the Imperial Manifesto: "All internal differences will be forgotten... and Russia, rising like one person, will boldly push back the enemy."

Den', July 23/August 5, 1914, p. 1

Editorial

In certain periods the people are tested in their civic maturity. Russia has just passed precisely this test. Many in number, composed of many different languages, divided into hostile classes, Russia threw to the side its internal conflicts and came together in a great feeling of defense of the motherland. In Russia there are no longer peoples and groups of the population—in this is our strength, and to this the future of Russia is indebted.

It had long been acceptable to accuse all these peoples and all these groups of the population of a lack of love for Russia, to accuse them of everything up to treason to the motherland, but in the fateful moment they turned out to be the model of great love toward their rising nation, and [they turned out] to be prepared to accept any sacrifice for the glory of their country.... All turned out to be serious citizens, full of concern for the fate of the motherland.

Nevertheless, there are those who start from the presumption of the irrationality of those who live in Russia and from a suspicion of minority sons of the fatherland, those who for a long time have opposed our embarking on a new path, the path of deep and free reform. This is why they struggled against the very existence of the State Duma, and this is why as a result of this struggle the development of Russia has gone at a slow pace.

Maybe, with the existence of legislative institutions among us for the first time, the government will today go to the State Duma to get support for the war from a peoples' government (*narodnoe pravitel'stvo*). For the first time "they" will not put themselves in opposition to "us." Since now "they" and "we" are not enemies. In the situation where "we" and "they" are not enemies, Russia can and should live on. The danger has been revealed as a mistake, as the conceptions of the "undeveloped" sense of citizenship and about the "ill-intentioned" minorities. Russia passed the exam wonderfully. It is united. And, united in thoughts and feelings, it waits for today['s meeting of the Duma] with concern and seriousness. It expects from the government a firm declaration that the sun will rise on a new free life in our motherland.

NOTES

All dates and periodical references are given first according to both the Julian calendar, then the Gregorian. The Julian calendar was used in Russia at the time and was 13 days behind the Gregorian calendar.

1. Among many studies of the tensions of the prewar period, see Joan Neuberger, *Hooliganism: Crime, Culture, and Power in St. Petersburg, 1900–1914* (Berke-

ley: University of California Press, 1993); Barbara A. Anderson, *Internal Migration during Modernization in Late Nineteenth-Century Russia* (Princeton, N.J.: Princeton University Press, 1980); W. Bruce Lincoln, *In War's Dark Shadow: The Russians before the Great War* (New York: Dial Press, 1983); Judith Pallot, *Land Reform in Russia, 1906–1917: Peasant Responses to Stolypin's Project of Rural Transformation* (Oxford: Clarendon Press, 1999); Geoffrey Hosking, *The Russian Constitutional Experiment: Government and Duma, 1907–1914* (Cambridge: Cambridge University Press, 1973); Christopher Read, *Culture and Power in Revolutionary Russia: The Intelligentsia and the Transition from Tsarism to Communism* (Houndmills, Basingstoke, and Hampshire, England: Macmillan, 1990).

2. For the most influential elaboration of this argument, see Leopold Haimson, "The Problem of Social Stability in Urban Russia, 1905–1917," *Slavic Review* 23:4 (1964), pp. 619–642; 24:1 (1965), pp. 1–22.

3. Quoted in *Rech'*, 22 July/4 August 1914, p. 1.

4. On the symbol of domestic unity in 1914, see Jeffrey Verhey, *The Spirit of 1914: Militarism, Myth, and Mobilization in Germany* (Cambridge: Cambridge University Press, 2000); Robert Wohl, *The Generation of 1914* (Cambridge: Harvard University Press, 1979); Martha Hanna, *The Mobilization of Intellect: French Scholars and Writers during the Great War* (Cambridge: Harvard University Press, 1996).

5. Benjamin Rigberg, "The Efficacy of Tsarist Censorship Operations, 1894–1917," *Jahrbücher für Geschichte Osteuropas* 14:3 (1966): 335; B. I. Esen, *Iz istorii russkoi zhurnalistiki nachala xx veka* (Moscow: Izd. Moskovskogo universiteta, 1984), 12.

6. The only major exception was *Novoe vremia*, but its fall in circulation was likely due to the difficult transition within the A. S. Suvorin publishing empire after the death of the senior Suvorin and the breakup of the company into several parts headed by his "less talented sons." Louise McReynolds, *The News under Russia's Old Regime* (Princeton: Princeton University Press, 1991), 257; Nikolai Vasil'evich Snessarev, *Mirazh Novogo vremeni: pochti roman* (St. Petersburg: Tip. M. Pivovarskogo i A. Tipografa, 1914), 134. *Novoe vremia's* street sales fell from 4.6 million in 1912 to 3.9 million in 1914. But the war eventually helped the paper achieve a remarkable comeback and expansion, recording sales of 6.2 million in 1915. McReynolds, News, table 5, p. 296.

7. N. I. Ulianov, "Pochtovyi den' v sele (Vesti s voiny)," *Istoricheskii vestnik* (1916), 456–57.

8. For an excellent overview of the role of the press, focusing on the liberal papers, see McReynolds, *News*; Jacob Walkin, "Government Controls over the Press in Russia, 1905–1914," *Russian Review* 13:3 (July 1954): 203–9.

9. Rossiiskii gosudarstvennyi istoricheskii arkhiv [Russian state historical archive] (hereafter RGIA), f. 778, op. 1, d. 1; see also T. S. Ilarionova et al., eds., *Vlast' i pressa: K istorii pravovogo regulirovaniia i otnoshenii, 1700–1917* (Moscow: Izd. RAGS, 1999), 204–10; *Pravo*, nos. 30, 32, 44, 45 (1914); O. I. Averbakh, *Zakonodatel'nye akty, vyzvannye voinoiu 1914 goda* (Vilna: 1915), 17–39.

10. A. F. Berezhnoi, *Russkaia legal'naia pechat' v gody pervoi mirovoi voiny* (Leningrad: Izd. Leningradskogo universiteta, 1975), 18.

11. RGIA, f. 778, op. 1, d. 2, l. 9.

12. RGIA, f. 778, op. 2, d. 4.

13. Orlando Figes and Boris Kolnitskii, *Interpreting the Russian Revolution: The Language and Symbols of 1917* (New Haven, Conn., and London: Yale University Press, 1999).

14. Rigberg, "Efficacy," 341.

15. RGIA, f. 776, op. 32, razdel 2, d. 118–120.

16. Berezhnoi, *Russkaia legal'naia pechat'*, 25.

17. "Declaration of the Social-Democrat Deputies of the IV State Duma in Connection with the Beginning of the War, 26 July 1914," in *Men'sheviki: Dokumenty i materialy, 1903—fevral' 1917 gg.* (Moscow: Rosspen, 1996), 350–51. See also *Rech'*, 27 July/9 August 1914, editorial, p. 1.

18. There was also an active but small antiwar group within the Socialist Revolutionary party. For an overview of antiwar political groupings, see Michael Melancon, *The Socialist Revolutionaries and the Russian Anti-War Movement, 1914–1917* (Columbus: Ohio State University Press, 1990).

19. Funding for the reptile fund increased to 1.6 million rubles in 1916. Berezhnoi, *Russkaia legal'naia pechat'*, 25.

20. Iv. Tobolin, "Reptil'nyi fond 1914–1916 g.g.," *Krasnyi arkhiv* 105 (1941): 332–38.

21. RGIA, f. 776, op. 1, d. 44, ll. 39–39ob.

22. Ibid., ll. 40–40ob.

23. Berezhnoi, *Russkaia legal'naia pechat'*, 30.

24. Lead editorial, *Novoe vremia*, 12 July/25 July 1914, p. 1.

25. *Vechernee vremia*, 17 July/30 July 1914.

26. Effie Ambler, *Russian Journalism and Politics, 1861–1881; the career of Aleksei S. Suvorin* (Detroit, Wayne State University Press, 1972), p. 175.

27. *Novoe vremia*, 14 July/27 July 1914, p. 3.

28. For a book based on a collection of articles by the leading *Novoe vremia* journalist on this topic, see A. Rennikov, *Zoloto Reina: O nemtsakh v Rossii* (Petrograd: A. S. Suvorin–*Novoe vremia*," 1915).

29. For more on this campaign, see Eric Lohr, "Enemy Alien Politics within the Russian Empire during World War I" (Ph.D, diss., Harvard University, 1999), especially 23–59.

30. The anti-Jewish leanings of the paper were most clearly expressed during the Beilis case in the years prior to the war. Even in the weeks before the war, after the travesty of the case against Beilis had long been revealed, the paper continued to polemicize with his defenders in the liberal press, and the paper was not above such practices as referring to the liberal daily *Rech'* as a "Kadet-Jewish paper" because one of the editors was Jewish. *Novoe vremia*, 1 July/14 July 1914, p. 3; editorial, *Novoe vremia*, 13 July/26 July 1914.

31. The 1914 annual report of the Petrograd censorship committee reflected no awareness of this potential problem, describing *Novoe vremia* in straightforward terms as "one of the most serious and important papers in the Russian Empire with wide circulation. Sympathetic to the national party and its ideas.... The clearly nationalist orientation of the paper was expressed with particular strength with the declaration of war. *Novoe vremia* undertook a systematic trampling of everything German and raises Russian consciousness in a wide public." RGIA, f. 776, op. 10, d. 1915, l. 167.

32. Lead editorial, *Russkoe znamia*, 20 July/2 August 1914, p. 1.

33. On the pressures from the extreme Right in Germany, see Roger Chickering, *We Men Who Feel Most German* (London and Boston: Allen & Unwin, 1984). It had always been difficult for the Russian right wing to accept alliance with the constitutional republics of Britain and France; the conservative German and Austrian monarchies were ideologically more compatible. D.C.B. Lieven, "Pro-Germans and Russian Foreign Policy, 1890–1914," *International History Review* 2 (1980): 34–54.

34. The tsar sent messages of thanks to branches of the Union of Russian People for telegrams of support that he received from them in the first weeks of the war, and was known to support the organization from its earliest days. RGIA, f. 1284, op. 3, d. 707.

35. Gosudarstvennyi arkhiv Rossiiskoi Federatsii [State archive of the Russian Federation] (hereafter GARF), f. 215, op. 1, d. 174, l. 28. This important circular stated, "In the general rise of healthy popular sentiments, we need to seek the forces to maintain state order and peace in the empire. We need to preserve this unification of all the population in a common patriotic attitude, and not distance the population from the authorities."

36. Hans Rogger, *Jewish Policies and Right Wing Politics in Imperial Russia* (Berkeley and Los Angeles: University of California Press, 1986), 218.

37. RGIA, f. 776, op. 10, d. 1915, l. 167.

38. The centerpiece of the critique and a major intellectual controversy over it was based a collection of articles by many of the leading Russian intellectuals: *Vekhi Landmarks: A Collection of Articles about the Russian Intelligentsia*, trans. Marshall S. Shatz and Judith E. Zimmerman (Armonk, N.Y.: M.E. Sharpe, 1994); Christopher Read, *Religion, Revolution, and the Russian Intelligentsia, 1900–1912: The Vekhi Debate and Its Intellectual Background* (London: Macmillan, 1979).

39. Dominic Lieven, *Russia and the Origins of the First World War* (New York: St. Martin's Press, 1983).

40. Alfred Fischel, *Der Panslawismus bis zum Weltkrieg. Ein geschichtlicher Überblick* (Stuttgart und Berlin: Cotta, 1919).

41. *Vechernee vremia*, 17 July/30 July 1914.

42. McReynolds, *News*, 230.

43. "On the Eve of War," *Golos Moskvy*, 12 July/25 July 1914.

44. *Birzhevye vedomosti*, 12 July/25 July 1914, p. 1.

45. *Birzhevye vedomosti*, 13 July/26 July 1914, p. 2.

46. Melissa Stockdale, *Paul Miliukov and the Quest for a Liberal Russia, 1880–1918* (Ithaca, N.Y.: Cornell University Press, 1996), 218.

47. McReynolds, *News*, 243.

48. For an elaboration of the argument that a new "nation"—or at least a new national discourse—did suddenly coalesce with the mobilization of 1914, see Josh Sanborn, "The Mobilization of 1914 and the Question of the Russian Nation: A Reexamination," *Slavic Review* 59:2 (summer 2000): 267–89; and his "Military Reform, Moral Reform, and the End of the Old Regime," in *Military and Society in Russian History, 1450–1917*, ed. Marshall Poe and Eric Lohr (Leiden, the Netherlands: Brill, 2002), 507–24.

49. Lead editorial, *Rech'*, 22 July/4 August 1914, p. 1.

50. The liberals not only stressed the importance of the fact that Russia was allied with the most democratic countries as a means to support the war, but also

as a means to argue that this was the direction Russia had to move if it were to win. Many stories praised the virtues of the involvement of parliament and society in the mobilization of French and British society. The liberal papers also loved remind their readers that many on the right side of the political spectrum had favored alliance with Austria and Germany—right up to the eve of the war— because of their directly opposite ideological preferences. The none-too-subtle implication was that the liberals were more patriotic, more in tune with the national interests of the country, than the Right.

51. Editorial, *Den'*, 6 August/19 August 1914, p. 1.

52. This polemic took explicit form in the editorials of *Den'* already in the first two months of the war.

53. *Tushino* refers to the infamous camp outside Moscow where a pretender, then a Polish candidate to the Russian throne, set up court (1608–12) during the chaos and war of the Time of Troubles. Later Russian historiography excoriated those from the Muscovite elite who serve these courts as traitors to Russia.

Chapter 4

German Propaganda: The Limits of *Gerechtigkeit*

Troy R. E. Paddock

Did we have anything you could call propaganda?
I regret that I must answer in the negative. Everything was so inadequate and wrong from the very start that it certainly did no good and sometimes did actual harm.

The form was inadequate, the substance was psychologically wrong: a careful examination of German war propaganda can lead to no other diagnosis. The receptivity of the great masses is very limited, their intelligence is small, but their power of forgetting is enormous. In consequence of these facts, all effective propaganda must be limited to a very few points and must harp on these in slogans until the last member of the public understands your slogan. As soon as you sacrifice this slogan and try to be many-sided, the effect will piddle away, for the crowd can neither digest nor retain the material offered.
Adolf Hitler, *Mein Kampf*

Adolf Hitler was not the first to comment on the effect of propaganda in World War I. Numerous monographs in the 1920s were dedicated to the effect of war atrocity stories. Nevertheless, Hitler was one of the first to make an effort to understand the psychology behind propaganda in an attempt to determine what kind of propaganda was effective and what was not. In his judgment, the propaganda of Germany's enemies, especially England, was vastly superior to German efforts during the war. British propaganda was unequivocal in its position: England was good, Germany was evil. For Hitler, the superiority of British propaganda (or the failure of German propaganda) was the main cause for Germany's demise.[1] German propaganda consciously appeared to eschew this kind of approach as simplistic and disingenuous. This chapter will examine how German newspapers discussed the origins and first few months of the war: who was at fault for causing the war, how the war was conducted, and why Germany was involved in the war. Such an examination reveals a dynamic that has been overlooked to this point. In the beginning, Russia, not Great Britain, was viewed as the cause of the war and as the greatest threat to Germany. The shift of emphasis to Britain occurred in late September. By mid-October, there are clear attempts to influence newspapers and public opinion before the creation of a government office to coordinate such efforts. The examination also reveals that in spite of the unity of cause that surrounded the so-called *Burgfrieden*,[2] the criticisms of Russia and Great Britain betray the domestic concerns and aspirations behind disparate political agendas.

During the month of July 1914, the German political press did its part to keep the international situation in the forefront of its pages and its readers' minds. As one historian has noted, "The initial mobilization of opinion came spontaneously in August 1914, and it required neither official encouragement nor compulsion."[3] From the radical Left to the conservative Right, newspapers used editorials and reports to make their positions unequivocal. This chapter will look at 10 newspapers that span the political and geographical spectrum of imperial Germany:[4] *Norddeutsche Allgemeine Zeitung, Kölnische Zeitung, Kreuzzeitung, Münchner Neueste Nachrichten, Kölnische Volkszeitung, Frankfurter Zeitung, Berliner Tageblatt, Vossische Zeitung, Vorwärts,* and *Leipziger Volkszeitung.*

The first three papers listed had various connections to the German government. Coming out of Berlin, *Norddeutsche Allgemeine Zeitung* was considered to be the mouthpiece for the German government for domestic affairs. Other newspapers acknowledged this relationship by noting some articles picked up from *Norddeutsche* with the word "official" (*amtlich*) in parentheses. *Kölnische Zeitung* had been recognized as the government organ for foreign affairs until March 1914, when an article entitled "Russia and Germany" claimed Russia was preparing for a war against Germany.[5] The article caused such a stir that the government severed its official relationship with the paper. Nevertheless, *Kölnische Zeitung* remained an important commentator on foreign affairs. *Neue Preussische Zeitung,* universally referred to as the *Kreuzzeitung* because of the Iron Cross that adorned its banner, was considered both inside and outside of Germany to have semiofficial status. Founded in response to the 1848 revolution, *Kreuzzeitung* represented the interests of the conservative German nobility (*Junkers*). The fact that the *Junkers* wielded much of the authority within the German government led many to believe that *Kreuzzeitung* represented the real views of the government.[6]

The socialist perspective, often the antithesis to the government's point of view, could be found in *Vorwärts* and *Leipziger Volkszeitung. Vorwärts* was the official organ of Germany's Socialist Party (Sozialdemokratische Partei Deutschland, or SPD).[7] *Leipziger Volkszeitung*, which proudly displayed across its banner, "Organ for the interests of all working people," represented the views of the left wing of the SPD.

Various liberal perspectives were also well represented. While nominally independent, *Vossische Zeitung* usually mirrored the position of the German Progressive Party (Deutsche Fortschrittspartei).[8] *Frankfurter Zeitung* followed the line of the German People's Party (Deutsche Volkspartei, or DVP).[9] *Berliner Tageblatt* did not follow any particular liberal perspective. It had supported Bismarck's foreign policy of maintaining the balance of power, but had condemned Kaiser Wilhelm II's "New Course."[10]

Catholic concerns were represented by *Kölnische Volkszeitung* and *Münchner Neueste Nachrichten*. *Kölnische Volkszeitung* came out of Bismarck's *Kulturkampf* as the leading voice of the Center Party, supplanting *Germania*.[11] The national-liberal *Münchner Neueste Nachrichten* was the leading Bavarian daily paper.[12] These 10 papers provide a good cross section of German political discourse in the weeks before and during the first months of World War I.

NEWSPAPERS AND CENSORSHIP

Before the outbreak of hostilities, the German press agreed that Germany was facing a world-historical moment.[13] On July 31, 1914, Wilhelm II declared a "state of war" (*Kriegszustand*) within the Reich. According to the "Gesetz über den Belagerungszustand vom 4. Juni 1851" ("Law on the State of Siege from June 4, 1851"), the government had the right to censor the press if it was in the interest of public security.[14] At this time, the government released a catalog containing 26 points relating what the press could not print about the impending war effort. The 26 points contained no surprises. The press was not permitted to reveal the location or strength of troops, nor could troop movements or logistical details (e.g., the condition of harbors and railroads or ammunition supplies) be printed. Reports of damage to naval vessels and their repairs as well as letters from the front had to be cleared through military channels.[15] Military leaders felt that it was necessary to have a close relationship between the military authorities and the press. Major Walter Nicolai, the *Chef der Nachrichtenabteilung (III B)* [Head of the News Department] and the man theoretically responsible for the press policy of the military, was reported to have said that the press was an "indispensable means in warfare."[16] The press was the one instrument that could clarify and transmit the message of the war to the German people.[17] However, the relationship between the press and the military was not that simple. Nicolai's was just one of several departments involved in press policy. The Secretary of the Imperial Navy, Admiral Alfred von Tirpitz, erected his own press bureau for the Imperial Navy. The Foreign Policy Office had its own Press Department headed up by Otto Hammann. There was also a "Literarischen Büro" for the Prussian Ministry of the Interior as well as a press department in the Imperial Post Office under Secretary Stephan.[18] Germany did not have a united propaganda office until August 1916.[19] The absence of a central federal office to coordinate official policy toward the press and the war left the press with a fair amount of leeway in what it could print.

Military officials met with representatives of the major papers in Berlin on August 3, 1914 and informed them of the plans of the General Staff. The principle laid down by the military was "We will not always be able to say everything, but what we will say is true."[20] Nicolai may have recognized that the press was an asset in conducting the war, but the above statement disclosed the government's, especially the military's, attitude toward the press. The military expected the full cooperation of the press in the reporting on the war. This included not only not printing sensitive military information, but also refraining from any criticism of the conduct of the war.[21] The military's distrust of the press was understandable considering the numerous attacks it had received in liberal and socialist newspapers before the war. At the same time, the military's high-handed treatment of the press confirmed the latter's suspicion that the military wanted the press to simply rubber-stamp the former's views and actions. As a result, the German press and the German government were never able to establish a positive cooperative effort such as occurred in Great Britain, where publishers of leading papers were involved with government officials in the planning of propaganda.[22] English propaganda was so successful that Nicolai claimed it strove not just for a military victory, but also for the total destruction of Germany.[23]

Evidence that the government did not get the kind of support from the press that it wanted can be found in the actions of Friedrich Wilhelm von Loebell, the Prussian minister of the interior. Just over a week into the war (August 9, 1914), Loebell told the other ministers and secretaries (confidentially, of course) that the current steps taken to influence the population had not produced the desired results.[24] What exactly displeased Loebell is not clear. Nevertheless, by October 5, 1914, a 16-page "Note on the Improvement of the Press Organization" signed by Loebell was circulating in the Prussian Ministry of the Interior. Loebell advocated the renewal of an agreement from April 16, 1898, in which all ministries without their own press offices were required to maintain regular contact with the Interior Ministry's *Literarischen Büro*. Other recommendations that Loebell put forth were (1) that the Prussian Interior and Foreign Offices and their Bavarian counterparts work together to influence the press with regard to Prussian domestic policy; (2) that other higher offices cooperate with the Interior Ministry and distribute relevant material that the ministry approved; and (3) that press organizations of the Foreign Office, War Ministry, and Imperial Navy Office not be disturbed, but that the Foreign Office and Interior Ministry maintain a good cooperative working relationship.[25] It was not until August 1915, when a cabinet order authorized the creation of a War Press Office (Kriegspresseamt), that the basic prerequisites for a positive press policy by the government were created.[26]

The lack of a coordinated press policy and regulations in the opening months of the war is important. It suggests that newspapers had a certain amount of freedom in defining the war. Certainly the *Burgfrieden* had its restrictions. Nothing directly related to the actual war effort was printed without prior military approval. Preventative censorship of military news fell to local police.[27] The discussion of important domestic issues was discouraged. This especially affected the socialist press. *Vorwärts* was shut down twice in September by the Berlin police (September 22–24 and 28–30). But newspapers were allowed to define the significance of the war and to characterize the enemy.

RUSSIAN RESPONSIBILITY FOR THE WAR

According to the German press, Russia was responsible for both the increase in international tensions and the opening of the war. On August 2, *Kölnische Zeitung* proclaimed that Russia had begun the war.[28] The article maintained that Russia had attacked Germany first, thus initiating the war. Within two days, similar stories had appeared in a number of other papers.[29] On August 4, *Kölnische Zeitung* published an article entitled "France as Attacker."[30] The point of the article was to demonstrate that in spite of Germany's violation of Belgium's neutrality, Germany was, in fact, the victim, not the aggressor.[31] The provocateur was Russia. Two months after the war began, *Münchner Neueste Nachrichten* ran an article from the Swedish paper *Dag* that noted that the state that mobilizes its troops towards the border is the one responsible for the war.[32] Although Great Britain's entrance into the war got wide attention in the press—this will be discussed later—the focus during the opening weeks of the war was clearly Russia. The Catholic *Kölnische Volkszeitung* maintained that the guilt for starting the war lay with Russia.[33] The liberal *Frankfurter Zeitung* declared that Germany was fighting a defensive war.[34] Even *Vorwärts* characterized the war as "a struggle against tsarism."[35] The socialist daily's characterization of the war could be found in newspapers spanning the entire political spectrum. This agreement masked significant differences in the nature of the threat and what the newspapers (and political parties) hoped the war would ultimately achieve.

Vossische Zeitung, before the war began, claimed that Russian plans had been clear since Peter the Great. Russia wanted to control Constantinople and southeastern Europe, which meant the destruction of Austria-

Hungary. The liberal Berlin daily offered a favorite saying of the pan-Slav-ists: "The road to Constantinople must be laid through Berlin and Vienna."[36] *Kreuzzeitung* noted that Russia had simultaneously attempted to expand in East Asia while stirring up agitation in the Balkans.[37] *Münchner Neueste Nachrichten* reported that the Slavs wanted to weaken Germany in order to rule the world.[38]

Both *Leipziger Volkszeitung* and *Vorwärts*, which had originally campaigned vigorously against the war, denounced Russia's aggressive intentions.[39] A *Vorwärts* article by Eduard Bernstein, SPD member and leading revisionist theorist, sounded as if the conservative Russophobe Theodor Schiemann had been his ghostwriter.[40] In the article "Abrechnung mit Russland" ("Reckoning with Russia"), Bernstein blamed Russia for the war, calling it "Russia's War."[41] Russia, he maintained, had always tried to prevent *Deutschtum* from becoming too strong, and to that end Russian policy had always been willing to cede to France the—"pure German"—left bank of the Rhine in exchange for territory on the Danube and Vistula.[42] Bernstein also claimed that hatred of Germans was greater in Russia than in any other land and was an integral part of Russian chauvinism and the pan-Slavic agenda, which was behind the Russian agitation for war.

Bernstein noted that as a layman he would not argue with the army's decision to attack the West first rather than the East. However, he observed that the political consequences of violating Belgian neutrality had cost Germany much goodwill abroad, a loss the value of which is hard to estimate. Bernstein continued with remarks that revealed just how sharply he differed from both conservative and liberal supporters of the war and how the SPD was also engaging domestic issues. If Germany were to win over foreign opinion, it must state its war aims. There would be no sympathy for Germany if it defeated both democratic France and England and annexed French and Belgian territory, but left autocratic Russia unaltered. If Germany were a democracy, there would be no doubt about what could be achieved. Germany could lead a revolutionary war to the east and free the people form the yoke of Russian autocracy. The German military would be greeted as liberators and Germany would win world favor. But since Germany was not a democracy, it would be utopian to expect such a policy. Nevertheless, it would not be unreasonable to demand that "tsarism and its nationalist oppressors" bear the cost of the war. "It is not only the command of justice, it is also the command of political wisdom." If tsarism remained intact, then the suffering of this war would have been for naught.[43]

The closing installment of the article demonstrated just how far away from conservative Russophobes the socialist view stood. The first two installments, which essentially covered nineteenth-century Russian foreign policy, mimicked the conservative line and acknowledged the role of anti-German sentiments among pan-Slavs. Yet Bernstein explicitly rejects the racial war analysis of conservative Russophobes. Bernstein argued that anti-German sentiments among the Russian elites and bourgeoisie were not responsible for the anti-German foreign policy. Bernstein contended, "Tsarism is not just the personal regime of the current bearer of the Russian crown, rather it is a system of Russian politics, whose representative and tool the current tsar is."[44] Bernstein does not fault the Russian people, nor does he see the war as the result of age-old racial antagonisms. He blames the Russian state. The war was not Germans versus Slavs; rather, it was a war against an autocratic regime.

The last installment of the article also revealed the rift inside Germany over war aims. Bernstein explicitly rejects all calls for annexation. The fact that he does so before the end of August 1914 indicates that at least some circles within Germany were pondering such actions. In order to maintain the moral high ground against Russia and to gain respect in the West after violating Belgian neutrality, Germany needed to liberate the various peoples in Russia from tsarism and pan-Slavism, not annex territory.[45] When it became clear in Bernstein's mind that Germany was not simply fighting a defensive war and that the German government bore the major responsibility for the war—not the Russian and Serbian governments, as he had originally thought—he regretted his voting for war credits.[46]

Berliner Tageblatt was explicit about the link between pan-Slavism and the war. In an article in the Berlin daily, Professor J. Jastow claimed that "the puerile, intimidated man, who through his lineage is condemned to sit on the tsar's throne, did not want the war."[47] Nor did the masses, which by and large were not informed or concerned about Russia's foreign policy. A class of people in ruling circles, members of the War Party (Kriegspartei), wanted the war. What was the War Party? Jastow answered:

It is the party, that the pan-Slavs see not as a cultural development, but as a military-political rule over the united eastern Slavdom, as rule abroad and at home with sabre in hand; the party, which is personally a thorn in the eye of the modest parliamentary system of the new Duma, which wants to suppress all free domestic feeling, in order to maintain the power united in their hands for pan-Slavic foreign policy goals.[48]

The pan-Slavic program included the advancement of Russia and the Russian language. *Leipziger Volkszeitung* noted that Russia forced, through penalty of law, usage of the Russian language even where the Russian element was slight. This resulted in the suppression of Poles and Baltic Germans.[49] Similarly, *Münchner Neueste Nachrichten* announced that in the Baltic Russia was battling not only Germany, but also *Deutschtum* (all things German).[50] The implicit assumption behind the Russian expansion in the Balkans, the Russification of the Baltic, and the general championing of "Slavic interests" by Russia was that non-Russian Slavs, inside and outside Mother Russia, approved of this. German newspapers took great pleasure in announcing the contrary.

"The Fiasco of Pan-Slavism" was the headline splashed across the top of the front page of *Kölnische Zeitung*. Contrary to the assumption that Russia's Slavic kinfolk would unite behind her in the battle against Germany and Austria, the paper pointed to Bulgaria's neutrality and Czech opposition to Russia as proof of the transparency of Russian claims. Russia claimed to be fighting for all Slavs, but was actually fighting for its own interests and would suppress individual Slavic peoples.[51] *Münchner Neueste Nachrichten*, *Kölnische Volkszeitung*, and *Frankfurter Zeitung* also noted with satisfaction that pan-Slavist propaganda was not having the desired effect.[52] The Catholic daily triumphantly proclaimed that the Slavs in Austria-Hungary were siding with the Habsburgs *against* Russia.[53]

The reason for the failure of pan-Slavism, as the German press saw it, was rather simple: Russia was an autocratic, Asiatic, backwards, and barbaric empire with virtually no moral authority. The bankruptcy of Russian character manifested itself in so many different fashions that the only difficulty newspaper editors may have had was choosing which one to highlight. Several newspapers mentioned the mistreatment of German officials and the plundering of the German embassy as the war began.[54] Others highlighted the brutality of the regime, with *Vossische Zeitung* noting, "Not without reason had one in Berlin earlier called a stockade, a 'Russian government advisor.'"[55]

The Russian military was also denigrated by the German press. During the second week of the war, *Berliner Tageblatt* ran an article on the Russian army by Major Moraht. Although he admitted that it was difficult to judge Russia, he would anyway. Moraht maintained that Russia had not improved since the Russo-Japanese War.[56] Similar claims appeared in other newspapers that noted various deficiencies in Russian equipment, tactics, morale, and morality.[57] Moraht observed that the character of the army is more important than the number of troops.[58]

The physical, technical, and spiritual fitness (or lack thereof) of the troops was the key to success. Military fitness was a part of cultural fitness. Paul Rohrbach, one of the most active anti-Russian publicists before and during the war, wrote a two-part piece for *Frankfurter Zeitung* entitled "Our Russian Opponent" in which he maintained,

We need only to look around us to let the experience of our splendid inner unity, of our moral and material performance, the order and composure and military confidence work on us, that goes through the nation—and without hearing what occurs beyond our eastern border, we may assume in every instance the opposite from us.[59]

It was inconceivable to Rohrbach that Russia could defeat Germany on the battlefield. The Russian soldiers were unfit and ill equipped. The officers were corrupt and in no way equal to their German counterparts. In terms of understanding of the military fundamentals, Rohrbach maintained that the Russian brigadier general was the equal of the average German lieutenant; moreover, the Russian staff officer and general staff lacked the initiative and ability to make decisions. As a result, the Russian army's mind-set had not changed since Catherine the Great and lacked the strategic ability to win a "European" war.[60]

This view of Russian martial ability was modified slightly as the war progressed. *Kreuzzeitung* printed a report of a talk by General Hindenburg in which he claimed,

The Russians are good soldiers and maintain discipline, and discipline, after all, decides the campaign. But Russian discipline is something other than German and Austro-Hungarian discipline. In our army it is the result of a moral spirit (*Geistesmoral*), in the Russian army more mute and dull obedience. The Russians had learned a lot since the war with Japan.[61]

The correspondent who reported Hindenburg's remarks noted that the general claimed that numerical superiority was Russia's main weapon. However, numbers were not as important as they had been in previous conflicts. "The Russians will not grind us down, on the contrary, the Russians are demoralized. All signs indicate that they will soon be finished."[62] As a result, the general could claim that the current war with Russia was, more than anything, a question of nerves (*Nervenfrage*).

Although granting that the Russian military had made some progress, Hindenburg's assessment of the war was essentially the same as that of the newspapers. The war with Russia was not about men or weapons; it was about spirit and culture. As long as Germans remained true to the values that had made Germany strong, they would win. The conservative call to remain true to German values was more than an appeal to patriotism. It was also an effort to stave off attempts at political reform. Conservatives hoped that a German victory would reinforce the monarchy and the power of the traditional elites against demands for reform from the Left, especially socialists. Conservatives could counter that Germany's rise to power and military success was the product of certain political and social traditions that put Germany at the pinnacle (in their view) of European power and culture.

Russia could not compete with a European power. "A war on behalf of Russia is a war against civilization," wrote *Berliner Tageblatt*.[63] In the German press, Russia may have been a European great power, but it was an Asiatic nation. Russia borrowed European (mostly German) institutions, yet remained a barbaric Asiatic nation. The Asiatic nature of Russia displayed itself most clearly on the battlefront where Russians committed, in the words of one newspaper, "deeds that Europeans held for impossible."[64] German newspapers were filled with the mistreatment of German soldiers and civilians by the French, British, Belgians, and Russians. The first three were almost always treated as violations of international practice or common decency; but on the eastern front, Russian actions were consistently described as barbaric. Tales of horror at the hands of Russian soldiers or Cossacks filled the pages of newspapers as the Russian army was pushed from German soil. To provide just one of dozens of examples in *Kölnische Zeitung* alone, an article related several accounts of atrocities at the hands of Russian soldiers: the corpse of a shackled policeman who had been stabbed to death was left in the town square, a farmer was killed for no apparent reason, and priests who complained about the quartering of Russian soldiers were shot in the mouth.[65] A *Kreuzzeitung* article written by Wolfgang Eisenbart noted,

And finally in Russia a people of Asiatic rawness; a land where no corruption extending to the highest circles is dirty or unworthy enough to be practiced shamelessly and, one might say, boldly in the light of day. A people, where the vain veneer of exterior civilization makes the inner rawness of barbaric un-culture (*Unkultur*) only more repulsive.[66]

Also working for *Kreuzzeitung* was Professor Theodor Schiemann, one of the most prolific and important Russophobes in the previous quarter century. The holder of the first chair in Russian history (Berlin) in all of western Europe, Schiemann contributed to *Kreuzzeitung* a weekly column, "Die äußere Politik der Woche," every Wednesday for 20 years before the war.[67]

The German–Austro-Hungarian alliance had maintained the peace in Europe for 35 years, Schiemann claimed, in spite of the revenge-happy French and the "envy and hatred" of Russia. Hate and envy were not the only engines driving the Russian juggernaut. The Slavic empire was also convinced that if Germany were defeated it would rule over eastern and east-central Europe; moreover, with the western side of its empire secure, it could then focus attention on the Orient, which must inevitably fall. Toward this end the Russian government had supported pan-Slavic agitation in the Balkans and Austria-Hungary. In 1908, Schiemann claimed that Russia had embarked on a new course, going in a new intolerant pan-Slavic direction; this new path was strengthened by "religion," a euphemism for the Russian Orthodox Church.[68] In this grand conspiracy, the tsar was seen as nothing more than a plaything, easily manipulated by the deceptive words of Rasputin or other magicians (*Wundermännern*).[69] Two weeks later, after Great Britain had joined the fray, Schiemann wrote of a decade-old plot concocted in Paris, London, and Petersburg against Germany, which after three heady weeks of battle had already proven itself to be the "decisive spiritual and political European power."[70] The Entente had hoped to wait until 1916–17 before beginning the war, but an impatient Russia could not wait to carve out its European empire from the Baltic Sea to the Adriatic Sea.[71]

For Schiemann, the war was a struggle between Russia and civilization. The Baltic émigré decried the abuse of women and children by Russian soldiers, a bunch of Cossacks who were "cruel to the defenseless and cowards before men."[72] Why France and Great Britain would side with such an uncultured nation, beyond desire for revenge and desire to knock out a major economic rival, respectively, was an issue that Schiemann, as well as most of his colleagues, failed to address. So continued Schiemann in his columns until his relationship with the conservative newspaper came to an end in September 1914.

As Rohrbach noted, in order to understand Russia, one needed only to imagine the opposite of Germany. Throughout the opening of the war, the positive attributes of the German people were emphasized and posited as reasons for Germany's ultimate victory. The truthfulness of the German people was one such attribute.

Theodor Schiemann declared, "All Russian Slavs always lie!"[73] Russian untruthfulness, as well as Slavic dishonesty in general, was another staple of wartime reports. Claims, by both Central and Entente powers, of exaggerations and outright lies by the enemy were commonplace. *Vorwärts* warned its readers against believing "hearsay."[74] The lack of truthfulness on the part of the Entente powers was virtually a daily occurrence in the German press. Complaints about slander (*Verleumdung*), conspiracy (*Verschwörung*), and lie factories (*Lügenfabrik*) abounded in the German newspapers. Whether it was an article concerning German victories,[75] the conduct of soldiers,[76] or just general misinformation,[77] the German press constantly cried foul about the Entente press and juxtaposed it with the "true to the truth German war reports."[78]

The juxtaposition of German uprightness with enemy deception was apparent in the discussion of the official accounts of the origins of the war. In the opening days of the war, the respective governments published documents that they claimed explained the causes of the war. The German press noted that Russia's publication of the Orange Book, which claimed that Germany's rejection of Great Britain's last-minute attempt to mediate the dispute was the cause of the war and that Germany had mobilized and declared war while negotiations were in progress, was simply wrong. The German government had supported mediation, but Russian mobilization had made such overtures illusory. Moreover, it was Russia, not Germany, that had mobilized troops towards the German border while negotiations were going on and after German authorities had been assured by Russian military officials that any mobilization on the part of Russia would be directed at the Austrian border in case of an Austrian attack on Serbia.[79]

The Russian government had intentionally misrepresented the facts in an effort to hide its culpability. Similarly, *Frankfurter Zeitung* noted how the British Blue Book did not represent the truth, but was simply an attempt to put British policy in a favorable light.[80] The German White Book, on the other hand, was treated as proof that Germany had tried to maintain peace and the international balance of power.

German moderation and levelheadedness were countered by Entente excesses and lies. The degradation of Kaiser Wilhelm II as "the New Attila" by the English press was just one example of how the Entente powers misrepresented the war and willfully slandered their opponent. *Norddeutsche Allgemeine Zeitung* noted that no German paper had done anything similar to Entente leaders.[81] The slandering of Wilhelm II was part of a larger systematic attempt by the English and French press to demonize Germans as barbarians.[82] *Kölnische Zeitung* published an article entitled "Presse und Pöbel" ("The Press and the Masses") that outlined how the English press methodically prepared its people for war and fanned anti-German sentiments against Germans living in England.[83]

The French press was also scorned. *Vossische Zeitung* noted "the German press fights for moral ideals, the French for materialistic values."[84] While the German press was honorable, French reports were deemed inaccurate to the point of lying and blinded by hate. The article noted that before the war, many of France's leading figures mocked their own press as a "pig sty" and a "blot on French culture."[85] The article notes with dismay that a press that could not be denigrated enough was now taken seriously by the same people who scorned it earlier. "They do not want to admit anymore that the Parisian press is incapable of being true and upright, ethical in the highest sense."[86] By permitting the press to constantly degrade Germany, the French leadership had revealed "the moral weakness of their culture and their unfitness for life in the future."[87]

During the opening weeks of the fighting, Russia was clearly the focus. Russian aggression fueled by the ideology of pan-Slavism and the War Party that had the tsar's ear was the cause of the war and the main threat to German existence. When newspapers carried articles about the war as a war for existence (*Daseinkampf*), it was a reference to the potential threat that Russia posed. However, even if the German press agreed about the cause of the war, there was not an agreement on what the causes revealed or exactly what Germany was fighting for. Conservatives maintained that it was a war between Germans and Slavs for the preservation of European culture and a conservative political order inside Germany. Socialists saw the Russian state as the enemy and hoped that its demise and the liberation of the peoples of Russia would have repercussions in Germany. Neither view would disappear over the course of the war; but, by the end of the summer, a clear shift in attention had occurred, and Great Britain had become responsible for the war and, in many of the papers examined here, the main threat to Germany. The shift westward does not change the main tenets of the German position: Germany and its allies had truth and integrity on their side, and German cultural fitness would translate into military success.

DAS PERFIDE ALBION: ENGLAND AS ARCHENEMY

Immediately after Great Britain's entrance into the war, the theme of British duplicity was introduced, and it remained a constant theme in German newspapers.[88] Whether it was Great Britain's conduct during negotiations before the war, its reasons for entering the war, or its conduct during the opening months of the war, German newspapers of all political stripes repeatedly maintained that the British government's stated position did not correspond with its actions or with actual events. In short, Germany was facing *Das perfide Albion* (the perfidious Albion).[89]

Before the war began, Great Britain claimed to desire to preserve the peace. In the days before the war, German newspapers noted that Great Britain could prevent a war. However, the land that had been tabbed as the only nation that could rein in Russia and prevent a war became the land that had secretly prepared for war while claiming to be interested in maintaining the peace. *Berliner Tageblatt* wrote that Great Britain had demanded certain conditions to remain neutral, but that the German government was not in a position to meet all of the demands. Germany could guarantee the neutrality of the Netherlands and promise not to attack the northern coast of France, but it could not vouch for the neutrality of Belgium. The Berlin daily speculated that Belgium was only a pretext for British involvement and that it would have joined the fray after Germany's first defeat, regardless of German guarantees. The condition of Belgian neutrality was only designed to hinder the German army and prolong this "terrible war."[90]

On the same day (August 5), *Vorwärts* and *Vossische Zeitung* published the same report from the Wolff Telegraph Bureau (the main German newswire agency) highlighting British duplicity. The British foreign minister, Sir Edward Grey, claimed to have tried to maintain the peace, yet was preparing British public opinion for war. Grey maintained that he had given the French only diplomatic support and could not enter any agreements that did not have the full support of British public opinion. However, he added, if the French were forced to go to war, British public opinion would support France.[91] In spite of the absence of any formal treaty, the organ for the SPD noted that the French and British had pursued identical foreign policies since the 1911 Moroccan Crisis.

Vorwärts observed that the current crisis was not something that originally concerned the French. In fact, no great power had less of an interest in the Austrian-Serbian quarrel than France. French involvement was due to its treaty with Russia. The socialist daily remarked, "We had a long lasting friendship with France, and to what degree that friendship modifies obligations—each person should consult his own heart and feelings and weigh the extent of the obligations."[92] Both *Vorwärts* and *Vossische Zeitung* noted that Grey's guarantee of the French coast helped to influence France's position before the war broke out. *Vorwärts* quoted from Grey's speech to Parliament on August 4: "If we take part in the war with our powerful navy which can protect our trade, our coasts and our interests, then we will have to suffer only a little more than if we remained passive."[93]

The next day, *Vossische Zeitung* followed up on the topic of Anglo-French cooperation by examining diplomatic meetings from August and September 1912. The paper recounts the exchange of letters on September 22 and 23 between Grey and Paul Cambon, the French ambassador to Great Britain, which concluded that both powers would consult each other if ever threatened by attack and discuss common actions.[94] This was the culmination of diplomatic meetings that began on August 9 when Raymond Poincaré, the French president, visited Russia and issued a joint communiqué with Russian foreign minister Sergi Sazonov reconfirming the Franco-Russian alliance. Just a few weeks after this visit, on September 12, Great Britain and France had a meeting to discuss their navies, with the result of France moving two Atlantic Ocean squadrons to Toulon to help offset the power of Austria-Hungary and Italy in the Mediterranean Sea. Great Britain took over the responsibility for protecting the channel and the North Sea. One week later (September 20) Sazonov met with Grey in London to discuss Persia and the Balkans.[95] Two days later, the exchange of letters occurred. The apparently innocuous comment that the two nations would consult each other appears in an entirely different light when seen as the culmination of nearly two months of diplomatic meetings. It is the result of a tripartite plan that commits Great Britain far more than Grey had publicly admitted.

This view is reiterated in *Berliner Tageblatt* when it notes that Lord Kitchener was named minister of war (*Kriegsminister*) and immediately traveled to Paris and that General John Dentom Pinkstone French, who had participated in maneuvers with the French army, was put in charge of the British Expeditionary Forces. Both actions indicated that the British had contemplated a war on the European continent and were preparing for such an event regardless of German actions.[96]

In addition to highlighting what they considered to be questionable British actions before the British declaration of war, newspapers also expressed doubt about Great Britain's justification for entering the war. *Münchner Neueste Nachrichten* noted that while Great Britain claimed that the violation of Belgian neutrality was the reason it declared war on Germany, who knows how often in the course of its own history Great Britain had violated the neutrality of another nation in similar or worse fashion?

It then pointed to Great Britain's support of France in 1870–71, support for the South in the American Civil War, and the bombardment of Copenhagen in 1807 as recent examples of British violations of international law.[97] British disregard for international law when it suited its own interest would be a constant theme for the German press. Less than a week after the *Münchner* article appeared, *Kölnische Zeitung* discussed the British seizure of a Dutch vessel in violation of international law.[98] The following month, the Cologne daily would lead its evening edition with the headline "Our Opponent and International Law" ("Unsere Gegner und das Völkerrecht"), featuring a lead article by Dr. Heinrich Triepel, a professor of law in Berlin. He opened the piece with an 1854 quote from an unidentified "famous English jurist": "A state which violates its treaties is the greatest enemy of nations, the disturber of their peace, the despiser of their fortune, the obstacle to their progress."[99] Triepel continues by noting that no other nation could compare to Britain in terms of violating international law or the breaking of treaties. Britain appears to have a double standard where it demands that other nations adhere to the letter of international law (note British reprimands of Russia during the Russo-Japanese War) while Great Britain, on the other hand, could sign two agreements at the Hague (1899 and 1907) that forbade the use of dumdum bullets and allow both itself and France to use the banned bullets.[100] The Entente's use of dumdum bullets is a recurring (and apparently false) complaint in the German press.[101]

The idea of an English double standard is reiterated in a *Vossische Zeitung* article claiming that Great Britain never conceded to neutral nations rights that it had demanded for itself. The Berlin daily maintained that the British seizure of ships and nonmilitary cargo destined for Germany on the open sea violated the rights of neutral nations. In fact, Britain "destroys the concept of neutrality and wants to replace it with the maxim: Whoever is not with me, is against me."[102] In an attempt to negate one of the most effective arguments of British propaganda, the German press tried to point out that Great Britain violated international law as well.

Even if German complaints about British violations of neutrals' rights and use of dumdum bullets had any merit, the violation of Belgian neutrality was the most egregious offense against international law, and one that clearly bothered the Germans. The idea of the German chancellor admitting that Germany was in violation of international law by invading Belgium[103] put Germany at a legal, as well as moral, disadvantage when trying to justify its actions.

One of the more interesting efforts to defuse this argument appeared in *Münchner Neueste Nachrichten* on September 13. In an excerpt from an article that appeared in the journal *Leipziger Zeitschrift für deutsches Recht* (*Leipzig Journal for German Law*) by Dr. Ferdinand von Miltner, the Bavarian daily proposed that Germany violated neither Belgian neutrality nor international law.[104] According to Article VII of the 1839 agreement, "Belgium constitutes…an independent and permanently neutral state. It is obligated to observe the same neutrality in relation to all other states."[105] In his August 4 speech to the Reichstag, Chancellor Theobald von Bethmann Hollweg did not deny that Germany had violated Article VII, but he argued that Germany was forced to march troops through Belgium because France was to do the same to attack Germany. According to Miltner, this raised the legal question of whether or not Germany was in a state of emergency (*Notstand*). It is not clear what the relationship between the "state of emergency" (*Notstand* or *Notrecht*) and international law (*Völkerrecht*) is. If international law has the same status as private law and criminal law in relation to the "state of emergency" or self-defense (*Notwehr*), then Germany was not guilty of violating international law. Germany was in a state of emergency, fearing an attack by France through Belgium. In this instance, the state of emergency allows Germany to override the 1839 agreement, just as France was prepared to do. "For him who will not concede that in these circumstances Germany acted in a state of emergency, nothing remains other than to put forth the monstrous proposition that Germany should have waited first for that invasion to take place."[106] However, during negotiations in the early days of August, it became clear that Belgium would not only not be able to prevent a French invasion, but also was working in accordance with France for just such an action. Belgium itself had abrogated the second sentence of Article VII "to observe the same neutrality with all other states." Thus, Belgium and France, certainly with Great Britain's consent, had violated both the 1839 agreement and the 1907 Hague Convention concerning the rights and duties (*Rechte und Pflichten*) of neutral powers. There was no violation of neutrality by Germany since Belgium itself had already forfeited its neutral status.[107] The issue of culpability was clearly a vexing one for the German press, as well as the German government. Bethmann Hollweg's concession that Germany's sweep through Belgium constituted a violation of international law (which he promised that the nation would atone for after the war) put Germany at a disadvantage in the propaganda battle that its opponents exploited fully.

There were no other efforts to defend Dr. von Miltner's claim that Germany's *Notstand* trumped its obligations to international law. However, the second part of the jurist's argument, that Germany did not violate Belgium's neutrality because it was no longer neutral, would become the centerpiece of a government press offense that virtually all German newspapers would adopt and support. In this offensive, Great Britain replaced France as Belgium's major coconspirator. The desired result was to prove that despite statements to the contrary, Great Britain not only desired war with Germany, but had actively planned for it. If any nation deserved the title *der Feind Europas* (Enemy of Europe), that nation was Great Britain, not Germany.

In early October in the pages of *Norddeutsche Allgemeine Zeitung*, one sees the groundwork for the official line against Great Britain. According to the government's mouthpiece, Great Britain's intentional irresolution was responsible for the outbreak of the war.[108] The reasons for Great Britain's inaction were clarified a week later. On October 13, *Norddeutsche Allgemeine Zeitung*'s headline read, "The Breach of Belgian Neutrality by England and Belgium." The article opens,

By Sir Edward Grey's own declarations, the claim of the English government that the German violation of Belgian neutrality caused England's intervention in the present war has already been proven untenable. The pathos of moral indignation utilized to turn the neutral nations against Germany finds a new and unusual illumination as a result of certain documents that the German military administration found in the archives of the Belgian General Staff in Brussels.[109]

The key documents were a map found with the writing (*Ausschrift*) "*Intervention anglaise en Belgique*" and a note (*Schreiben*) dating from 1906. The map was tied to plans for moving British troops to Belgium in the case of a second Franco-German war. The note, dated April 10, 1906, planned for a 100,000-man British expeditions corps that would work with the Belgian army against Germany. The British troops would land in Dunkirk, Calais, and Boulogne and then be transported by Belgium from France to Belgium. The Belgian authorities would supply the necessary accommodations and food for the troops. The fact that French harbors were involved was evidence that arrangements with France had already been cleared. "The three powers had established plans for a collaboration of a 'confederated army' as it is called in the document. That a map of the French deployment was found in the secret files also speaks for this."[110] The British military attaché in Brussels at the time, Lieutenant Colonel Barnardiston, noted that Holland's support could not be counted upon. He also noted that Great Britain intended to provide food for Antwerp "as soon as the North Sea was cleared of German warships."[111] Barnardiston also directed the establishment of a Belgian spy service in the Rhine province. All of this proved that Britain's claims were hollow. Belgian neutrality was not the issue because Belgium was not neutral. It had taken sides. The new revelations also appeared to vindicate the position of the German military that France intended to use Belgium as a base from which to attack Germany.[112]

Berliner Tageblatt and *Münchner Neueste Nachrichten* ran the *Norddeutsche* article verbatim.[113] *Kölnische Zeitung* ran the same story, noting that the government had released the documents the previous evening and concluded with the following statement: "The English's Word by now has become synonymous with the word lie."[114] *Frankfurter Zeitung* noted that publication in *Norddeutsche* comes from the German government. Taking a slightly different tack than the other papers, the Frankfurt daily notes that these plans are not a formal agreement, but it does indicate that an oral agreement (*mündliche Vereinbarungen*) existed between not only Great Britain and France, but also between the two powers and Belgium. In spite of British assurances to its own people that they were fighting for the little nations, "[T]oday one knows that for the last eight years Belgian neutrality was a mask that deceived Germany and the rest of Europe."[115] Similarly, *Münchner Neueste Nachrichten* declared that the Belgian neutrality was an exposed shadow.[116] After the publication of these documents, German newspapers maintain that Great Britain's claims of protecting the rights of smaller nations and the integrity of international law do not stand up to scrutiny.[117]

To further support this position, the German government, through *Norddeutsche Allgemeine Zeitung*, published a series of official documents relating to the prehistory of the war.[118] The documents are introduced as a response to enemy claims that the German *Militarpartie* (Military Party) and German militarism bears the guilt for the current war. The first documents addressed Anglo-French naval cooperation before the war and included an exchange between Grey and the French ambassador to Great Britain, Paul Cambon. The key point in the exchange is Grey's observation that while the current naval cooperation does not bind either Great Britain or France in any fashion, "if either Government had grave reason to expect an unprovoked attack by a third power, of something that threatened the general peace, it should immediately discuss with the other whether both Governments should act together to prevent aggression and to preserve the peace, and if so, what measures would be prepared to take in common."[119] The remaining dispatches outline the gradual alignment of British, French, and Russian interests. The result was, in the words of *Vossische Zeitung*, a "conspiracy against Germany."[120] Great Britain had the ability to influence the actions of both France and Russia in the summer of 1914, but chose not to do so—or at least chose not to exercise its influence in the interest of maintaining the peace. The next day *Münchner Neueste Nachrichten* confirmed *Norddeutsche*'s (and German government's) position that these documents, along with others regarding Belgian neutrality published previously, undermine Britain's earlier claims to be an honest broker in the efforts to avoid war and that the British government deceived not only Germany, but also its own citizens.[121] The contention that Great Britain had conspired against Germany became virtually an article of faith in the German press. Even the left-wing socialist *Leipziger Volkszeitung* would contend that Belgian neutrality was simply a pretext for British involvement in the war.[122]

To hide this fact, Great Britain would go to great lengths. The British cut the transatlantic cable in an effort to control information leaving the continent and launched a propaganda campaign to arouse feeling against Germany.[123] *Vorwärts* alleged that Great Britain was preparing public opinion for war.[124] German inability to get its message out and receive news from abroad was an early concern expressed in some newspapers. *Berliner Tageblatt* called on readers to pass on any information about reports in the foreign press that they may have received through connections abroad.[125] Shortly thereafter, through *Norddeutsche Allgemeine Zeitung*, the *Deutsche Werkbund* declared that it would combat the false reporting of Germany's foes and asked for people to send "newspapers in all languages which contained false reports (*Lügennachrichten*) about Germany and German conduct of the war (*Kriegsführung*)" and to provide names of trustworthy people living overseas to whom true information could be sent to fight misinformation.[126]

Spreading the German message abroad was a concern to the press, and reports of foreign newspapers agreeing with a German perspective were met with satisfaction. *Norddeutsche Allgemeine Zeitung* reported that Switzerland's *Neuen Zürcher Nachrichten* agreed that Germany's recent publications of documents proved that since 1906 Belgium was not in a neutral position.[127] Earlier, *Kölnische Zeitung* ran "The Change in Judgment about Germany," which quoted at length an article from Stockholm's *Dagblad*. The article claimed that the British and French press were painting Germany in an unfair light and that Germans were not barbarians.[128] Unfortunately for the German press, there were few similar stories to report. Far more frequent were complaints about the circulation of false reports about German defeats or atrocities.[129] Several papers also accused British papers of intentionally rousing anti-German sentiment among the general population, which resulted in the abuse of German nationals living in hostile nations or the mistreatment of German prisoners of war.[130]

In the view of German newspapers, the hostile anti-German rhetoric and posturing about Belgian neutrality was a smoke screen to hide Great Britain's true motivation for war: self-interest. Great Britain was not directly threatened by Germany militarily, but it stood to lose a great deal if Germany won the war and could reap significant benefits from a German defeat. *Kreuzzeitung* reminded its readers of Clauswitz's dictum "War is politics by other means" and that England's policy held that the suffering of a land war could be transferred to its allies without hurting its interests.[131] In a dramatic turnaround, *Kreuzzeitung* had changed its position on the war and shifted its focus to Great Britain as the organizer of an "economic battle of annihilation without precedent against us [Germany]."[132] The following day, the conservative daily claimed that Germany was fighting the world domination (*Weltherrschaft*) of Great Britain.[133] *Vossische Zeitung* concluded that Great Britain wanted the war and used France and Belgium to help destroy German trade and power and ultimately finish off Germany's navy.[134] *Frankfurter Zeitung* asserted that even though Russia was the greatest threat to Great Britain's world empire, English self-interest dictated supporting France and Russia. It claimed that *The Times* stated quite openly that Great Britain's self-interest (*Eigeninteresse*) was "the most important and decisive reason for England's position."[135] Germany was becoming too powerful.

German strength as the casus belli for British intervention was a recurring theme in the German press. *Vossische Zeitung* depicts Edward Grey as a detached calculator of Great Britain's material interests. The English people did not want war; they wanted "peace and friendship with Germany and the world, only a half dozen men sat and calculated—calculated that the war would bring England advantages, and hurries its people into bloody battle."[136] The growth of German industry benefited England as long as Germany was dependent upon England for raw materials; however, the growth of German colonies made them less dependent upon foreign raw materials and that made England nervous.[137] Grey concluded that the cost of war was cheaper than the cost of neutrality. A short victorious war could give Britain Germany's colonies, destroy Germany's navy, and weaken the political power of Germany.[138] The costs of the war for Great Britain were relatively minor. *Kölnische Zeitung* noted that the continent destroyed itself for Britain's benefit. Great Britain's power depended upon European disunity; it may be a part of the European continent, but Britain, due to its global reach, was not a part of European politics.[139]

Global versus European politics played a role in evaluating British motives and possible consequences of the war. *Vossische Zeitung* declared that Germany needed to united Europe against Great Britain.[140] *Kölnische Zeitung* called the island empire a world tyrant, and asserted that it was the German mission to free the world from English rule.[141] The conflict between Great Britain's traditional balance-of-power policy toward the European continent and its role as the leading world power was the subject of a speech by the historian Erich Marcks, a summary of which appeared in *Münchner Neueste Nachrichten*. Marcks argued that Germany's opponents were looking at it through old-fashioned political paradigms: France saw Germany through the eyes of 1870, Russia saw Germany in relation to Bismarck's actions, and England was fighting over European hegemony. Germany did not want to fight Britain, nor did it threaten Britain's existence, but Britain had become the deadly enemy (*Todfeind*).[142] Marcks was part of a generation of historians who attempted to take Leopold von Ranke's notion of the balance of power and apply it on a global scale.[143] For Marcks, war and expansion were natural and served as both a test and expression of a nation's inner vitality. This was Germany's test.

WAR AND VALUES

The cultural meaning of the war was an important topic in the German press. Just as Russia's barbarism was contrasted to Germany's superior cultural status, Great Britain's crass material motives were contrasted with Germany's higher ideals. "England has never fought for cultural ideas, but rather only for the sake of material interests, about which, to be sure, its non-conformist conscience often draped the threadbare cloak of narrowly defined standard morality."[144] Not all papers were quite as harsh in their assessment of Great Britain. *Münchner Neueste Nachrichten* recalled a speech at the 1878 Berlin Congress by Lord Beaconsfield in which he concluded, "if England remains true to itself, never extinguishes its honor, its power will never sink."[145] However, Great Britain had lost its honor, for, according to the Bavarian daily, if it had remained true to itself, there never would have been a war. Fear and envy caused Great Britain to lose its way and sell out to baser forces (by siding with Russia). As a result, Great Britain's balance sheet did not add up. It is not an accident that the title of the article is, as with the Gustav Freytag novel, "Soll und Haben" (Credit and Debit).[146]

In a different article, *Münchner Neueste Nachrichten* avowed that while war was destructive, it also had an aspect of renewal for a people and a culture.[147] Approximately six weeks later, Erich Marcks's speech hailed the war as "the moment of truth, if we will become our own world nation (*Weltvolk*) in power, economics and culture."[148] *Kreuzzeitung* hailed the war as the reason for Germans returning to traditional values, honoring the emperor, military, and God in a way that had been seen too seldom before the war.[149] For *Kreuzzeitung*, the maintaining of traditional values included preserving the traditional political order, against both foreign and domestic attack. The emphasis on values and cultural ideals over crass material interests would be the key to German victory. The economist Werner Sombart, who in an earlier article lauded the deep-seated hatred of England that he found in Germany,[150] wrote, "I call England simply a commercial firm. The entire manner in which England conducts war strikes one quite like a struggle that an unscrupulous business fights out with the competition."[151] Sombart quoted Churchill as saying, "England will win because it has the last million to spend." Sombart concluded, "Now we see clearly what is at stake in this struggle. Now we see clearly who is fighting whom: the warrior with the merchant. Now we also know the battle cry under which both warring parties take to the field. 'We will fight to the last Mark,' they say. 'We will fight to the last man,' we answer."[152]

It is appropriate to conclude with Sombart's article. The piece itself is noteworthy in that the editors of *Berliner Tageblatt* felt compelled to state that they disagreed with some of Sombart's characterizations. While they understood that Great Britain posed a threat to Germany, the editors clearly maintained that Russia was a greater threat to German security. The position of the editorial staff of *Berliner Tageblatt* is made clear when they inserted *in the middle* of an article by Professor J. Jastow, "The Russian World Empire," "(We think it is still premature to consider the manner in which the absolutely necessary and emphatic weakening of Russia should come to pass. But we believe that the goal of the war must be to push Russia as far as possible out of Europe and away from Germany's borders. Editor.)"[153] The liberal *Berliner Tageblatt*'s view of Russia was in the middle of the conservative and socialist positions discussed earlier. It accepted the fault and threat of Russia, but did not subscribe to the clash-of-races theory that marked conservative views, nor did it support the "liberation" of the Russian peoples. The claim that Russia must be "pushed back" can support both annexationist aspirations and the creation of independent states for ethnic minorities. What is perhaps even more noteworthy is the fact that the editorial staff would continue to assert that Russia should be the chief concern even after it was clear that the German government was trying to shift attention to England. The editors welcomed the response from Wolfgang Heine, an SPD delegate to the Reichstag, who chided Sombart for deriding England, stating that Germany should not mock any of its enemies, but rather rely on its own power.[154] "And the nature of the German demands reason and fairness (*Vernunft und Gerechtigkeit*)."[155] Heine deplored Sombart's enthusiasm for hatred of England. He maintained that hatred toward other nations served no purpose and that the only emotions that he wanted were "love for our threatened people and Fatherland and the thankfulness for a fighting brothers."[156] The only hatred he would tolerate and advocate was a hatred of any signs of untruthfulness, bondage, or unfairness (*Unwahrheit, Unfreiheit, Unrechtigkeit*) inside of Germany.[157]

The editorial position of *Berliner Tageblatt* and Heine's article are noteworthy for a couple of reasons. It is the only example that I have found of the editorial staff inserting its opinions in the middle of an article, although commenting before or after was a fairly frequent practice. Moreover, the position of the editorial board was clearly in opposition to that of the German government. By the end of September the German government was unmistakably trying to change the focus of the war from Russia to Great Britain. The exact reasons for the shift may never be known for certain, but there are several factors that are suggestive. The decisive victories at Tannenberg and the Masurian Lakes had stopped the Russian advance, and by mid-September there would no longer be Russian troops on German soil. Simultaneously, the failure to secure a quick victory in the West was apparent.[158] Moreover, the effects of the British naval blockade made Britain more than just a foe on the battlefield.

The transformation of *Kreuzzeitung* is the clearest indication of the change by the German government.[159] The most Russophobic of all the major German newspapers in the two decades before the war, the conservative daily, led by Theodor Schiemann, had advocated better relations with Great Britain and a harder stance toward Russia. The same stance was taken in the opening weeks of the war by Schiemann and other writers on the staff. However, in September, for reasons that may never be known, Schiemann was dismissed and replaced by Otto Hoetzsch, a student of Schiemann's. Hoetzsch had always maintained that Russia was Austria's mortal enemy, not Germany's, and that Germany's chief enemy was Great Britain.[160] The release of government documents in *Norddeutsche Allgemeine Zeitung* was part of a concerted effort on the part of the German government to make Great Britain the main enemy in the eyes of the German people. Even though the articles did not always bear the mark of an official release, other German newspapers had no difficulty distinguishing between the work and opinions of the editorial staff at *Norddeutsche* and those of the German government.[161] The fact that most of the newspapers adopted the line of the government does not reflect the coercive power of the government (witness the position of *Berliner Tageblatt*), but more likely the belief that Great Britain did represent the most formidable opponent. This view may have been influenced by events on the battlefield, where Germany was having greater success in the East than in the West. It also may have been influenced by the fact that Great Britain was having greater success with its propaganda, and German newspapers, as well as the government, felt that combating Great Britain and its propaganda may be the most difficult task facing the Fatherland.

Wolfgang Heine's plea for "Reason and Fairness" was emblematic of much of the German propaganda that was not looking for "proof" of Russia's or England's culpability for the war. More noble than most of the propaganda that defended the German perspective in the contest of nations for victory, Heine's call for equanimity was not heeded by either side. There were attempts on the German side to offer complex answers to the question of war and to acknowledge that the other side had legitimate concerns—even if said concerns were deemed selfish or crass. From the other side, the Germans only saw the kind of simple single-mindedness that Hitler envied. Stories of German barbarism and atrocities were the staple of enemy propaganda and put the Germans on the defensive. Perhaps the clearest manifestation of this defensiveness and frustration was the manifesto of German intellectuals that appeared in October 1914. In an effort to preserve the honor of German *Kultur*, dozens of Germany's leading minds were reduced to a series of defensive claims beginning with the phrase "Es ist nicht wahr... " ("It is not true... ").[162] This is not to say that only the Entente powers lied. As *Vorwärts* noted, both sides certainly exaggerated atrocity stories.[163] Nor is it simply a matter of interpretation.[164] Nevertheless, calls for "*Vernunft und Gerechtigkeit*," claims of complicated conspiracies, or discussions of the balance of power on the world stage were no match for enemy propaganda depicting a powerful Germany illegally attacking and destroying a smaller neighbor.

It is clear that between August and October 1914, the majority of the newspapers examined here had switched their positions from a focus on Russia as the cause and major foe in the war to Great Britain inheriting both titles. The line of argumentation in the papers remains fairly consistent. Stated succinctly, Germany had remained truthful and true to itself throughout the July Crisis and the outbreak of war. Duplicity characterized the other side. The consensus on the most basic level of blame did not translate into uniformity of beliefs. The characterization of the war in the political press allowed for some differences of opinion to be expressed. Both conservatives and socialists could blame Germany's eastern neighbor for the war, but they faulted different aspects of Russia while doing so. Conservatives claimed it was the final struggle in an age-old conflict between Germans and Slavs. Socialists saw the ever-expanding appetite of an autocratic behemoth that oppressed all peoples. Implicit in the socialist position was a critique of the German government that had more in common with Russia than it did with the western powers.

As emphasis shifted to Great Britain, conservatives could point to British jealousy of German economic and military power, the product of a conservative order that they wished to preserve. Liberals and socialists could concur; however, the latter would point to economic interests overpowering the interests of the English people to the point where liberal Britain would side with the most repressive power on the continent to preserve its own privileged position and those of British business interests. Liberals would chastise Britain for caring only about material interests at the expense of "higher" ideals.

Still, in the efforts to justify their actions, Germans started out at a disadvantage; Chancellor Bethmann Hollweg had already conceded that Germany had violated international law with the invasion of Belgium. This gave the Entente powers the upper hand, one that Great Britain did not relinquish. The German government also committed the cardinal sin of propaganda in the eyes of Adolf Hitler: it conceded that the enemy could have a point. All of the attempts to undue that damage by "proving" that Belgium was not neutral were too complicated and too late.

SELECTED READINGS FROM THE GERMAN PRESS

The following article ran in socialist newspapers as the war began. German socialists opposed war in principle, but supported this effort even though they feared that their constituency would bear the heaviest burden. This statement reflects the fine line that German socialists tried to walk.

Vorwärts and *Leipziger Volkszeitung*, **August 1, 1914**

Party Comrades!

A state of war has been declared. The next hour can bring the outbreak of a world war. The toughest test will be forced upon not only our own people, but also the entire continent.

Up to the last minute, the international proletariat has done its duty, and beyond our borders all strained to preserve the peace and to make war impossible. If our earnest protests, our constantly repeated efforts were unsuccessful, have the conditions under which we live become still once again heavier, than our and our working brothers' will, then now we must resolutely take what may come with eyes wide open.

The awful self-mutilation of the European people is the cruel confirmation of what we have been shouting admonishingly to the ruling class, if only in vain, for more than a generation.

Comrades, we will not live through coming events with fatalistic indifference. We will remain true to our cause. We will stick together, inspired by the exalted greatness of our cultural mission.

Women, especially, upon whom the weight of events will fall twice and thrice as hard, have in these earnest times the task, in the spirit of socialism to work for the high ideals of humanity so that the repetition of the unspeakable calamities will be prevented and so that this war is the last. The severe regulations of martial law hit the workers' movement with terrible sharpness. Rashness, useless and falsely understood sacrifice harm at this time not only the individual, but also our cause.

Comrades, we call upon you to persevere in unshakeable confidence that in spite of everything, the future belongs to international socialism, justice and humanity.

Berlin, 31 July 1914   The Party Executive Committee

The following statements from the German emperor and empress was reproduced in part or completely in most German papers.

Norddeutsche Allgemeine Zeitung, August 7, 1914

To the German People!

For the forty-three years since the founding of the Reich [i.e., German unification], it has been my and my predecessors' hardest effort to maintain peace in the world and to pursue our development in peace. But our opponents envy the success of our work.

All public and secret enmity from east and west, from beyond the sea, we have borne up to now conscious of our responsibility and strength. But now they want to humiliate us. They demand that we watch with folded arms as our enemies arm themselves for an insidious invasion; they will not tolerate that we stand with resolute loyalty by our ally, who fights for its reputation as a Great Power. And with their debasement, our power and honor is also lost.

So the sword must be unsheathed. In the middle of peace, the enemy attacks us. Therefore, up! To arms! Every fluctuation, every hesitation would be treachery to the Fatherland.

It concerns the existence or non-existence of our nation that our fathers founded anew. The existence or non-existence of German power and German essence.

We will defend ourselves until the last breath from man and steed. We will survive this fight, even against a world of enemies. Never has Germany been overcome, when it was united.

Forward with God, who will be with us, as he was with our fathers!
Berlin, 6 August 1914   Wilhelm

To the German Women!
At the call of the Emperor, our people arm themselves for a struggle without compare, that it had not conjured up and that it conducts only for its defense.

Those who can carry weapons will hurry to the flag with joy and with their blood answer for the Fatherland.

The fight will be a horrible one and the wounds to be closed countless. Therefore, I call upon you, German women and girls and everyone who does not have the privilege to fight for the beloved homeland, to help. It falls to everyone, according to their strength, to make the fight easier for our husbands, sons and brothers. I know that in all circles of our people without exception, the will exists to fulfill this high duty. May the Lord God strengthen us for this sacred labor of love that calls also us women to consecrate our complete strength to the Fatherland for its decisive battle.

Due to the gathering of voluntary helpers and gifts of all sorts, further announcements have already been issued from the various organizations for whom these tasks fall to first and whose support above all is needed.

Berlin, 6 August 1914   Auguste Victoria

The following article presents a conservative view that the war could spark a rebirth of traditional political and spiritual values in Germany. It also reflects the position that Germany had remained morally superior to its enemies and that would be the reason for its victory.

Kreuzzeitung, **August 12, 1914, pp. 1–2**

*"The German People in a Struggle for Its Independence and Its Future" by
Wolfgang Eisenhart*

When in the 1880s, the French envoy in Berlin once expressed the opinion to Prince Bismarck that the increasing political splintering of parties in Germany was a sign of its decline and inner decomposition, the great statesman replied with his unique brilliant foresight: "Do not believe that! Our domestic political party struggles are just superficial. If the Fatherland should really be in danger, the Germans will come together from all corners to protect its sacred ground, so that the Emperor Frederick Barbarossa, if he could come back to this Earth, would marvel at how little his people have changed in seven centuries."

In our day this powerful man's prediction has been fulfilled in marvelous fashion. His words about the Austrian Emperor, whose people would all follow him as soon as he mounted his horse, have proven themselves to be the true prophecy of a statesman equipped with an almost superhuman vision.

What a great, powerful change in our people today! The Germans, who just a few months earlier were in a bitter party struggle, stand there today again in a wonderful decisive unity, that in the long years of peace we had yearned for in vain. All party hatreds have disappeared like a ghost in the night; no Right and no Left anymore, only a united, earnest people prepared for the highest sacrifice....

In the recent years, filled with concern, we have often asked whether those signs of moral decline, which in most recent time proclaimed themselves, did not mean the beginning of decay of our national life. We had to see, with pain and deep sorrow, our people's increasing irreligiosity and turning away from God. We were forced to witness how the drive for luxury and rising joy in ever more ostentatious fashions diverted our people from the old sacredness of its renowned ideal world view. We saw how the pursuit of material wealth and all around greediness increasingly filled their hearts. And then we wondered fearfully, if a people who have erred in their highest convictions could still have a great future?

Today stands before us a completely changed people. The Germans would have to not be Germans, if they felt themselves satisfied in the long run, like the French, through the shallow teachings of the so-called scientific materialism. The time had to come when the people of the Reformation, for whom like few others religious questions have been among the deepest matters of the heart, again recalled the roots of their strength. The nation that had brought forth a Goethe and Schiller, a Kant and Schliermacher, must sooner or later strive to return to the high earnestness of the world view that above all illuminated the splendid works of our classical writers.

The hard steel of emergency strikes the German heart, and again as so often in the great days of our history, a spark springs out that we had in vain attempted to awake through admonitions and teaching, through persuasion and preaching. We experience again the old truth that once became clear to the noble Queen Luise in flight from the same enemy that threatens us today, that *trials and tribulations are God's blessings*. That they are the eternal means through which He raises the people to Himself.

We hope for victory, but we do not know the outcome of the war. But we can indeed predict one thing, that an inner, deepened and ennobled German people will come out of this terrible fight for its existence. Let the enemy from without threaten us as dangerous, we have already overcome the far more dangerous enemy from within that threatened to corrupt our people. The days when unbelief, doubt, materialism and moral frivolity threatened Germany are gone.

And when we see, how in dynastic loyalty the German people assemble around their emperor and princes today, how the monarchical sense so splendidly preserves itself, then one can with joy pronounce, that today along with the great Bismarck's words to which we referred to at the start, the prophecy of another noble German patriot also holds true. The words that Heinrich von Trietschke once pronounced: "The coming twentieth century will be Christian and monarchical!"

And these German people, that today once again in their greatness raise themselves, that lays down in the opening battles the complete profundity, the complete noble courage of its *Weltanschauung*, the complete power and strength of strong idealism, they should be toppled by foreign enemies? And by what sort of enemies! Beyond the channel an originally brave and high striving people, that today have completely fallen for the curse of materialism, that no longer knows the honor of armed service who fights wars with mercenaries—a modern Carthage. In France a people without religious belief, without a sense of right, without shame and without cultivation. A nation that has already for centuries fulfilled the sad calling to be the teacher of moral frivolousness to other peoples. A people, that had long unlearned, to kneel before God; a nation of vanity and self deception, a land whose so-called fine literature virtually stinks from uncultivation. And finally in Russia a people of Asiatic rawness; a land where no corruption extending to the highest circles is dirty or unworthy enough to be practiced shamelessly and, one might say, boldly in the light of day. A people, where the vain veneer of exterior civilization makes the inner rawness of barbaric un-culture [*Unkultur*] only more repulsive.

And these three morally corrupt people believe that they can treacherously attack and destroy one of the noblest cultural peoples [*Kulturvölker*] that the earth has seen! No, as long as there is a divinely ruled world, as long as an eternal unchanging will administers the destiny of men, that will not happen. God does not select the morally corrupt people as his instruments, rather the noble, ethically heightened people. If our people turn once again to God; so God will not let them down, rather lead them to new great deeds.

The poet says, that on German essence the world will be healed. But to fulfill this mission, the German essence must first heal itself. The terrible war will purify and heighten us, the refuse that in the long years of peace had laid itself around the noble core of the German national character will jump off, and the pure gold, the broad and splendid treasure of the German spirit and heart will reveal itself again before the eyes of the world, as it has so often in our history.

In our breast is our star of destiny!

The following is the concluding part of a series of articles that Eduard Bernstein had written in support of the war. While he clearly supported the war and blamed Russia for causing it, he is also critical of his own government and warns that it must be viewed in the East as liberators if they have any hope of justifying their action. It is worth noting that he did not feel that it was his place to comment on military strategy because he was a layman.

Vorwärts, August 28, 1914 (Beilage, p. 1)

"Reckoning with Russia: A Legacy of Our Rival" (part 3) by Eduard Bernstein

In 1879, Bismarck brought about, as a counter-defense against the Russian machinations of the time, an alliance treaty with Austria and expanded it in 1883 to the Dreibund. He took the edge off the threat through a secret neutrality treaty with Russia in 1884. In 1885, he allows Russia free reign against the Bulgarians who had fallen in disfavor in Petersburg; he permits Battenberg to fall to please Russia; for the same reason he opposed Kolberger; in order to put the French in a favorable mood he supported their colonial undertakings. And with all that did not prevent that the French idea of revenge continues to be fueled by Russia and in the second half of the 1880s flared up to a bright flame in the form of Boulangismus. Fortunately, in France's democracy this finds strong resistance: the war will be avoided. But the anti-German tug of the tsarist diplomacy in the meantime lead Bismarck to feel compelled to forbid the lending of Russian assets through the Reichsbank and sea trade, and thereby blocking Russian loans on the German market. A measure whose factual justification was not to be argued, but its results led Russia tightening its hold on France more firmly. Russia pressed France into the service of its policy, that it becomes in the growing measure its debtor, and the keeping alive of the idea of revenge becomes also a financial interest of Russia's.

All later efforts by Bismarck and his successors to win back Russia's friendship through diplomatic favor failed because of these circumstances. In addition, there exists in the circle of Russian nobles, the higher civil servants, and broad levels of the Russian bourgeoisie a traditional hatred of Germans that no other land can surpass. That is the reason why the same slice of parliamentarianism that Russia has today could not alter the anti-German course of its foreign policy. Tsarism is not simply the personal regime of the current bearer of the Russian Crown, rather it is a system of Russian politics whose representative and—as the case may be, instrument the current tsar is. This system, however, in reference to Russian foreign policy is not weakened by a parliament in which the nobles and bourgeoisie of Russia have the most influence, but rather has only been intensified.

The German warfare has directed the first attack not to the east, but rather to the west against France, who one could say is forged to Russia through financial chains. As a layman, I will not argue about the strategic expediency of the action from a military stand point. Politically, however, because it was tied with the breach of Belgian neutrality, it has brought bitter opposition to Germany, also in countries that had previously been well disposed toward Germany. What Germany has lost thereby cannot be lightly valued by those who think about how Germany's economic life should be constructed after the war. In the eyes of Europe's democracies, Germany's military strategy will only be justified when it shows itself as merely the *prelude to the political reckoning with Russia* that had become unavoidable due to the state of affairs.

What advantages do we gain from a defeat of France and a successful defense against England's maritime attack if tsarist Russia comes out of the war intact? They will fall light as a feather on the scale, in as much if they, following the cries of the pan-Germans, translate into the annexation of French or Belgian territory, Germany will achieve only ruin. We must attempt to close such a peace with the western Nations that promises a peaceful community, if not an immediate reconciliation. We must strive for it and we will achieve it all the sooner the more thoroughly we hold tsarist Russia to account.

If Germany were democratically ruled, no doubt would exist about how that would be achieved. A democratic Germany would lead a revolutionary war to the east. It would call upon nations oppressed by Russia to resist it and give them the means to fight earnestly for their liberation. It would make the peasants take an interest in a German victory to seek the democracy [enjoyed by] the cities—in short, it would bring the latent domestic war out into the open. Driven by the same strength as happened in France in the early part of the French Revolution, and to this day has garnered great sympathy toward France from the people in Belgium, Holland, Italy, etc., such a campaign would quickly have eliminated the Russian peril for Germany and Europe from the world.

However, Germany is no democracy, it is therefore utopian to expect from it such a policy with all of its consequences. But it is not too much to demand from its rulers that they take as examples the political warfare against Russia of Napoleon in 1806 and Bismarck in 1866. Through the conduct of the German Poles, that have so much to forget, it is made easy for them to embrace the Russian

Poles as liberators. The Germans advancing must bring salvation to the Poles, the Finns and the other nationalities oppressed by Russia due to their language or religion, from the political yoke that burdens them. And indeed, not simply a liberation on paper. Because we know how tsarist Russia keeps its promises. Not the French, the great majority of whom went to war against us with very heavy hearts as dictated by the rhetoric form Petersburg among which a growing number of responsible politicians sincerely and with longing strove for a reconciliation with Germany—tsarism and its nationalistic drivers must be made to carry the costs of the war. That is not only a command of justice, it is also a command of political wisdom. If tsarism remains unaltered in control or if one leaves it to temporarily come to terms with its domestic opposition with sundry concessions, as defeated governments are wont to grant, then once again let it be said, *the enormous sacrifices of this war have been made for nothing.* (We have reproduced this explanation without agreeing with all of the particulars. Editor of *Vorwärts.*)

The following is a typical report of Russian atrocities in the East. Russian actions were consistently depicted as barbaric and foreign to the European. Brandt was one of the few reporter granted access to the front. He sent reports to numerous papers. Some were later published under the title *Funf Monate an der Ostfront...Kriegsberichte (Five Months of the Eastern Front...War Reports).*[165]

Norddeutsche Allgemeine Zeitung, **September 19, 1914, p. 1**

"From the Eastern Theatre" by Rolf Brandt

1st Army High Command, 14 September. The German Army pursues [General] Rennenkampf's defeated Russian Army with all the strength that man and steed can possibly give. In these days, our infantry has marched fifty and sixty kilometers and had to acquire quarters in the evening with the bayonet. This unparalleled accomplishment of our Eastern Army was achieved after an exhausting three-day battle, after a tremendous march a week earlier to encircle the Russian Narew Army.

Yesterday, we drove in an automobile along side our troops for sixty-five kilometers almost to the Russian border.

They march forward (the strong rain had changed the fabulous provincial streets into little morasses). They march thoroughly covered and dirty, and they sang soldier's songs. And suddenly a company began to sing "Deutschland Deutschland über alles." In the last days before I departed Berlin, I had heard that song sung in so many cafes, that I thought I would never want to hear that song again. One sang it like one sang "Puppchen" before, as a fashionable patriotic song. Here it became fresh and bright again, and the Thuringian and Hessian marched to it as night fell. One must repeat it in every report. One must write it twice every day: this Eastern army, assembled from all corners, over taxed and exhausted, is splendid, splendid beyond all measure. The East Prussian Army Corps, that since the beginning of the campaign have been here on bitter and difficult work, have earned the warmest thanks of Germany. In our German Armies in West and East everyone certainly does his duty; but they have achieved more than one could assume, that even German soldiers themselves could muster.

Now East Prussia is free. The Russians have withdrawn from our embrace at the right time. Our troops that marched through the Masurian Lakes against the southern Russian flank had to overcome stronger resistance than one would have believed. Rennenkampf pitched the 22nd Finnish rifle corps against them, that our corps had to clear out first. That gave the northern Russian flank time to retreat. It abandoned its ingeniously constructed position before Gerdauen and marched out. For nine days Rennenkampf had prepared for the German attack. One could see artillery positions that were tidily built and that the old Russian reputation as good defensive troops was thoroughly confirmed as far as the fortification of positions was concerned. The trees for kilometers along the magnificent eastern tree lined streets from Gerdauen to Nordenburg were felled on the German side of the approach and every branch and every twig had been cleanly sharpened. Infantry trenches had been provided with covered pathways. They did not even make an earnest attempt to hold the position. We have driven the Russians out of East Prussia with such a superior strategy, that the old veteran Rennenkampf only attempted to salvage the retreat.

This last attempt to bring the Russian army over the border somewhat intact was shattered as a result of our unparalleled pursuit. Rennenkampf's Russian Army no longer withdraws, it runs in pure flight and our operations against them are, as I write these lines, in full swing.

East Prussia is free; it is liberated from robbers and murderous thugs. In the last report I wrote that so much was proven that hardly anything else remained. It is certain that there is hardly a vulgarity that the Russian soldiers in East Prussia have not committed. I could convince myself through first hand experience of deeds that the European simply held for impossible. From the country road across the flat land as far as one can see tower the burnt ruins of the farmers and estate owners. Only the larger cities remain spared. Little Nordenburg (3000 inhabitants), where we spent the night, was left by the soldiers of the Emperor of all Russians in such a condition that no one can believe, that no one can imagine. War is war, and that excesses occur is sad, but understandable; but this has nothing to do with excesses but rather the *planned destruction of a flowering land through banditry and deadly arson*. From top to bottom, building by building was ransacked and soiled in such a bestial fashion that one would think that herds of swine had been housed in these merchant's businesses, pharmacies, grocery stores and homes. One must emphasize that here every expression is not an invective, but the only designation that our language was for such occurrences. In order to describe the Russian conduct correctly, our rich German language must invent new words, our stock is not sufficient to describe the vulgarity and bestiality. We Europeans and German could not yet imagine these things until now.

This article is one of many that appeared on this or the following day that attempted to prove that England's reasons for entering the war were phony. Many papers printed large excerpts from the *Norddeutsche* article and wrote lengthy commentaries. This is the clearest attempt on the part of the German government to change the focus of the war from Russia to England. It was successful. From October 1914 onward, the majority of German papers focused on England as the chief threat to Germany.

Vossische Zeitung, **October 16, 1914, p. 1**

"Conspiracy against Germany" (editorial)

Norddeutsche Allgemeine Zeitung is publishing a series of official documents that reveal the English-French-Russian attack against Germany. We provide detailed excerpts from these documents in the third supplement.

The outbreak of the war was not the first time that they who have forced the war against us have raised complaints against "German militarism," against "the German Military Party." In all the years of a long peace, while accepting challenges and threats calmly in a feeling of strength, we have heard the same charges: that we strengthened our defense of peace in order to maintain the peace that they wanted to disturb for us, proved our desire for war. The scolding against war-like Germany became louder and louder. And because this Germany never attacked, one thought that they felt too weak to do so, and from Paris and Petersburg came the ridiculing calls that they were only waiting for the completion of the arming that would finally secure the superiority of our opponents. Public opinion in France and Russia was prepared with all means for the war. What was of necessity hidden until the last moment—i.e. they expected war with certainty in 1916—was only the nearness of the point in time, in which the decision would be brought out. At the same time in England, the public still had the feeling, even with the strong anti-German current, that one had the freedom to decide; and German willingness during the Balkan Wars to concede to Sir Edward Grey a leading role as mediator seemed to confirm that England was still unallied. Since then we have learned how firmly it was already allied, and as the pre-history of the war becomes clearer, the more frequently the question hung on German lips: whether our diplomacy in the last years was up to the task. We could not be taken be taken by surprise militarily; has it not happened to us diplomatically?

Both of these legends, that of our lust for war and defiant preparation for war and that of our diplomatic unpreparedness, are simultaneously destroyed by the recent publication of documents concerning the pre-history of the war in the *Norddeutsche Allgemeine Zeitung*. These are intelligence reports to the Berlin Foreign Office, produced from secret files, in order to show how the threads were gradually pulled together around us and how we marked it. In March 1913, a highly important report arrived at Wilhelmstraße: the ambassador reminds that a military arrangement between England and France had already been known and imparts the essential contents of a since concluded Anglo-French maritime convention. He can also reveal, what the situation is with these army and navy conventions *before* the conclusion of an alliance—they otherwise usually follow. The alliance has in fact been formed since 22 November 1912. Only not formally; because the English constitution does not permit a secret alliance, and the English practice must therefore find a form to circumvent the constitution. That happened through the exchange of letters between Sir Edward Grey and Ambassador Paul Cambon, the essence [of the exchange]: Each confirms to the other that the common plans of the General and Admiral Staffs of England and France have not obligated them to proceed in common. However, if the occasion arises, as soon as one decides to proceed in common, those plans should be brought forth. No alliance treaty, this correspondence! One is simply covering all possibilities like the man who in the evening goes into the forest with a loaded weapon—after all, he could be attacked there. That was England's freedom of movement! At the least since March 1913, our Foreign Office has known about the Anglo-French alliance. One can picture the events of that month. Before mid-March 1913, notice was given by the German government, that the necessity of strengthening of the army has become acknowledged unanimously in the consultation with leading figures and that they agreed about the principles for covering the costs of the Army Bill. Simultaneously (12 March) an official declaration was released in which a calm judgment over the European situation closed with: As long as the eternal world peace is not yet guaranteed, Germany must reckon with a war for its very existence on multiple fronts. For such an eventuality, that Germany can be forced against its will, the new Army Bill should make provisions.... The conviction that it is our duty to make these provisions is so commonly held by the entire people that this baseless warmongering can only distort it. Resolved to preserved the peace as long as possible, the German government emphatically rejected apprehensions, which the visible machination of our enemies aroused, and remained on guard.

It learned about the conclusion of the Anglo-French alliance in a timely fashion, and it was in the last month before the war completely instructed about the realization of the Anglo-Russian alliance. The further published documents show this. During King George's and Grey's visit to Paris (May 1914), Iswolski stimulated military-political arrangements between England and Russia. Grey is won over and wins the entire English cabinet for it. England, which had made itself to be the tool of French thoughts of revenge, now plays into the hands of tsarism without Parliament or public suspecting anything. French indiscretion permitted information about the Anglo-Russian naval convention to make its way into the public. Questioned in Parliament, Grey responded with the ambiguous truthfulness of the oracle, in essence: that England was not bound to Russian and will not be bound. The naval convention should be merely a contingent treaty, like the one with France. But on 26 May in St. Petersburg, the plan of this convention was solidified in a conference by the Chief the Russian Naval Staff. And this plan that has been relayed today, even if there was no time for its realization, is of particular interest for one reason. Namely, it states: "In the area of the Bosphorus and Dardanelles, temporary undertakings in the straits should be considered as Russian strategic operations in the event of war." And further: "With the consent of England, Russian ships must be permitted to use English harbors as bases in the eastern Mediterranean Sea, just as the French maritime convention allows the Russian Navy to base itself in French harbors in the western Mediterranean." The result of that is that the passage of Russian warships through the Dardanelles, which could be compelled in emergency situations [breaking Turkey's neutrality], had long been a part of a common Franco-Russian plan and had also become a common Anglo-Russian plan. And it is understood what roll the English marine mission played in the Bosphorus and why Turkey had to rid itself of it and had to close the straits.

We were encircled under George V as under Edward [VII]. England has allied itself with France, Russia, Belgium and Japan, and put itself in the service of foreign hate and ambition and placed foreigners again in the service of its brutal selfishness in order to bring down Germany; as usual, it considered the strongest as its enemy and has attempted to bring it down. After documents, like the ones published today, one must stop speaking of a German War Party.

This last selection, from Werner Sombart, is representative of German attempts to claim the cultural high ground. Germans are fighting for higher values than mere crass materialism, and for that reason, Germany will win.

Berliner Tageblatt, **November 21, 1914, pp. 1–2**

"What We Are Fighting For" by Werner Sombart

(This is the conclusion of an article that appeared on 2 November under the title "Our Enemies.")

If we had not yet known why we are fighting, the enemies, especially England, would have told us as they issued the battle cry: The battle against Germany is about the destruction of "militarism." Therewith, they have with unerring instinct the hostile principle recognized and have simultaneously opened our eyes to what they are defending against "militarism," that is what constitutes the opposite of this. It is nothing other than commercialism, mercantilism, capitalism or however else one wants to identify this type of disposition, out of which England conducts this war.

This like all its previous wars. Because whether it pursued Spain in the sixteenth century, Holland in the seventeenth, France in the eighteenth as the main enemy; whether it conducted in the nineteenth century against China the Opium War, against the Boers the Gold-Diamond Wars: its behavior always follows the same line. With almost frightening clarity, also in this war, this pure mercantile orientation again comes to light: in the view of the sense and goal of the war not less than in the art and manner of its conduct.

Above all: the war has a "Goal!" And this goal is purely commercial in nature: that their high level of trade and industry profits that are threatened by Germany's competition must be maintained. In other words, the same motivation, that is at the base of every capitalistic undertaking. So then the war itself will also be seen as nothing other than a capitalistic undertaking and as such organized. There is the overriding thought: one does not conduct war himself. But one has war conducted. As one buys a cotton mill, production equipment, and labor on the market for its business, so according to the principle of the mercenary army, cannons and soldiers. It is the old viewpoint of shopkeeper's warfare, such as Carthage in antiquity and the Italian banking states in the Middle Ages. Still better and from a mercantile stand point more correctly considered, is it to conduct the war in no way at your own cost or risk, but simply to take part with a capital investment in the undertaking: that was the procedure of England in the eighteenth century when it flooded the European states with their subsidies. Unfortunately, nowadays it is no longer so convenient to close this deal. Today, the deals in general are hard to make: that is indeed the trademark of our time, and also here the "damned Germans" have made life sour for the poor British, just as they have by trade in the commercial market.

Today a more artful process must have been employed in order to get foreign nations to fight for England's trade interests: if one cannot give them the order like branches and bureaus of the home office "to deliver" so and so many men: so one proceeds with the colonial people, who are naturally for the English in England also foreign, with vassal states like Egypt and Portugal: so one must either enter into a partnership, that is appropriate for similarly disposed nations on the order of the Japanese, or—where one still must reckon with a certain law of decency and chivalry, as with the French and Belgians, there one must understand how to deftly exploit their weaknesses in order that they also participate in the undertaking.

So once the undertaking is set in motion the eye of the careful salesman has to watch (to see) that it is carried out with the highest possible benefit and with the slightest possible loss. Foreign troops cost England nothing: they can therefore be sacrificed as one wishes: also foreign cities can be bombed (Antwerp, Ostende with English artillery!). However, ones own troops must be paid in cash: consequently, they must be spared as much as possible. What happened not long ago in Antwerp in accordance with these mercantile principles screams to heaven. Without even a thought to duty and loyalty and decency, the English troops moved out of the besieged fort that they are supposed to defend, just in time to reach the ships in Ostende that bring the refugees to safety unscathed. I am convinced that it has not occurred even for a moment to the department heads, which preside as Ministers of the Commercial Firm England, Ltd., that it was an unspeakably dirty affair. They would, if one reproached them, answer: but it was more practical to handle it so. From their standpoint, they are completely correct.

I called England a commercial firm. The entire way and manner that England conducts the war strikes one completely and totally like a struggle that an unscrupulous firm wages against its competition. Since its participation with troops plays basically no role, the most important means of battle that England itself employs are immediate commercial oppression and chicanery, that are above all certain to damage our material interests: boycotting, patent theft, harming customers, privateering—the English business managers appear hardly to think about anything else. Yes, it is known that England alone is to be thanked for the fact that there is still privateering today in which also nations hostile to England of necessity must participate. It reveals the most inner essence of its warfare, which it considers this shabby form of fight as fundamentally one of the most important components, which it, as it declared at a recent international conference, "cannot forego."

But one also frequently has the impression as if a businessman is playing out a new trump against the competition, if one reads the official English war reports: so for example, when the arrival of Indian troops in France was announced: "a wonderful, wonderful article that surpasses all previous arrived today and is on display in the window." Advertising, commercial boosting, depreciation of the opponents: it all fits the picture. Also the purely quantitative observations of the war come from the same spiritual ground. How often have we heard now about the millions of soldiers of the noble Lord Kitchener and that so and so many troops come from Canada, from India, from Portugal. Always numbers and only numbers. From the standpoint of the entrepreneur who sees in the high turnover the surest sign that business is flourishing, this was thought out in a very thorough going way. With shameless openness, Churchill also declared: England will win because it has the last million to spend. Here is also the pure capitalistic conception of things not cloaked with any cape. It is frankly spoken: For us, the war is a business like any other. And because we live in the Age of Capitalism, the business with the greatest capital will carry the victory.

There were some of us, who before the war thought: this spirit that fills England is the general spirit of the people in whom the capitalist economic system has come to prevail. Many nations could not conduct the war in any other spirit than the capitalist spirit. The events of the last months have set straight all who thought that belief was better. We, who were alive at this time, have experienced in the innermost part of our souls that there is another war than England's. That is the war that is conducted by Germany and we could easily add Austria-Hungary. No war for external successes, no war for money and possession, no war for a goal; rather a war for the life of our Fatherland, for the existence of our people and states.... The entire people are a single steel plated warrior, inspired by one will, no longer by the will of the individual, but the will of the whole. The individual is a part of the whole, serves only it, like the individual part of our body serves the entire body. In battle, true, aware of duty, devoted, fit, prepared for sacrifice: that is that "militarism" that you shopkeepers hate. That is heroism, that is simple German heroism.

Now we see clearly what is at stake in this struggle. Now we see clearly who fights whom: the warrior with the shopkeeper. Now we know the battle cry under which both warring parties take to the field of battle. "We fight to the last Mark," they say. "We fight to the last man," we answer.

NOTES

1.The superiority of British propaganda has gone virtually unquestioned. David Welch is the first to seriously challenge this view. He argues that in some respects, Germany's propaganda was superior to Great Britain's. See David Welch, *Germany, Propaganda, and Total War, 1914–1918* (New Brunswick, N.J.: Rutgers University Press, 2000).

2. *Burgfrieden* literally means "fortress of peace" and was the term associated with Wilhelm II's claim that he no longer recognized political parties, only Germans. Implicit in this position is that all opposition to the war and government should be muted in the interest of German unity.

3. Roger Chickering, *Imperial Germany and the Great War, 1914–1918* (Cambridge: Cambridge University Press, 1998), 47.

4. For a good brief overview of the various political tendencies of the German press, see Klaus Wernecke, *Der Wille zur Weltgeltung. Außenpolitik und Öffentlichkeit im Kaiserreich am Vorabend des Ersten Weltkrieges* (Düsseldorf: Droste, 1970), 11–25.

5. The article, "Russland und Deutschland," appeared in the midday edition on 2 March 1914. Risto Ropponen sets the prewar circulation for the *Kölnische Zeitung* between 70,000 and 75,000. See Risto Ropponen, *Die russische Gefahr. Das Verhaltnis der offentliche Meinung Deutschlands und Österreich-Ungarns gegenüber der Außenpolitik Rußlands in der Zeit zwischen dem Friedens von Portsmouth und dem Ausbruch des Ersten Weltkrieg* (Helsinki: Suomen historiallen seura, 1976), 24.

6. Meinolf Rohleder and Burkhard Treude provide a good brief introduction to the history and political influence of *Kreuzzeitung*; however, they do not provide prewar circulation figures. See Meinolf Rohleder and Burkhard Treude, "Neue

Preussische (Kreuz-) Zeitung," in *Deutsche Zeitungen des 17. bis 20. Jahrhundert*, Hrsg. Heinz-Dietrich Fischer (Pullach bei München: Verlag Dokumentation, 1972), 209–24.

7. Volker Schulze, "Vorwärts," in *Deutsche Zeitungen des 17. bis 20. Jahrhundert*, Hrsg. Heinz-Dietrich Fischer (Pullach bei München: Verlag Dokumentation, 1972), 336. The increase in the paper's circulation in the early twentieth century reflected the growth of the SPD. The number of papers printed daily grew from 56,000 in 1902 to 112,000 in 1906 and 165,000 in 1912 (337).

8. Klaus Bender, "Vossische Zeitung," in *Deutsche Zeitungen des 17. bis 20. Jahrhundert*, Hrsg. Heinz-Dietrich Fischer (Pullach bei München: Verlag Dokumentation, 1972), 37. According to Bender, the paper had 25,000 subscribers in 1914; although a relatively small number, the high quality and intellectual tradition of the *Vossische Zeitung* made it a "Prestigeblatt" (38).

9. Kurt Koszyk, *Deutsche Pressepolitik im Ersten Weltkrieg* (Düsseldorf: Droste Verlag, 1968), 156. Before World War I the paper's circulation was well over 100,000. It reached a high of 170,000 copies daily in 1917. See Kurt Paupié, "Frankfurter Zeitung," in *Deutsche Zeitungen des 17. bis 20. Jahrhundert*, Hrsg. Heinz-Dietrich Fischer (Pullach bei München: Verlag Dokumentation, 1972), 248.

10. Gotthart Schwarz, "Berliner Tageblatt," in *Deutsche Zeitungen des 17. bis 20. Jahrhundert*, Hrsg. Heinz-Dietrich Fischer (Pullach bei München: Verlag Dokumentation, 1972), 318, 321. Recovering from a low of 55,000 in 1895, from 1900 on the number of subscribers rose steadily, reaching a high of 245,000 in 1916 (320).

11. Rolf Kramer, "Kölnische Volkszeitung," in *Deutsche Zeitungen des 17. bis 20. Jahrhundert*, Hrsg. Heinz-Dietrich Fischer (Pullach bei München: Verlag Dokumentation, 1972), 261. Kramer states that from the turn of the century to 1914 the paper's circulation grew from 20,000 to close to 30,000 (260). The other leading Catholic paper was *Germania*. Centered in Berlin and more liberal in its approach, *Germania* will not be included in this discussion. After the *Kulturkampf*, *Germania* lost its position of primacy as the leading voice of the Center Party, and the spectrum of liberal foreign-policy approaches is adequately covered by the other liberal Berlin papers.

12. Klaus Wernecke notes that one Prussian official, in a letter to the Reichs Chancellory, described the paper as practically indispensable in Bavaria. See Wernecke, *Der Wille zur Weltgeltung*, 12. Risto Ropponen puts the prewar circulation figure at somewhere between 140,000 and 160,000. See Ropponen, *Die russische Gefahr*, 28.

13. See *Vorwärts*, 30 July 1914; *Leipziger Volkszeitung*, 1 August 1914; *Berliner Tageblatt*, 1 August 1914; *Kreuzzeitung*, 2 August 1914; and *Münchner Neueste Nachrichten*, 3 August 1914. Further citations of these newspapers will be abbreviated to their initials: *V, LV, BT, K,* and *MNN*. Unless otherwise noted, all stories appear on page one of the edition cited.

14. Koszyk, *Deutsche Pressepolitik*, 20–21. On the same day, Bavaria, through royal decree, also declared a state of war in accordance with Article 1 of the "Gesetz über den Kriegzustand vom 5. November 1912."

15. For the complete list of restrictions, see Koszyk, *Deutsche Pressepolitik*, 22–23.

16. Koszyk, *Deutsche Pressepolitik*, 28.

17. Walter Nicolai, *Nachrichtendienst, Presse und Volksstimmung im Weltkrieg* (Berlin: E. S. Mittler und sohn, 1920), 168.

18. Koszyk, *Deutsche Pressepolitik*, 24–25.

19. Walter Nicolai, "Nachrichtwesen und Aufkläung," in *Der Grosse Krieg 1914–1918*, Hrsg. M. Schwarte, Bd. 8, *Die Organisationen der Kriegsführung*, (Leipzig: J. A. Barth, 1923), 489. See also chapter 2 of Welch, *Germany*.

20. Nicolai, "Nachrichtwesen und Aufkläung," 489.

21. A good example of this attitude is the reaction of the Reichs Marine Amt to criticism of its *U-bootkriegs* policy. See Abschrift: Schreiben des Kreigspresseamte von 29.3.16. and Nr. 433 Geheim 23.4.16., Abschrift: Nr. 3694/J. Nr.1511 b. Geheim, in RM 5/3722 in BA Freiburg.

22. See Steven Koss, *The Rise and Fall of the Political Press in Britain*, vol. 2, *The Twentieth Century* (Chapel Hill and London: University of North Carolina Press, 1984) for examples of cooperation between the British officials and publishers.

23. Nicolai, "Nachrichtwesen und Aufklärung," 486. Nicolai's writings about the *Nachrichtwesen* during the war are useful, but must be used cautiously. For example, he charged Entente propaganda with putting the blame for the war on Germany. He also condemned the *Berliner Tageblatt* and *Frankfurter Zeitung*, which he called *"ausgesprochen jüdische Blätter,"* for helping to undermine morale with their liberal and democratic tendencies. Nicolai, *Nachrichtendienst*, 172; see also 71. He remarked that it could be said that during the war the press failed in terms of the result of their work—that is, if one defined success in terms of keeping domestic morale high regardless of reality (166). By laying the blame for the decline of domestic morale on the press, especially the "Jewish" press, Nicolai was contributing to the "stab in the back" theory, which maintained that Germany was not defeated on the field of battle, but lost due to a domestic subterfuge.

24. Koszyk, *Deutsche Pressepolitik*, 58.

25. Ibid., 59–60.

26. Ibid., 68.

27. Welch, *Germany*, 36.

28. *Kölnische Zeitung*, 2 August 1914. Further citations of this newspaper will be abbreviated as *KZ*.

29. See *MNN* and *B*, 3 August 1914; and *Norddeutsche Allgemeine Zeitung*, 4 August 1914. (Further citations of this newspaper will be abbreviated as NAZ.) The story also appeared in smaller regional papers: see *West-deutsche Zeitung* and *Breisgauer Volkszeitung*, 3 August 1914.

30. *KZ*, 4 August 1914.

31. The question of who crossed the other's border first is difficult to ascertain with complete confidence. In his monumental work on the origins of World War I, Luigi Albertini writes, "A detailed analysis of the mutual accusations and rebuttals would not only be tedious, but would be of no importance." Luigi Albertini, *The Origins of the War of 1914*, vol. 3, *The Epilogue of the Crisis of 1914: The Declaration of War and of Neutrality* (London: Oxford University Press, 1952), 204. He then notes that the French had ordered their troops to withdraw at least 10 kilometers from the border and appears to discount German claims of French encroachment while noting that there was one confirmed incident, by Moltke himself, of Germany violating French borders. The only French violation that Albertini acknowledges is the accidental drift of a French plane into the German Alsace (see

204–8 for a the full discussion). However, on the basis of materials in the Bavarian War Archives, Karl Deuringer claims that "Im Bereich des XXI. A.K., das in Lothringen östlich vom Delmer Rücken den Grenzschutz zu übernehmen hatte, rückte das 3. b. Ch.R. an seine Plätze vorwärts Duß. Die 2. u. 3./5. b. Ch.R. gingen zum gleichen Zweck von Saargemünd in den Abschnitt Delm—Château Salins ab. Allen Truppen, die an die Grenze rückten, wurde peinlichste Zurückhaltung und Vorsicht eingeschärft. Es war untersagt worden, zu schießen oder gar französisches Gebiet zu betreten. Dagegen überschritten schon am 30. Juli französische Streifen bei Ste. Marie aux Chênes nordwestlich von Metz die Grenze." See *Die Schlacht in Lothringen und in den Vogesen 1914: Die Feuertaufe der Bayerischen Armee; Bd. 1 Friedensgestalt der Armee. Mobilmachung. Ereignisse bis 22. August.* Herausgegeben von Bayerischen Kriegsarchiv (Verfaßt auf Grund der Kriegsakten von Karl Deuringer) (Munich: M. Schick, 1929), 11. My thanks to James Knechtmann for bringing this last citation to my attention.

32. *MNN*, 8 October 1914.

33. *Kölnische Volkszeitung*, 2 August 1914. Further citations of this newspaper will be abbreviated as *KV*.

34. *Frankfurter Zeitung*, 4 August 1914. Further citations of this newspaper will be abbreviated as *FZ*.

35. "Der Kampf gegen Zarismus," *V*, 3 August 1914.

36. *Vossische Zeitung*, 30 July 1914. Further citations of this newspaper will be abbreviated as *VZ*. Cf. Graf A. von Mont, "Der russische Feind," *BT*, 16 September 1914. See also *FZ*, 3 August 1914.

37. *K*, 12 August 1914.

38. *MNN*, 30 August 1914; cf. *BT*, 7 August 1914.

39. The last days of July witnessed an aggressive campaign by the official organ of the Social Democrats to whip up popular sentiment against the war. The front page of the 27 July issue of *Vorwärts* loudly proclaimed itself to be "Still against the War!" (*Immer wieder gegen den Krieg*). Two days later the paper would claim that the declaration of war was "against reason and Volk."

40. A Baltic émigré, Schiemann held the first chair in Russian history in Germany. For background on Schiemann's Russophobic credentials, see Klaus Meyer, *Theodor Schiemann als politischer Publizist* (Frankfurt and Hamburg: Rütten & Loening, 1956). A discussion of Schiemann's "Rußlandbild" can be found in Loren K. Campion, "Behind the Modern *Drang nach Osten:* Baltic Emigrés and Russophobia in Nineteenth-Century Germany" (Ph. D. diss., Indiana University, 1966). For an account that places Schiemann's "Rußlandbild" in a broader intellectual context, see Troy R. E. Paddock, "Historiker als Poltiker," in *Russen und Rußland aus deutscher Sicht. Band 4: 19./20. Jahrhundert: Von der Reichsgründung bus zum Ersten Weltkrieg,* ed. Mechthild Keller, in the series *West-östliche Spiegelungen,* ed. Lew Kopelew (Munich: Wilhelm Fink Verlag, 2000), 298–348.

41. Eduard Bernstein, "Abrechnung mit Russland," *V*, 26 August 1914.

42. Ibid. The following day Bernstein would claim, in the second part of his article, that Russia's chief diplomatic talent lay in the ability to use the conflict of other great powers for personal (i.e., territorial) gains. (Beilage, p. 1.)

43. Ibid., *V*, 28 August 1914, Beilage, p. 1.

44. Ibid.

45. The liberation of the peoples of Russia would be a familiar theme in socialist papers. On 12 October 1914, *Vorwärts* ran an article about how the British press was hoping that the war will push Russia toward political reform. The socialist daily responded that victory would only strengthen the Russian state. This latter view would be reiterated 13 days later (see *V*, 25 October 1914, pp. 1–2). Amid reports that the war was gaining popularity in Russia, *Leipziger Volkszeitung* restated that its initial fear, that war would strengthen the tsarist regime instead of bringing about revolution, was being realized. See *LV*, 13 November 1914.

46. Susanne Miller, "Bernstein's Political Position, 1914–1920," in *Bernstein to Brandt: A Short History of German Social Democracy*, ed. Roger Fletcher (London: Edward Arnold, 1987), 97.

47. J. Jastow, "Wer ist Russland," *BT*, 8 August 1914.

48. Ibid. For similar observations, see *FZ*, 1 August 1914; and *VZ*, 31 July 1914. The *Kölnische Zeitung* also declared, on 11 August 1914, that the War Party in Russia has been itching for a war with Germany for quite some time.

49. *LV*, 5 August 1914. In addition to the suppression of Poles and Baltic Germans, newspapers also reported the long history of Russian anti-Semitism and oppression of the Finns. For examples of the former, see *NAZ*, 19 August 1914; *NAZ*, 15 September 1914; and *MNN*, 3 September 1914.

50. *MNN*, 20 September 1914. The *Frankfurter Zeitung* also claimed, on 22 August 1914, that Russification was due to the Russian hatred of Baltic Germans. For further examples of this theme, see *FZ*, 2 September 1914; *BT*, 8 September 1914; and *MNN*, 17 November 1914.

51. "The Fiasco of Pan-Slavism," *KZ*, 13 August 1914.

52. *MNN*, 11 August 1914; *KV*, 13 August 1914; *KV* 16 August 1914; and *FZ*, 30 August 1914.

53. *KV*, 10 August 1914. The *Frankfurter Zeitung* noted on 30 August 1914 that Slavs inside Austria-Hungary were "Austrian, anti-Russian, and above all anti-Tsar." For similar observations concerning Slavic support for the Habsburg monarchy inside Austria-Hungry, see *VZ*, 14 August 1914; *VZ*, 18 August 1914; *BT*, 8 August 1914, p. 2; and *NAZ*, 19 September 1914.

54. *BT*, 7 August 1914; *NAZ*, 7 August 1914; and *KZ*, 8 August 1914.

55. *VZ*, 7 August 1914. For similar characterizations, see *V*, 3 August 1914; *V*, 12 October 1914; and *BT*, 8 September 1914.

56. Major Moraht, *BT*, 13 August 1914.

57. For a more detailed discussion of this theme, see Troy R.E. Paddock, "Still Stuck at Sevastopol: The Depiction of Russia during the Russo-Japanese War and the Beginning of the First World War in the German Press," *German History* 16:3 (1998): 358–76.

58. Major Moraht, *BT*, 13 August 1914.

59. Paul Rohrbach, "Our Russian Opponent," *FZ*, 18 August 1914.

60. Paul Rohrbach, "Our Russian Opponent," *FZ*, 19 August 1914.

61. *K*, 20 November 1914.

62. Ibid.

63. *BT*, 7 August 1914.

64. *K*, 18 September 1914.

65. *KV*, 6 August 1914.

66.   *K*, 12 August 1914. For a more detailed account of Russian atrocity stories, see Paddock, "Still Stuck at Sevastopol."

67.   For an account of Schiemann's career as a journalist, see Meyer, *Theodor Schiemann als politischer Publizist*.

68.   Theodor Schiemann, "Die äußere Politik der Woche," *K*, 5 August 1914; for an almost identical analysis of Russian designs, see *K*, 12 August 1914.

69.   Ibid., *K*, 12 August 1914.

70.   Ibid., *K*, 26 August 1914.

71.   Ibid.

72.   Ibid.

73.   Ibid., *K*, 5 August 1914.

74.   *V*, 24 August 1914.

75.   *K*, 17 August 1914.

76.   *KZ*, 7 October 1914; and *VZ*, 20 October 1914.

77.   *NAZ*, 18 August 1914; *KZ*, 18 August 1914; *K*, 19 August 1914: *BT*, 11 August 1914; and *MNN*, 27 November 1914.

78.   *BT*, 24 August 1914. Examples cited in the three are just an extremely small sample of the kind of reports, observations, and complaints that appeared in the German press. Few were the days when the reader could not find an article or report about enemy misinformation in at least one of the 10 newspapers examined here.

79.   See *NAZ*, 9 August 1914; and *FZ*, 9 August 1914. Both newspapers carry the identical report from Wolff, the most important wire service in Germany at this time.

80.   *FZ*, 11 August 1914.

81.   *NAZ*, 8 October 1914. This claim of German virtue is not entirely true. Nicholas II was constantly belittled in the German press as an ineffectual leader both before and during the opening months of the war.

82.   *KZ*, 7 October 1914.

83.   "Presse und Pöbel," *KZ*, 21 October 1914. For a similar depiction of British hostility to Central Power citizens living in England, see *V*, 12 November 1914.

84.   *VZ*, 20 October 1914.

85.   Ibid.

86.   Ibid. "Sie haben nicht mehr zugeben wollen, dass Parisier Presse unfähig ist, wahr und aufrichtig, sittlich in höchsten Sinne zu sein."

87.   Ibid.

88.   It is worth noting that German newspapers almost never referred to England as Great Britain. Newspapers use "England" and "English" where "Britain" or "Great Britain" and "British" should be used. My thanks to my colleague Polly Beals for bringing this point to my attention.

89.   *Kölnische Zeitung* was the first to run "Das perfide Albion" as a headline (29 August 1914, and again on 12 November). Both articles contain various stories about British deception, treachery, and duplicity. While this particular slogan does not appear often in the headlines, similar sentiments are expressed routinely in all the German press. As with the anti-Russian sentiments just discussed, these anti-English sentiments draw from sometimes long-standing prewar views. For two

examples with good, but now perhaps dated, bibliographies, see Charles E. McClelland, *The German Historians and England: A Study in Nineteenth-Century Views* (Cambridge: Cambridge University Press, 1971); and Paul M. Kennedy, *The Rise of the Anglo-German Antagonism, 1860–1914* (London: Allen & Unwin, 1980). For a recent study on Anglophobia during the war, see Matthew Stibbe, *German Anglophobia and the Great War, 1914–1918* (Cambridge: Cambridge University Press, 2001). Much of the discussion in the rest of this chapter confirms Stibbe's conclusions about the kinds of arguments made against England. However, Stibbe's discussion of the nature of the initial Russophobia of the German press underestimates the complexity of the ideas at work. Contrary to his assertion, after the opening weeks of the war Russia was never treated with "benevolent sympathy" (12).

90.   *BT*, 5 August 1914.

91.   *V*, 5 August 1914. See also *VZ*, 5 August 1914.

92.   *V*, 5 August 1914.

93.   Ibid. On the same day, *Vossische Zeitung* also commented on Grey's remarks: see *VZ*, 5 August 1914, p. 2.

94.   *VZ*, 6 August 1914.

95.   Ibid.

96.   *BT*, 7 August 1914.

97.   *MNN*, 9 August 1914.

98.   *KZ*, 14 August 1914.

99.   Heinrich Triepel, *KZ*, 15 September 1914. The English jurist was not identified.

100.   Ibid.

101.   On the false accusation of the use of dumdum bullets, see H. Binder, *Was wir als Kriegsberichtestatter nicht sagen dürften!* (Munich: 1919), as noted by John Horne and Alex Kramer, "German 'Atrocities' and Franco-German Opinion, 1914: The Evidence of German Soldiers' Diaries," *Journal of Modern History* 66:1 (March 1994): 13 n. 14.

102.   *VZ*, 3 October 1914.

103.   Bethmann-Hollweg did so in an address to the Reichstag, 4 August 1914.

104.   Dr. von Miltner was the Bavarian justice minister from 1902 to 1912 and later served as editor for *Leipziger Zeitschrift für deutsches Recht*. For a brief biography, see Walther Killy and Rudolf Vierhaus, eds., *Deutsche Biographische Enzyklopädie*, Bd. 7 (Munich: K.G. Saur, 1998), 146.

105.   *MNN*, 13 September 1914.

106.   Ibid.

107.   Ibid.

108.   *NAZ*, 6 October 1914.

109.   "Der Bruch der belgischen Neutralität durch England und Belgien," *NAZ*, 13 October 1914.

110.   Ibid.

111.   Ibid.

112.   Ibid. The idea that France would use Belgium as an avenue of attack was not new to the war. In 1901 Schlieffen had put the German army through an exercise that had the French attacking through Belgium and Luxembourg. See Terence Zuber, *Inventing the Schlieffen Plan: German War Planning 1871–1914* (Oxford:

Oxford University Press, 2002), 171. Zuber notes that the possibility of a French attack through Belgium had been considered by the German General Staff even before the 1901 exercise.

113. See *BT*, 13 October 1914; and *MNN*, 13 October 1914.

114. *KZ*, 13 October 1914.

115. *FZ*, 13 October 1914.

116. *MNN*, 13 October 1914. Niall Ferguson argues that if Germany had not violated Belgian neutrality in its war against France, Britain would have. Ferguson makes no reference to the documents published by *NAZ* but rather focuses on a 23 August 1911 meeting of the Britain's Committee of Imperial Defense, the decisions of which would entail violating Belgian neutrality. See Niall Ferguson, *The Pity of War: Explaining World War I* (London: Basic Books, 1998), 64–67.

117. In fact, *Kreuzzeitung* will suggest that England was using the war to divert attention from domestic troubles in Ireland. See *K*, 19 September 1914. The benefit of war diverting the attention of Britons abroad was not lost on some members of the British elite. See Holger Herwig, *The First World War: Germany and Austria-Hungary 1914–1918* (New York: St. Martin's Press, 1997), 30–31.

118. *NAZ*, "Amtliche Aktenstücke zur Vorgeschichte dea Krieges." 16 October 1914, pp. 1–2. *Kölnische Zeitung* also published the same collection of dispatches on the same day.

119. Ibid., quoting a letter from Sir Edward Grey to Ambassador Paul Cambon, 22 November 1912. The letter was published in English. A German translation of the letter will appear in *Münchner Neueste Nachrichten* the following day.

120. *VZ*, "Verschwörung gegen Deutschland." 16 October 1914, pp. 1–2. The article discusses the revelations published in *Norddeutsche* and comes to the conclusion that the British government circumvented its constitution in order to arrange an agreement between Great Britain and France.

121. *MNN*, 17 October 1914.

122. *LV*, 3 December 1914. "Nach der Darlegungen des Reichskanzelers bestünden jetzt keine Zweifel mehr daüber, daß England in der Lage gewesen sei, den Ausbruch des Krieges zu verhindern. Die englische Entrüstung über den Bruch des belgischen Neutralität durch Deutschland sei ein heuchlerische Vorwand, denn wie die durch die deutsche Regierung veröffentlichten Dokemente beweisen, habe England schon lange vorher Belgiens Neutralität durchbrochen und seine Beteiligung am Krieg gegen Deutschland vorbereitet."

123. *NAZ*, 18 August 1914.

124. *V*, 5 August 1914.

125. *BT*, 7 August 1914.

126. *NAZ*, 18 June 1914.

127. *NAZ*, 27 October 1914.

128. "Die Wandlung im Urteil über Deutschland," *KZ*, 7 October 1914.

129. For just a few examples of this kind of complaint, see *KZ*, 18 August 1914; *KZ*, 16 September 1914; *KZ*, 23 September 1914; *KZ*, 21 October 1914; *VZ*, 16 October 1914; *VZ*, 3 November 1914; and *V*, 26 September 1914.

130. See *MNN*, 13 September 1914; *LV*, 17 October 1914; *KZ*, 30 October 1914; *KZ*, 12 November 1914; and *V*, 12 November 1914, pp. 1–2.

131. *K*, 13 September 1914.

132.　Ibid. This is a turnaround because in the years before and the opening weeks of the war, *Kreuzzeitung* had maintained that Russia was the main threat to German existence. More will be said about this later.

133.　*K*, 15 September 1914. In a slightly different form, a parody of Schiller's *Die Räuber* portrays England as the world tyrant, and it is the German mission to free the world form British rule. See *KZ*, 29 September 1914.

134.　*VZ*, 28 October 1914, p. 2.

135.　*FZ*, 9 August 1914. *Berliner Tageblatt* would also claim that Great Britain's only reasons for getting involved in the war were economic. See *BT*, 29 September 1914.

136.　*VZ*, 27 August 1914. 2. Beilage, p. 5. The article concludes, "Wenden wir das Wort auf die Engländer an und sagen: Das Volk ist all right, aber die Regierung ist übel." The theme that the British government was responsible for the war and that the common people were against it was mentioned in a number of papers. See also *V*, 6 September 1914, pp. 1–2.

137.　*VZ*, 27 August 1914. 2. Beilage, p. 5.

138.　Ibid.

139.　*KZ*, 27 August 1914. It will reiterate the claim that Europe devastates itself for Great Britain's benefit two days later.

140.　*VZ*, 14 August 1914.

141.　*KZ*, 29 September 1914.

142.　*MNN*, 14 October 1914.

143.　For a discussion of the views of Marcks and like-minded contemporaries, see Ludwig Dehio, "Ranke and German Imperialism," in *Germany and World Politics in the Twentieth Century*, trans. Dieter Pevsner (New York: Knopf, 1959), 38–71. The essay appeared originally in *Historische Zeitschrift* 170:2 (1950), 307–328.

144.　*VZ*, 27 August 1914.

145.　"Soll und Haben," *MNN*, 15 November 1914.

146.　Ibid. Freytag's *Soll und Haben* extols the virtues of the honest and industrial middle class over the decadent aristocracy. In this comparison, Great Britain is the aristocracy that has grown soft and lost touch with the values that made it worthy, and Germany (it is implied) is the rising class that will replace the old regime.

147.　*MNN*, 30 August 1914.

148.　*MNN*, 14 October 1914.

149.　*K*, 21 October 1914.

150.　Werner Sombart, *BT*, 2 November 1914, p. 2. For a brief biography of Sombart, see Killy and Vierhaus, *Deutsche Biographische Enzyklopädie*, Bd. 9, 367–68.

151.　Werner Sombart, *BT*, 21 November 1914, p. 2.

152.　Ibid.

153.　J. Jastow, "Das russische Weltreich," *BT*, 3 October 1914. "Wir halten ein Eingehen auf die Form, in der die absolut notwendige nachdrückliche Schwächung Russlands zu erfolgen hat, allerdings noch für verfrüht, glauben aber auch, daß das Zeil des Krieges sein muß, Russlands möglichst weit aus Europa heraus und von den deutschen Grenzen abzudrängen. Die Redaktion." The editorial staff will still claim that the weakening of Russia must be the necessary goal (*notwendige Endziel*) of the war in its disclaimer before Sombart's first article. See Werner Sombart, *BT*, 2 November 1914.

154.   Wolfgang Heine, *BT,* 13 November 1914. For the disclaimer on Sombart, see the opening of Sombart's article in *BT,* 2 November 1914. For a biography of Heine, see Der Historischen Kommission der Bayerischen Akademie, ed., *Neue Deutsche Biographie,* Bd. 8 (Berlin: 1969), 296.

155.   Wolfgang Heine, *BT,* Duncker & Humboldt, 13 November 1914.

156.   Ibid.

157.   Ibid.

158.   Terence Zuber argues that the failure on the western front was not due to Moltke's mismanagement of the Schlieffen Plan. Instead he offers the provocative thesis that there was no Schlieffen Plan and that the failure at Marne was due to poor decision making by field officers. See Zuber, *Inventing the Schlieffen Plan.*

159.   Neither Koszyk, *Deutsche Pressepolitik,* nor Welch, *Germany,* even mention a change in policy or any discussion of propaganda themes at this time. Leo Loewensen claims that Schiemann's virulent anti-Russian sentiment became too extreme for his conservative *Junker* readership, which was more inclined to view England as the main villain—which Loewensen calls the "Gott strafe England spirit"—and that this led to his disappearance from the *Kreuzzeitung.* Loewensen offers no documentary proof for this position. However, the ideological position of Schiemann's replacement, Hoetzsch, lends considerable weight to Loewensen's position. See Leo Loewensen, "Karl Stahlin: 1865–1939," *Slavonic and East European Review* 28 (1949): 154.

160.   Schiemann and his supporters did not go quietly into that good night. See Johannes Haller, "Die russische Gefahr im deutschen Hause," in *Die russische Gefahr,* vol. 6, ed. Paul Rohrbach (Stuttgart: J. Engelhorns, 1917). In this 94-page pamphlet, written in response to the second edition of Hoetzsch's *Russland: Eine Einführung auf Grund seiner Geschichte von 1904 bis 1912* (Berlin: G. Reimer, 1913; 2nd ed., 1915), Haller criticized Hoetzsch's theoretical assumptions (e.g., that one can talk about a European Russia and an Asian Russia), his scholarly omissions, and his historical analysis of the origins of Russia as a whole. In the foreword to the pamphlet, Paul Rohrbach thanked Haller for writing this pamphlet and correcting the dangerous perception that Hoetzsch's was an informed opinion. How Haller, a medieval historian, could be more informed about Russia than Hoetzsch, a student of Schiemann's, is a question that Rohrbach chose not to address. For a brief biography of Hoetzsch, see Der Historischen Kommission der Bayrischen Akademie der Wissenschaft, *Neue Deutsche Biographie,* Bd. 9 (Berlin: Duncker & Humboldt, 1972), 371–72.

161.   Koszyk notes that Interior Minister Loebbel had arranged with newspapers a series of signals to indicate the status of the information distributed that would prevent newspapers from simply becoming a second edition of *Norddeutsche Allgemeine Zeitung.* See Koszyk, *Deutsche Pressepolitik,* 60–61. It is worth noting that release of the documents found in the Belgian General Staff archives and others relating to the prehistory of the war did not bear any of these symbols. German newspapers did not indicate any difficulty in reprinting articles from *Norddeutsche,* nor did they refrain from commenting on what was appearing in other newspapers inside and outside Germany.

162.   Many of the German newspapers carried this manifesto. See *KZ,* 4 October 1914.

163.   *V,* 26 September 1914.

164. In an interesting article, John Horne and Alex Kramer maintain that German soldiers, leadership, and public opinion could justify Belgian and French civilian casualties because they were not innocent bystanders but rather *Francs-Tireurs* and thus not protected by international laws. See Horne and Kramer, "German 'Atrocities,'" 1–33.

165. Rolf Brandt, *Funf Monte an der Ostfront...Kriegsberichte* (Berlin: E. Fleischel, 1915).

Chapter 5

The Empire without Qualities: Austro-Hungarian Newspapers and the Outbreak of War in 1914

Andrea Orzoff

In Robert Musil's peerless novel *The Man without Qualities*, it is 1913, and Austria-Hungary has once again been caught napping. The German empire, its upstart neighbor, is already amid plans for a 1918 celebration of 30 years of rule by Kaiser Wilhelm II. Hastily, burdened by typical feelings of guilt and inadequacy as well as the desire to trump the Prussians, the Austrians begin their own plans for a celebration of Emperor Franz Joseph's 70th birthday. It will take place that same year. The Austrians' grandiose hopes, however, are betrayed by their unfortunate choice of a title for Franz Joseph's celebration, which they name "the Parallel Campaign."[1]

This title neatly represents the prevalent themes in Austro-Hungarian newspaper coverage of the early months of the Great War, for two reasons. First, the term *Parallel Campaign* is emotionally empty, providing no connection between its audience and the monarchy, and creating no portrayal of the monarchy as an entity worth celebrating. Second, the term situates the monarchy as "parallel" to, and thus defined by reference to, the German empire.

Similar lacunae emerge in a reading of Austro-Hungarian press coverage between August and December 1914. As is widely known, the Dual Monarchy's conflict with Serbia lit the European powder keg. Nevertheless, Austria's efforts were generally represented—in its own press—as parallel to the war being waged by Germany, both in the West and East. When the Austrian press bragged about the bravery and ability of the Central Powers, it was Germany they lauded, and 1870 the historic victory to which they referred. At the least, this was historically awkward, given that Germany's 1870 victory over France followed an equally effortless defeat of Austria itself. Nonetheless, Austro-Hungarian newspapers tirelessly sang the praises of the victors of Sedan.[2]

Moreover, Austro-Hungarian wartime press coverage said relatively little of the monarchy as one of Europe's last supranational powers. When it did, the pages of the wartime Austro-Hungarian press tried to create the kind of cooperative multiethnic state that had almost never existed in fact. But much more pervasive, albeit subtly, was intense concern about the monarchy's subject nationalities and the effect of the war on their attachment to the monarchy. Would the empire's "subject peoples" support its war efforts? Which of them, if any, could be trusted? How would they be controlled? Would the increasingly important "national question" affect the war itself, and if so, how? Both Austria-Hungary and its opponent the Russian empire were conservative multinational empires. Austro-Hungarian press coverage of tsarist Russia referred often to the "yoke" under which its peoples labored. But what about the Austro-Hungarian "prison-house of nations"?[3] Thanks to general enthusiasm for the war as well as censorship, this question was not often posed in 1914. The year 1918 would prove quite different.

Meanwhile, Austria's nationalities responded to metropolitan papers in their own local presses. Some chose overt declarations or demonstrations of loyalty; others opted for coded references to injustice and oppression, as well as a refusal to denigrate the monarchy's enemies. These gambits were common in newspapers under tight censorship rein, particularly those published by suspect nationalities such as the Czechs. Reading the "suspect" newspapers sheds light not just on Austro-Hungarian censorship but on the ways it was evaded, and the ways Austrian nationalities were able to use the press even during wartime as a means of real, if cryptic, public communication.

Finally, the early war coverage offers a revealing glimpse of Austro-Hungarian insecurity within a newly hostile Europe in which former allies had turned foe. Initially, the Austro-Hungarian papers concentrated their ire on Russia, as the head of a pan-Slav conspiracy aimed at destroying the monarchy and dominating Europe. Serbia was viewed as a mere tool of the tsar, himself personified as alternately evil and hapless. By October, Austro-Hungarian newspapers directed their ire at the Western Allies, particularly at their "War of Lies" about supposed German atrocities. In return, the Austrian papers printed atrocity stories and divisive reports about the Western powers—the cruelty visited upon guileless young German soldiers by Belgian women, the lies told by the French, the unreliable nature of the British as allies. By the end of 1914, then, Austria was isolated within Europe, claiming, along with Germany, to be the sole bearer of its values and legacy even as its press made clear its distance from most European powers and peoples.

The title of this volume is particularly apt in describing the relationship of most Austro-Hungarian newspapers to the state for the first two years of the war: that is, the empire's main papers, and particularly its German-speaking press, became willing instruments of state propaganda. Papers published by oppositional organizations or ethnic minorities had two choices: to mute their criticism of the state or to feel the heavy hand of the censor. Historians of the Austrian press have noted that even steadfast loyalists turned against the empire by 1917.[4] But in 1914, the empire's newspapers rushed to serve as its voice, not as its critic. Even the socialist *Arbeiter-Zeitung* followed Social Democratic leader Viktor Adler in supporting the war effort, at least initially.[5]

This chapter will analyze Austro-Hungarian press coverage of the war between August and November 1914. I will focus on three main newspapers: the liberal Viennese *Neue Freie Presse*, the semiofficial Budapest German-language daily *Pester Lloyd*, and the Prague Czech nationalist *Národní listy* (*National Pages*). These papers differed subtly but significantly in their attitudes towards the war, their relationships to the state (and the censor), and their presentation of the war's events and issues.

Given the generally partisan nature of European newspapers, even an impressionistic glance at the Austro-Hungarian press in 1914 grants scholars a window into the empire's political culture. Analyzing the Austro-Hungarian press means analyzing a splintered and fragmented public sphere, riven by political and national divisions. German-language papers in Vienna did not necessarily reflect the views of German-speakers in Prague, Ljubljana, or the Bukovina. Nationalist Czech, Slovak, and South Slav newspapers battled those willing to support the empire. Poles and Hungarians were relatively more unified, aligned with the imperial regime, but not entirely. Within these national divisions, different political parties and groupings interpreted the situation of the empire and their group's ethnic future differently in the pages of their partisan press.

As was generally true of the European press at the time, the Austro-Hungarian press was deeply fragmented. Each city had its own newspapers, few of which pretended to offer general coverage of the empire as a whole. The closest thing the empire had to a paper of record was the *Neue Freie Presse*, based in Vienna. The different ethnic groups within each city generally preferred, by 1914, to read about the day's news in their own language. Further division occurred along party lines. A German-speaking socialist living in Krakow, therefore, would not necessarily read the same newspapers as socialists in Vienna. In sum, the empire's overall provincialism was reflected in its press.

The papers described in this essay are among the empire's most important, in different ways. Historian Arthur May has dubbed the *Neue Freie Presse*, one of the papers considered here, as the single best published source of information on the Dual Monarchy. The *Neue Freie Presse* was published twice a day and reached 110,000 subscribers, about a fifth of which was circulated abroad. The *Neue Freie Presse* possessed an international standing unique in the Austro-Hungarian press. It was also unabashedly supportive of the imperial administration, as well as old-school liberal politicians and "Austrogerman business interests."[6] The desires of subject nationalities for autonomy—or simply an end to government repression—did not mar the *Neue Freie Presse*'s pages.

Nor did those desires appear in the pages of the *Pester Lloyd*, one of Hungary's foremost papers, although German-language and often regarded as the voice of the Ballhausplatz—the imperial foreign ministry in Vienna—as well as business and financial interests.[7] Some historians refer to both the *Neue Freie Presse* and the *Pester Lloyd* as semiofficial, noting that the *Pester Lloyd* was rumored to have received government subsidies. Nevertheless, even semiofficial papers published alarmist reports and rumors alongside official communications.[8]

The Czech-language paper *Národní listy* had once represented the progressive or liberal wing of the Czech national movement. By 1914, it had fallen far from that peak; its eventual domination by the Young Czechs, a Czech nationalist parliamentary party, had bled *Národní listy* of its critical populism and journalistic quality.[9] Nevertheless, it remained the preeminent Czech-language daily in Bohemia and Moravia from 1861 until the First World War, in terms of its popularity, its literary quality, and its importance for the Czech national cause. Its reputation was built not just on the prominence of its writers but also on its consistent defiance of Austrian authoritarian imperial policies. The paper had campaigned on behalf of patriotic Czech causes such as raising funds to build the National Theater, or the monument to Jan Hus, fifteenth-century religious martyr and Czech national hero, in Prague's Old Town Square.[10] *Národní listy* was also one of the most important sources of the Young Czech party's strength.[11]

AUSTRIA-HUNGARY, ITS PRESS, AND WARTIME CONTROL

An assessment of the Dual Monarchy's political culture must precede any analysis of its press. Recent scholarship on the Habsburg empire has reversed the conclusion drawn by scholars in the 1920s that nationality conflicts were the main reason the empire did not survive the war. On the contrary, it appears that most of the monarchy's peoples were relatively content in its last few years of life, maintaining their allegiance to the monarchy rather than working for its dissolution or the creation of national states.[12] For a few years prior to 1914, peace had settled on the empire. The major political parties supported the monarchy even when they opposed its government. Even social democracy in Austria-Hungary was relatively less internationalist, and therefore looked more positively on the maintenance of the empire, than elsewhere in prewar Europe.[13] The words of one Czech writer might be taken to speak generally for most of the empire's peoples in 1914:

We could not possibly be tempted...by the creation of an independent Czech statelet, which would find itself at the mercy of its more powerful neighbors. And if world events gave us such a state against our will, it would certainly be the first concern of all reasonable Czech politicians to incorporate it...into a powerful Austria-Hungary, justly reorganized.[14]

All this is not to say, however, that the monarchy did not possess fault lines along which chasms might erupt at times of stress. The monarchy's modern foundation was the Compromise of 1867, which made the Hungarian, or Magyar, aristocracy equivalent in their half of the empire to the German dynasty in its own. But this division precluded equal treatment for all nationalities in the empire. The Hungarians imposed stringent Magyarization on their minority nationalities, save the Croats; the Germans were forced to compromise with "their" Slavic peoples in order to strengthen their own rule. In the past, Czechs, Ruthenes, Transylvanian Romanians, South Slavs, and Italians had at various times chafed against the Habsburg system, and different variants of Russophilism or pan-Slavism had struck a chord with Austria's Slavic nationalities.

The Austro-Hungarian press in 1914 was highly developed; at least one of its newspapers, the *Neue Freie Presse*, had a reputation for reliable reportage and scintillating feuilletons not just within the monarchy but in Europe. In Vienna, 25 German-language dailies, and at least 3 in Slovene and 2 in Czech, were published in 1915: the number of weekly, biweekly, and monthly papers, journals, and magazines was of course much higher. For Budapest, exact numbers are harder to come by, but in 1910, 39 periodicals of various kinds were published, in German, Hungarian, Slovak, English, French, and Romanian.[15] That situation was mirrored in the empire's provincial capitals: Prague, for example, boasted of "seventeen dailies, one four-times-weekly, two thrice-weekly, thirty twice-weekly, and seventy-five weekly papers coming out in the Czech language" in 1890. There were 418 periodicals and magazines published in all of Bohemia that same year, 253 in Czech and 157 in German.[16] This vibrant journalistic exchange also involved sincere differences of opinion, particularly evinced by the socialist newspapers. In each region of the empire, different newspapers defended different stances, particularly along the dividing line of loyalty to the empire. For example, in Slovenia, *Resnica* demonstrated loyalty to the empire, whereas *Slovenec* and *Slovenski Narod* were more nationalist; likewise, the reliable Croat *Hrvatska* soon competed with the Yugoslav-national *Glas Slovenica Hrvata i Srba*.[17]

Long before war was officially declared, however, the emperor and his military advisers were concerned about ensuring the existence of a loyal press. In fact, the Kriegsüberwachungsamt (KÜA), described in detail below, had been designed—quite illegally, according to constitutional historian Josef Redlich—as early as 1912, as part of confidential contingency plans should war break out.[18] Even before war broke out in late summer 1914, the Austro-Hungarian press first received "official instructions" about their portrayal of the diplomatic note that the monarchy addressed to Serbia on July 23: "that although the Monarchy's demands were severe, they were completely justifiable and necessary, left no room for discussion, and did not exclude the hope of maintaining peace."[19] Historian John Ewart Wallace Sterling notes that from this point almost the entire Viennese and Budapest press, barring the socialist papers, "chorused approval of the Monarchy's action."[20] Just days later, on July 25, Prime Minister Count Karl Stürgkh suspended most civil rights and imposed censorship of the press.[21]

On July 31, 1914, as the army mobilized for war, the Army High Command (Armeeoberkommando, or AOK) announced the official creation of the Kriegsüberwachungsamt (KÜA), a supervisory body for the Austrian part of the empire to monitor any activity designated subversive under the new laws.[22] The KÜA afforded the AOK a great degree of control over the provinces, and in particular over the provincial press. The KÜA was also representative of a larger battle between civil and military authorities, one in which, at least at first, military discipline—and paranoia—gained the upper hand. Not that authoritarian rule was entirely unfamiliar to the Dual Monarchy: Prime Minister Count Stürgkh had been ruling by decree since March 1914, having dissolved the Reichsrat (Parliament). But the precept of wartime security granted the military authorities more legitimacy. Even when Stürgkh was able to rein in the extremities of the KÜA, resentment still festered among the empire's nationalities, especially those deemed to be politically suspect (see below).[23]

Hungarian censorship was structured slightly differently. In the Hungarian lands, Parliament continued to meet, having declared a political truce (*Treuga Dei*) in the name of defending the homeland. With the exception of Croatia, the military was prohibited from exercising on Hungarian soil the powers it possessed in the Austrian lands (and even Croatia's Diet was allowed to function for the majority of the war).[24] However, the Hungarian state imposed emergency powers similar to the situation in Austria. The Hungarian press was supervised by the Hadifelügyeleti Bizottság (HFB), which coordinated its policy with the KÜA.[25]

Austro-Hungarian censorship remained severe for the first two years of the war. Regional censors supervised each issue of even the smallest local paper, forcing the Austro-Hungarian press to operate under extremely tight deadline pressure. Censors could examine papers a mere three hours before going to press, and could excise any items deemed harmful to the war effort: sentences, passages, even entire articles.[26] The reader was aware of the presence of the censor, since deleted copy left large white spaces in the text of already-formatted pages. Yet the Habsburg wartime censors seem particularly to embody socialist Viktor Adler's deathless epithet about the monarchy as a whole: "Absolutismus, gemildert durch die Schlamperei" ("Absolutism made gentler by sloppiness"). There was almost no way to maintain total surveillance given the need for close reading of periodicals in 11 official languages: German, Hungarian, Czech, Slovak, Polish, Ruthenian, Italian, Romanian, Slovenian, Croatian, and Serbian.[27] Writer Alfred Polgar noted that in fact, it was often the case that a story would be banned in one paper but run in another.[28]

Papers that tended to defend the imperial administration also attempted to excise the traces of its censor. The *Neue Freie Presse*, for instance, apologized to its readers for those spaces that remained, explaining that "in the more important cases we have repeatedly closed up with white spaces in the paper in order not to disturb our readers by intrusions on the part of the censors."[29] However, not all papers were able or willing to efface the censor's work. Jan Hajšman, a Czech journalist writing for *Čas*, a paper that opposed the regime, reports that newspaper vendors in Prague would call out, "What is white is the truth—what is black is lies!"[30] Historian Maureen Healy also notes that the white spaces could unpredictably politicize more imaginative, and nationalistically inclined, readers, citing the words of Pole Katarzyna Titz of Vienna: "The Polish nation cannot be deterred by any power in the world, not least by the censor…I'm telling you, I have the censor to thank—the white spaces and so forth—for the fact that I've acquired full national consciousness."[31]

Another important element of Austro-Hungarian control over the press was the Kriegspressequartier (KPQ, War Press Office), a part of the AOK, which filtered the military's approved version of the war to both domestic and foreign correspondents.[32] Domestic and foreign journalists covering the war from Vienna were housed at the KPQ, which also produced its own daily official reports, the *Höfer Berichte*. Correspondents had to apply for express permission to visit the actual fronts; permission was denied if the Austro-Hungarian forces were doing badly.[33] The correspondents at the KPQ could either simply embellish the KPQ's reports or write their own articles, which were frequently vetted by the KPQ even before reaching the KÜA or HFB censors.[34] The KPQ was particularly concerned about disloyalty or lack of patriotism, but also scanned the correspondents' reports for any impression of Austro-Hungarian weakness, any nationalist or socialist implications, any criticism of the government, and any nod to rumors or pacifist messages afloat within the monarchy.[35] Newspapers were not even allowed to print casualty lists, "which quickly became too long (and demoralizing) to print."[36] Nor were the KÜA/KPQ censors interested in public response. Hugo Ganz, a Viennese journalist, informed the authorities of popular irritation at censorship in 1914. He was told, "the people's job in wartime is to shut up and obey."[37]

Moreover, various KPQ correspondents wrote for more than one paper, further ensuring homogenization of the war as presented to the monarchy's readers. For example, the *Neue Freie Presse*'s war correspondent, Alexander Roda-Roda, also reported for the Budapest *Az-Est*; Dr. Karl-Hans Strobl's wartime writings appeared in not just Austro-Hungarian papers (Vienna's *Die Zeit* and *Fremdenblatt*, and Budapest's *Az Újsag* and *Neues Pester Journal*) but also German dailies such as the *Leipziger Neueste Nachrichten* and Berlin's *Vossische Zeitung* and *Berliner Tageblatt*.[38] During 1914 the KPQ was characterized by one of its own leaders as largely "indifferent" or passive, mainly supervising and censoring rather than producing its own "positive" propaganda, as it did later in the war.[39]

Austro-Hungarian war coverage demonstrated a few overall tendencies. First, news from the front made its way to the front pages slowly and incompletely. Reports were often a full week or more behind actual events: for example, on September 12, the *Neue Freie Presse* ran stories on the German victory over the British on August 25 and 26 as well as on life in emptied Paris, awaiting the German onslaught. But by September 12, the Germans had lost Paris and were retreating to near the river Aisne, where they began to dig trench lines. No word appeared in the *Neue Freie Presse* to indicate a German defeat: rather, subsequent issues simply announced a change of battle venue.[40] This example demonstrates a second general tendency: an overwhelmingly positive vagueness. The Austro-Hungarian press dwelt at length on the Central Powers' victories and whenever possible described even retreats as "favorable positions." Also, details of life on the battlefield or strategy were minimal compared with hagiographic coverage of the two kaisers as well as their military advisers. In his wartime memoirs, Czechoslovak president Tomas G. Masaryk recalled being unable to understand the nature of the war's momentum from Prague newspaper coverage. "Not until I went abroad was I able to consult the soldiers and get details. Then I understood that on the Marne the Germans had really been beaten."[41]

Individual newspapers' responses to censorship naturally differed. The most extreme responses were closure, either self-imposed or forced by the authorities, though few closed as early as 1914 (*Národní listy*, for example, was closed by the KÜA as late as spring 1917, despite its many previous conflicts with the wartime censor). Many papers, particularly those put out by the "suspect" nationalities, walked "the censorship tightrope," as one historian has put it, testing the abilities of both the censor and their own readerships to draw inferences and read between the lines.[42] Yet at least initially, most papers—even those traditionally hostile to the k.u.k. (*kaiserlich und königlich*, "imperial and royal") authorities such as the socialist press—agreed to an internal peace for the good of the empire.

This relative lack of criticism for much of 1914 was universal among the German and Magyar press, ranging from semiofficial papers such as the Viennese daily *Neue Freie Presse* to even the Budapest radical weekly journal *Nyugat*, though a few Viennese papers did openly chafe against the censor.[43] Even among the "suspect" nationalities, most political organizations declared loyalty to the empire, as expressed in this editorial from the Czech Social Democratic *Právo Lidu:* "The Czech nation, because of its international position, has to rely on Austria in the future."[44]

Over the course of the war, however, a fragmented and repressive wartime press apparatus resulted in, as historians of Austria-Hungary have been wont to put it, centrifugal forces within the empire. Metropolitan newspapers' relative lack of coverage of events and developments in the hinterland meant that, for example, Vienna readers remained almost totally oblivious of Prague's or Ljubljana's concerns, as well as of general anti-Austrian sentiment among the subject peoples. The empire's traditional provincialism was magnified by its wartime censorship, which exaggerated the already existing distrust among Austro-Hungarian peoples by the end of the war. But these tendencies were already apparent in the empire's press by the end of 1914.

It is, however, important to note that newspapers were far from the only source of information Austro-Hungarian subjects had. Historian Maureen Healy notes that the Catholic Church was an important source of pro-state information and propaganda, but also that information "circulated among the population in the form of rumors; and it flowed from the population back to the state through the widespread practice of denunciation."[45] Healy also notes that the government used its censorship of the post as another means of informing itself about public opinion, a practice Peter Holquist has dubbed "perlustration."[46] Since we have relatively little information about the responses by Austro-Hungarian subjects to the newspapers they read, this presentation of Austro-Hungarian press content should be read as a single voice amid a pluralist wartime conversation between state and society. Although the press tended to reflect the government's presentation of information, it was far from alone or even being dominant.

ENEMIES AND FRIENDS: AUSTRIA-HUNGARY AND WARTIME EUROPE

Given the interwoven nature of Austrian and German press culture as the war began, it is unsurprising that Austro-Hungarian papers raised themes and issues similar to those found in the wartime German press. But similarity does not imply heedless repetition—at least not entirely. Like their German peers, Austro-Hungarian papers discussed the Russian fault for the war and the threat of pan-Slavism; they indignantly denied charges of atrocities in Belgium; they lauded German greatness. All that said, the Austrian imperial press did far more than recycle stories from the Wolff Agency of Berlin.

One of the most profound differences was the ambivalence with which even the most loyal Austro-Hungarian papers greeted the outbreak of war. Even the most pro-war editorials were often laced with foreboding and doubt, some of which seems to have come from Austria-Hungary's surprise that France and England would enter the war as its enemies. Their willingness to fight the Central Powers meant a changed and dangerous Europe, and rendered Austro-Hungarian claims to represent Western culture against Russia somewhat hollow: after all, France, the cradle of European civilization, was fighting the monarchy. Marx's famous comment "All that is solid melts into air" might well come to mind when examining the Austro-Hungarian press portrayal of the war; the old Europe had vanished, and in its place a far more dangerous, less predictable, less stable Europe had come to be.

By August 1, the metropolitan Austro-Hungarian papers had dismissed any possibility of localizing the Austro-Serb conflict; this war, they wrote, would be both widespread and world-shattering.[47]

The events of recent days are too great for...human powers of comprehension. Thoughts swirl through our heads, gloomy, uncertain, refusing to be measured by the standards of our experience; the examples of history have become frail, providing no protection, and only the feeling speaks within us that the world stands before experiences which will not be comparable to any others.[48]

The following day brought similar rhetoric, calling forth a modern Sophocles as the only one capable of describing the tragedy about to befall humanity and Europe.[49]

However, in the first few months of the war, the Austro-Hungarian press hurled the blame for that change at the Russian empire. Even at the end of July, Austro-Hungarian papers noted Russia's ominous role in contemporary Balkan politics, and admonished the tsarist empire not to meddle in Serbian affairs or claim the role of Serbia's protector.

Would it bring even the smallest profit to Russia's interests, authority, or honor, if our Monarchy were to cultivate a country...whose generals lead instruction in bomb-throwing and assassination, [merely] to keep order on [our] borders? Would it be contrary to the interests of the Tsarist Empire if this professionally-arranged royal murder were to be punished? ...Serbia is an independent state, which does not stand under any foreign patronage. Thus also [it is] not [under] Russian [patronage]. Consequently Russia surrenders the right to shield Serbia from the punishing hand of our Monarchy.[50]

Once Russia announced its general mobilization, the Austro-Hungarian press concluded immediately that the failure to localize this conflict, and thus the responsibility for a war that would ignite Europe and perhaps the world, was Russia's.[51] Budapest's *Pester Lloyd* chose as its headline on August 1 "Russia Calls Forth the European War." It commented,

Russia has mobilized, and tomorrow from the Thames to the Danube and from the Neva to the Seine, many, many million men in the prime of life will have to leave their families and jobs to hasten under the flag...because Russia, unhindered by scruples or notions of culture, wants to show the world its power and impose its will on humanity. Britain's sons should bleed, the French should risk their lives, the German nation should throw the blood of its young men into the murderous mess of modern war... : and for what? for what? So that Russia prevents the disbandment of the Serbian *Narodna Obrana*, so that the university of state-theft and princely murder, taught by Serbia in the Csupria, will thrive as the glory of European civilization.

Much was made of the German kaiser's personal correspondence with the tsar in efforts to stave off war, with blame laid squarely at the tsar's feet. Just as the German minister of war and chief of staff were working to bring about discussions that might slow military preparations, suddenly the Russians mobilized. "The German emperor felt himself deceived and wants his contemporaries to know of his disappointment, and that a chasm divides Russian from European civilization."[52]

Serbia was just as much to blame for this conflict, the paper added, and deserved the drubbing she would face at the hands of the Dual Monarchy: "Now for the first time one understands whence little Serbia called forth the courage to challenge Austro-Hungarian power in such audacious ways.... Serbia was directed by Russia, [or it would not have] allowed itself to so completely and so brazenly [turn] against us. Serbia must have become a tool in Russian hands."[53]

This theme of Serbian connection to and dependence on Russia was sounded loudly during the month of August by various Austro-Hungarian papers. The most generous epithet used for Serbia was "Russia's adopted child."[54] Far more writers agreed with the *Neue Freie Presse* in dubbing Serbia a poison, an illness, an

outpost of Russian policy...obeying a hollow instinct for powerlust without morality and without a sense of justice, which threatens the world with a fall backward into barbaric conditions.... Serbia is Russia. It has given itself as a lackey in the service of the Tsar, it creeps before him in doglike obedience.[55]

The threat Russia posed was not merely a question of the Austro-Hungarian empire, the papers argued. Russia threatened Europe overall; it threatened European culture and indeed the entire developed West. The

Neue Freie Presse harked back to Austria's historical role as the protector of Europe against the infidel Turks in the seventeenth and eighteenth centuries, in particular the siege of Vienna in 1683, and wrote,

European civilization [was defended] on the walls of this city. At that point, such was our historic fate, and so is it again today.... We fight...for the wholeness of [our] culture, even when France, exactly as in the days of the Turks, [fights] on the side of barbarism.[56]

Russia threatened the West's most treasured ideals: liberty, honor, purity, and trust in public dealings. And despite the threat it posed, Russia itself as a state was "powerless, unfit, and miserable."[57] In short, this war was not simply a war of Great Powers: it was a war for Europe's soul. "Thus this world war will be and must be a war of worldviews [*Weltanschauungen*], a battle of cultures [*Kulturkampf*] in the highest and deepest sense."[58]

It could not be otherwise, for, as represented in the Austro-Hungarian press, Russian culture was dangerously different from that of the rest of Europe. Russia was Sarmatian, Cossack, aggressive, Oriental. Even the subject peoples of Russia, and even those who had previously believed in Russia's Europeanness, now had to take note:

Now the dreadful...decision is that of Western culture or Sarmatian servitude of spirit and body, to which the world is called and which will determine the direction of its history for centuries.... Whose mind and consciousness yet bars them to the inner necessity of this war of titans, let it to them be said: that no settlement or reconciliation is possible between civilization and Tsarism, between the ordained self-determination of creative national force and the hollow dreamworld of Cossack theocracy.[59]

Nor was the chasm between Russia and Europe merely symbolic or political: it could be seen in the physical landscape. An Austro-Hungarian journalist traveling near the Russian border reported that there was something disturbingly foreign about it.

There is something Asiatic about [their] clothing, and also about the silence.... The wind blows sharply, crossing the steppe unhindered.... One notices a different cultural zone, a lower one.... One sees in the figures on the road the living models...from Russian literature: the problematic, the passive, the desperate, the depraved and secretly revolutionary.... Barely half an hour away lies Austria, lies the first Austrian city. For the inhabitants of this little border town, this is where Europe begins.[60]

At no point, however, did the Austro-Hungarian press deprecate or minimize the military abilities of Austria's foes—quite understandable given the monarchy's significant difficulties on the battlefield throughout

1914. Rather, Austria's enemies were generally described as real threats and rivals, as reflected in the *Neue Freie Presse*'s reprinting of an address given by Army Commandant G. D. von Boroevic: "From here on the war is a technical problem. If the Russians had our infantry, they would be in Vienna now. If we had their artillery groupings, we would be positioned in Kiev."[61] Given the difficulty Austro-Hungarian troops faced for most of 1914, both on the eastern front and in Serbia, this respect granted their foes seems appropriate, if startlingly honest.[62]

Both the Russians and the Serbs were, in the first months of fighting, accused of atrocities. A report from the *Neue Freie Presse* from August 28 reports the following occurrences from the Serbian front:

Our dressing/first-aid stations were shot at. Serbian regular troops hoisted flags of peace and, after we halted our fire, cunningly attacked our troops.... On dead *Komitatschis* were found cartridges loaded with nails and with pieces of [the chemical] blue vitriol. The Serbian Civil Defense, among them females and children, shot and threw bombs surreptitiously and from behind our army.[63]

Likewise, the Russians—often equated with Cossacks—were depicted as lightheartedly shooting Austrian military doctors kind enough to treat their wounds.[64]

And yet one of the charges leveled against Russia must have echoed uneasily in Austria-Hungary. Among Russia's many offenses, such as "crime, treachery, oath-breaking and fraud," were also "destruction of peoples and confessions".[65] That is, Russia was the oppressor of peoples, and that in the end would inevitably doom its war effort. The Russian war effort was portrayed as under threat from its own people, who experienced "inner dissatisfaction, rebellions, misery, and hunger."[66] And, at least in the opening sallies of the war in Galicia, Austria-Hungary and Germany were their potential liberators. As in Europe, so too in central Asia and the Middle East. The Austro-Hungarian papers joyously reported a force of 300,000 Afghani troops marching against Russia and 400,000 against Russia's ally, the British colony India. Likewise the Shiite spiritual leader of Persia was reported to have called a meeting in which he demanded Persia be free of the "Russian yoke."[67] Even in 1914, the theme that would later dominate the discussion of the Dual Monarchy's destruction was pervasive in its coverage of its wartime enemies.

By contrast, and particularly in the war's first weeks, Austro-Hungarian papers were delirious in their praise for their ally Germany. Germany, the papers exulted, was proving itself still the victor of the battle of Sedan in 1870; Germany was the protector of European culture and values against bloody Russia and its callous allies. Throughout the month of August, Germany was looked at as Austria-Hungary's, and Europe's, savior.

Germany rises! Germany, with its sixty-five million inhabitants, with its stored power from decades of peaceful work, with its wisdom and with its ability, rises! Germany with the health of its people, with its honorable way of life, with its reliability and capability at all levels, rises! The finest, the most magnificent, the most well-formed army that has ever before been equipped, will [fight] on the side of our soldiers.[68]

Even the *Arbeiter-Zeitung*, Socialist party daily organ, saluted German participation in the war (and the German Social Democrats' vote to approve war credits) with an editorial praising "Germany's Day" as one which "displayed the dignity, grandeur, and sublimity of the German spirit."[69] The *Neue Freie Presse* greeted the German armies with "admiration.... It has never had an equal and nothing can happen to it, even when the gates of hell open."[70] On August 8, after the successful siege of the Belgian city Liège (Lüttich), the *Neue Freie Presse* wrote, "Everyone had the feeling that the German *Volk* is still the same one that once pushed through to France, to fight for the right to unification with the sword."[71] And again a few weeks later, as the Germans besieged Paris, the *Pester Lloyd* began its lead editorial with references to the battle of Sedan in 1870, and crowed, "History repeats itself."[72]

Interestingly, the Austro-Hungarian papers did not rush to acclaim their own army or to assure their readers of easy victories to come. Austria was portrayed as resigned but resolute, forced into war by Russia's treachery and Serbian political murder, to defend its own borders but also Europe at large. Austria's army was described in far cooler terms than that of Germany: it was "equal to every duty."[73] Save the occasional enthusiastic feuilleton, Austro-Hungarian newspapers refrained from bragging about the certain victories that awaited their forces; their lack of comment is notable. In late November, after months of silence on the subject, the *Neue Freie Presse* printed comments by a German major which ran in the *Berliner Tageblatt*: "Our brave allies have...already proved again their undiminished ability on the battlefield [*Kampfkraft*]." The *Neue Freie Presse* also printed praise from the *Norddeutsche Allgemeine Zeitung*:

The Austro-Hungarian troops led assault upon assault against the [enemy] in the south.... In victorious progress the enemy was thrown back to the Drina and the victory was brought deep into enemy territory. Here, as everywhere, the Austro-Hungarian troops fought with splendid courage and with unwavering perseverance.[74]

But not until a German newspaper praised the Austrian forces did the *Neue Freie Presse* join the chorus.

And yet the papers hoped, at least at first, that war would bring the empire to a new, higher unity. As war became increasingly inevitable at the end of July, the *Pester Lloyd* wrote optimistically that overnight, out of the…tired, apparently resigned Dual Monarchy, a new community with new goals and new problems [has emerged].… The energies of cohesion which held this monarchy together have expressed themselves with such force that no reasonable person seriously concerns himself with the spectre of division.… This Monarchy, so often underestimated and so often pushed aside…Europe must [now] with bated breath recognize its greatness.… Unified Hungary and unified Austria have, in the [face] of a common danger, found a new, higher spiritual unity.[75]

Egon Zweig, writing in the *Neue Freie Presse*, envisioned the Austro-Hungarian army, traditionally a means of overcoming national divisions, as the core of this new empire, now assuredly known as "Austria-Hungary—not Austria and Hungary as in…days that will [now] be forgotten."[76] Soon enough, however, the old national enmities broke out again, encouraged by the military's cracking down in parts of the empire it viewed as suspect, such as Bohemia and Bosnia-Herzegovina. Austria's purported new spiritual unity was mainly for the Germans and Magyars.

Nor would the empire's enemies be shown any mercy. The Austro-Hungarian press openly discussed the idea that total destruction ought to be visited on the losers of the war. Relatively early in the war Austro-Hungarian papers began using the rhetoric of total war to describe the conflict as well as its outcome. On September 16, the *Neue Freie Presse*'s lead editorial was headlined "Destruction as a Guiding Principle." Given the intensity of the war and the ferocity of the Central Powers' enemies, the paper intoned, the war could not pass without the military vision of "total war"—involving utter destruction of the enemy—being translated into the realm of politics. Certainly Russia would seek to crush Austria-Hungary and Germany should she win: therefore, the Central Powers would need to do the same if the tables were turned. "The war would be an unheard-of waste if it were not waged with the goal of preventing the return of pan-Slavism and revanchism, and protecting against future devastation. The political concept of destruction, oriented against revanchism and pan-Slavism, is the necessity in whose name the allied Empires fight."[77] By early October, Austro-Hungarian papers were referring to the eastern front as the "cleansing" of Galicia.[78]

PERFIDY FROM THE WEST

As the war progressed, vituperation in the Austro-Hungarian press shifted targets. No longer were the Russians the primary enemy, despite the fact that Russian forces were still providing the Austro-Hungarian army a solid challenge. Rather, over time, the apparent betrayal of the Western powers, particularly France and England, seemed to gall the monarchy's press far more.

Austro-Hungarian papers expressed astonishment that the Western powers would side with tsarist Russia, haven of reaction, rather than with them. The first laments "as from bodily pain" were that France, the birthplace of liberty, would ally itself with Russia. The French, warned the *Neue Freie Presse* in early August, ought to think back to Sedan and Bismarck's comment that in the next European war, the defeated power would be struck such a blow that it would lose its entire life's blood.[79] Would England make the same mistake? The Austro-Hungarian papers decided first that England would no doubt remain neutral and wait out the war. Why would it join the pan-Slavist camp?[80] In fact, the *Neue Freie Presse* opined, for England to join the war against Germany would be *Brudermord*, murder among brothers. The *Pester Lloyd* reminded its readers of England's cultural achievements: the first constitution, religious freedom, institutions that are just and assure equality, philosophical positivism, empiricism in natural-scientific inquiry, principles of social-development theory, trade and commerce, industrialism. How could this England join hands with Russia, enemy of European culture?[81]

As it became apparent that England and France would oppose the Central Powers, Austro-Hungarian press coverage began openly discussing encirclement. But, once again, their discussion was of Germany, not of their own empire—that England and France wanted to constrain the German empire economically and politically, to keep it from matching British or French power. England had intended for years to test German will, they explained, and the German invasion of Belgium simply allowed the German-English rivalry onto the battlefield.[82]

A ridiculous joke, this war is nothing more than a ridiculous joke. German trade cannot be disrupted by it as long as the German chemist has the gift of invention, as long as Siemens does not become extinct and...the German businessman roves from land to land, welcome everywhere, since he is industrious, flexible, and dependable.... The Englishman does not hate the German: only an elite, which calls itself society, does that.[83]

Later in the war, the *Neue Freie Presse* noted that it was particularly disillusioned not just by Britain's decision to enter the war, but also by its failure to prevent that war in the first place. Sir Edward Grey, the British foreign minister, was accused of failing to apply sufficient pressure on Serbia or Russia. A word from Britain, and both Belgrade and Petersburg would have restrained themselves, reasoned the *Neue Freie Presse*. But that word never came.[84]

Once the war broke out, the Austro-Hungarian press played up all differences among the Entente powers. For example, in early September, the *Neue Freie Presse* ran the headline "Alliance with England a Disappointment for France." The paper claimed that militarily, France has had little use for its allies. The Russian push into East Prussia has been ended with the fearful defeat at Tannenberg by the army of General von Hindenburg. The English field army, brought to the mainland, has only proved that recruited mercenaries cannot hold ground against national armies [*Volksarmeen*].... the losses of the English are far greater than previously acknowledged.[85]

A similar story ran in late October, taken from the *Berliner Lokalanzeiger*, commenting on those substantial English losses:

For the inhabitants of the French departments Seine-Inferieure und Pas-de-Calais, the landing of the English troops is a bitter misfortune.... John Bull duly returns the generosity of the French [by commandeering] goods. He concerns himself above all with French agricultural production, undisturbed by the hunger which is spreading misery in almost every coastal town from Dunkirk to Saint-Malo. The Englishman acts as if France belongs to him. One often hears these words from officers: "without us, the French would be lost."[86]

When the Allies had little success convincing Italy to join them, the *Pester Lloyd* commented disdainfully, "Is there still a door on which the [Allies] have not yet knocked? The spectacle would be nauseating.... These once so proud powers brought to this, that they are constantly trying to recruit new allies."[87]

Austro-Hungarian papers also faithfully reported atrocity stories about the French, English, and Belgians mistreating German soldiers: in effect counter-atrocity stories, to stand opposed to the horrific tales emerging from German-occupied Belgium.[88] On August 3, the *Pester Lloyd* wrote that a French doctor had been accused of infecting Germans with cholera. "A French doctor with the help of two disguised French officers yesterday attempted to infect a well with cholera bacillae. He was shot on grounds of martial law."[89] Later in the conflict, the French captured German doctors traveling on a neutral Dutch ship and imprisoned them, according to *Pester Lloyd* reports from mid-September.[90] A month later, the Germans protested that the French were actively contravening the principles of the treaty of Genf of 1906, which stated that all combatants were to care for the wounded and ill regardless of which side they were fighting on. But French troops had "bestially mutilated and murdered. They have also attempted to harm those who carry the wounded."[91] Nor were the Belgians any better, stated the German chancellor in a speech published by the *Neue Freie Presse*:

How cruelly the population of...Belgium have [acted] against German soldiers. The behavior of the Belgian is one of the most painful, embarrassing surprises of this war.... your countrymen will be told that German troops have burned Belgian villages and towns to the ground, but no one will tell them that Belgian girls have stabbed out the eyes of defenseless wounded men on the battlefield. Belgian municipal officials have invited our officers to dine in their homes and shot them across the table.

The British were also repeatedly denounced for their alleged use of dum-dum bullets, soft lead bullets that exploded on impact and left particularly horrible wounds.[92] In contrast, the *Neue Freie Presse* proudly reported that *The Times* of London had printed a report attesting to the correctness of German behavior with regard to the laws of war. "The population was not terrorized. The houses and supplies were unharmed and undisturbed, [according to] the law."[93]

The Western powers were also castigated bitterly in the Austro-Hungarian press for their purported *Lügenkrieg*, literally a war of lies: Western propaganda against the Central Powers, especially that by Great Britain, was denounced as deeply unfair and even un-European. "Hypocrisy, lies, dum-dum bullets: those are England's weapons. In Africa, perhaps it is possible to win with such weapons. He who wages war in Europe and stands outside European civilization, to him no other fate save the final collapse can be granted."[94] Earlier in the war, Austro-Hungarian papers had reported such accusations as rather obvious attempts to sway as yet uncommitted powers and disquiet neutral countries. But as the war continued, the Austrian press grew more indignant.

It is a hard thing, to lie. Amateurs ought not to venture into this business. For awkward lies simply reveal themselves and do not even arouse irritation, but rather only amusement.... The lie, if it is to be halfway effective, must at least touch upon truth...whereas the counterfeit coins circulated to the international public by our enemies are of such...foolishness that they expose themselves at first glance.[95]

AUSTRIAN NATIONALITIES AT WAR

You cannot be impartial in a conflict between two pirate fleets if you happen to be aboard one of them.
George Bernard Shaw, *What I Really Wrote about the War*

Most of the Austro-Hungarian "subject peoples" in autumn 1914 were content with their own pirate fleet, as stated in this chapter's introduction. There were, however, a few exceptions, and their very existence bred an atmosphere of general paranoia towards the subject nationalities, particularly those in the Austrian half of the empire. Not all the suspicion was unfounded. Some of the empire's peoples had made clear their disloyal tendencies, such as Bosnian Serbs and Ruthenes in Galicia, against whom the administration possessed ample evidence of treason.[96] Short of treason, but still worrisome, émigré Czechs in Paris had pulled down the flag at the Austrian Embassy on July 27 and publicized their entry into the French army on July 29; on August 28, émigré Czechs in Russia formed the Družina, or League, which would later become the basis for the Czecho-slovak Legion, a military unit fighting on the side of the Entente powers.[97]

Still, from the war's outset, Stürgkh and the AOK regarded the Czechs and Serbs—and soon the other South Slav peoples, such as the Croats and Slovenes—with great suspicion. As Mark Cornwall notes, "This rapidly produced a mood of vigilance bordering on discrimination."[98] By the end of 1914, 950 inhabitants of Bohemia had been arrested, 46 newspapers had been closed down, and the emperor informed Stürgkh that the poor behavior of Czech soldiers was linked to "unhealthy political conditions" in Bohemia.[99] Even historically loyal peoples such as the Slovenes were designated by the AOK as dangerous, and alienated by repeated arrests (910 in the first four months of the war).[100] The Cyrillic script was banned wholesale thanks to its use by the monarchy's enemies as well as danger-ous ethnic groups such as the Serbs and Ruthenians.[101] Over time, the AOK's tendency to generalize its distrust had the opposite of its intended effect: it would radicalize ethnic groups who had begun the war evidenc-ing loyalty to the empire. This development, however, began in late 1916 after Emperor Karl succeeded to the Austro-Hungarian throne, and is out-side the scope of this chapter.

Austro-Hungarian press coverage of the war naturally reflected the growing distance between the empire's metropolises and its provinces. Vienna and Budapest papers were freer to editorialize about the war and its progress, as well as the war's effect on the empire. The relatively tightly censored papers published by the empire's subject peoples relied far more on factual reportage, much of it reprinted from imperially approved sources such as the Wolff Bureau in Berlin, or Austrian press agencies. This did not mean, however, that anti-Austrian provincial papers were unable to express their points of view. Their choices of subject matter, their manner of treatment, the stories they picked up from the wire services, and the parts of those stories they chose to run: all of these eloquently communi-cated the papers' stances to their attentive and like-minded readership.

Metropolitan newspapers wrote quite a bit about the empire and national issues for the first several weeks of the war, although only to por-tray the empire as single-mindedly united behind the emperor. The out-break of the war in Hungary, reported the *Pester Lloyd* with great (if somewhat paternalistic) satisfaction, had caused all nationalities to rally to the Emperor from whom all benefits came: "Where are the nationalities of Hungary...? Once the king's call went out to them, they hastened in their enthusiasm to the flag of this besieged country, that assures them bread, freedom, and the possibilities of western civilization [*Kultur*]."[102]

Nationality issues were valid, even important, the metropolitan papers conceded. But aggressive, fraudulent nationalism, in the service of sheer power, had caused world war. The *Neue Freie Presse* wrote about Serbian nationalism, "This is a fraud against the rights of peoples, which desired an independent Serbia [but] could not have intended to shift the balance-of-power relationships among the European powers in such a manner, that Russian stretched its greedy finger out to the Sava [River] and...murder and death spread to the Balkans."[103] Nor, warned the *Neue Freie Presse*, would dreams of pan-Slavism prove themselves for the monarchy's Slavic peoples:

Since Russia ascended out of the darkness of its mere mass existence [*Hordenexistenz*]...it has proved itself for all peoples of the earth to be a representation of sheer force in the most authentic, horrible meaning of that word...hundreds of examples of horrifying truth prove that blood is the mortar with which the fortresses of despotism are [built].[104]

Austro-Hungarian nationalities more generally ought to understand their debt to the empire, continued the *Pester Lloyd*.

The many peoples on both sides of the Leitha [River] are sated and made powerful through the venerable civilization for which they have their affiliation with Austria to thank. In Austria live those Slavs who are culturally advanced. In Austria, the most diverse races have the possibility to develop themselves culturally and politically.[105]

The metropolitan papers approvingly printed comments from the provinces asserting loyalty to the empire, such as this statement by the Czech paper *Hlas Naroda* (*Voice of the Nation*): "Austrian Slavs are linked to this empire, which is our present and our future. We will not allow ourselves to be duped by Serbian propaganda and Russian pan-Slavism."[106] Or this one, in the Ljubljana paper *Slovenec* (*Slovene*):

The western Slavs, who have developed far beyond the barbarism of Russian Tsarism and its corruption, reject the Tsar's call with outrage and contempt. The Tsar has lowered himself to the protector of a...murderer and thus has damaged Russian-ness before the entire world. Russian Tsarism has become an inglorious stain on the Slavic shield. Eliminating it is the holiest duty of the culturally advanced western Slavs.[107]

Once fighting began, the metropolitan papers evidenced a bit of concern about those suspect national groups wearing Austro-Hungarian colors. For example, the *Neue Freie Presse* reprinted an officer's speech to his largely Bosnian Serb corps: "Our weapons are directed not against the Serb people, not against the Serb ethnicity, to which so many in our rows [belong] who will faithfully perform their duty. To all such [Serbs] we extend our brotherly hand."[108]

The metropolitan papers even framed Austria-Hungary's success on the battlefield in ethnonational terms. The *Neue Freie Presse* referred to the war as a *Volkskrieg,* or "war of peoples," and noted that therefore

[it] must adapt itself to the characteristics and the temper of those millions called forth. The Austrian and the Hungarian love the advance—the happy and certain encounter with the enemy, and it is for [them] lighter on [their] heart, when through the attack [they] can [themselves] choose the conditions of the battle.

That same day, the *Neue Freie Presse* reported that the Central Powers' armies were becoming the tool of national awakening in Russian Poland, where much of the eastern-front fighting was taking place. Poles were evidently welcoming the Austro-Hungarian armies with open arms. "Is it not rare, this new awakening of a people who had been bent so deeply under Russian servitude?"[109] As they advanced through Polish territory, the Central Powers distributed leaflets exhorting the Poles to turn against the Russians:

To the Polish people! By the will of God, who determines the fate of peoples, and through the power of our supreme commanders, the allied German and Austro-Hungarian armies have moved over the border; we bring you liberation from the yoke of Moscow. Greet our flags with trust: they bring you justice! These flags are not foreign to you and your ethnic brethren; for centuries the Polish have been associated with the Danube monarchy as well as with the German empire, in which they have engaged in astonishing cultural development, and from the time of King Sobieski, the first to bring aid to the threatened Habsburg state, the glorious Polish traditions have been closely associated with those of their western neighbors.[110]

Similarly, Austrian papers happily noted Ukrainian anti-Russian sentiment, reprinting articles from the Czernowitz paper *Nowa Bukowina,* hoping that the Central Powers would bring about the creation of an independent Ukraine.[111] At no point did the Austrian papers indicate awareness that their own empire might fall prey to similarly centrifugal forces as the war continued.

After these initial comments, the metropolitan papers generally refrained from addressing nationality issues, in Austria-Hungary or elsewhere. Generally speaking, the *Neue Freie Presse* was barely concerned with the provinces at all, except insofar as they declared or demonstrated loyalty to the kaiser and the empire. Nor did the metropolitan papers' *Presseschau,* a typical feature of the region's papers that reprinted news from other papers, usually reprint news from the provinces. As many bylines were from Berlin as were from Vienna, and the *Neue Freie Presse* devoted considerable space to reprinting speeches and pronouncements from the Berlin Reichstag.

This issue was important for two reasons: first, because it meant that readers in Vienna were reading roughly similar news to that which Berliners or Müncheners were reading—that is, that Austria-Hungary's public was linked closely, in terms of information, to Germany's. Long before the two states joined their military and economic administrations in May 1917, their public spheres had already joined.[112] Second, it also indicates that Viennese readers knew relatively little about events in the provinces. Not even the most basic news reports made their way into the pages of the *Neue Freie Presse* or the *Pester Lloyd,* let alone anything resembling the truth about the nature of military administration and civilian resistance in these areas.

Neither did the provincial papers comment on these questions directly, probably because of censorship. Indirectly, however, they spoke volumes. The main provincial paper analyzed here is the Prague Czech-nationalist *Národní listy (National Pages),* owned by Karel Kramář, an outspoken opponent of the Stürgkh regime and Austria-Hungary more generally. *Národní listy* was under tight supervision even before the war began. Censored white spaces appeared in the paper as early as July 25, and the degree of censorship exercised over it was ratcheted up in late September, when far more issues bore the label "Po konfiskaci nové opravněné vydání" ("after confiscation, newly corrected edition"). (One possible reason for increased official attention paid to *Národní listy* and other Czech newspapers might be the mobilization of the 28th Regiment, largely drawn from working-class neighborhoods in Prague, which had been the targets of National Socialist propaganda.[113] As the 28th moved off, "soldiers were heard singing, 'We are marching against the Russians, but no one knows why,' and civilian onlookers shouted, 'Don't shoot your Slav brothers.'"[114] After defending the empire for eight months, the 28th deserted to the Russians en masse in April 1915.) In December 1914, *Národní listy* was banned from publication entirely for eight days, as punishment for several editorials criticizing government policy.[115]

Nevertheless, *Národní listy* adroitly managed to pass on its message. For example, for several days before and after the declaration of war against Serbia on July 28, *Národní listy* ran feuilletons and articles about Serbia. None of them declared the Serbs to be murderers, handmaidens of the Russian pan-Slavist threat, or a danger to Austria-Hungary's legitimate interests. Rather, the stories soberly analyzed Serbia's recent history; Serbian Christmas customs (not coincidentally similar in many ways to Czech Christmas traditions); Belgrade's past as a fortress city founded by the Romans and the difficulty of taking it militarily; a thoughtful, if ultimately negative, assessment of the Serbs as military opponents; and a long article repeating anti-Austrian comments in the Serb press dating back to 1910, probably provided to Austro-Hungarian papers by the KÜA/KPQ.[116] None of these reports are at all lurid; none of them are laden with anti-Serb vituperation or prideful predictions that the Central Powers' armies will carry all before them. They rely to a far greater extent than most stories from the metropolitan newspapers on precise and detailed factual content.

Their presence, however, is striking. Austria-Hungary had just declared war on this state, but rather than running glowing feuilletons about the empire and Germany, *Národní listy* ran sedate analyses of the enemy. And the anti-Austrian sentiments described in the final story were likely to strike a similar chord with at least some *Národní listy* readers, particularly one comment from *Tribuna:* "Pacifists have created a new slogan about European identity and patriotism. [Their] program, however, could only be realized if Austria were broken up."[117] Interspersed among the stories about Serbia was a pleasant feuilleton from *Národní listy*'s Paris correspondent about summer nights in Paris—the capital of France, another of the monarchy's enemies.

Likewise, after the war began, *Národní listy* continued to refrain from demonizing the enemy. In a story about Czechs trying to get from London to Prague, the author's tone is precise and factual. He notes that he found it hard to get room on trains and hard to get home; banks would not take kroner or marks, and so Germans and Austrians in London were going hungry; and the consulates and embassies had problems on their hands. He refrains completely from characterizing or smearing the British, as well as the Dutch, nor does he laud the Germans. The reader is allowed, or forced, to do all the interpretative work.[118] To wit:

Now began cruel times for our fellow citizens and especially Germans. The consulate did not want to, or could not, provide support, and many innocent victims of the war walked the long streets of London from hunger, without a penny in their pockets.... We met women of good families, who had sent them money which had been lost in transit. The addressee received only an announcement of the [lost] sum. At the German consulate, the consul himself, surrounded by a crowd of people requesting money and advice about their journey home, advised them to remain in England, look for employment, and to stop coming to the consulate. This was vain advice, for every German in the City [London's financial district] had been informed of the loss of his position.

The writer could have cast this story in far more lurid terms, larding it for example with depictions of the well-fed English brutally turning away from hungry, innocent German women. But the story contains nothing of that kind.[119] Perhaps the traditional Anglophilism of the Czech intelligentsia renders this factual, moderate account unsurprising. Similarly, when news of the German siege of Paris reached *Národní listy*, the paper's response was to publish a detailed map of Paris and its environs on the front page, noting its defenses and fortifications. At no point did the paper cheer on the Germans or analyze the weaknesses of the French.[120]

Somewhat more than the metropolitan papers, the *Národní listy* carried reports from the empire's trouble spots, such as the Bukovina, Bosnia, and Slovenia, all gleaned from imperial press agencies. For example, in early August, the *Národní listy*'s reports on patriotic gatherings contained details not found in the metropolitan papers about Sarajevo and Czernowitz. Also, regarding the potential cooperation of Russian Poles with the Central Powers, the *Národní listy* allowed the Poles to speak for themselves; the paper carried stories from various Lvov papers as well as statements by the Polish Central National Committee, founded by the nonsocialist Polish parties to counter the influence of the Temporary Committee founded by socialists in 1912.[121]

Also akin to Austro-Hungarian papers elsewhere, the Czech press expressed relief that the initial battles in Serbia went relatively well and quickly, and occasional exclamations of joy that Russian munitions did not seem to work very well. However, unlike the *Neue Freie Presse*, the *Národní listy* did not express any existential lamentation about what the war might mean for the continued existence of the empire or for Europe as it was. On the contrary. The *Národní listy*'s few forthright statements to its readers interpreted the war as a potential opportunity for the Czech nation, as in this opening editorial from August 4, written by Czech nationalist leader and *Národní listy* owner Karel Kramář:

The historic moment has arrived, the moment which so many feared and so many anticipated. The words of the German chancellor, regarding a battle between Germandom and Slavdom, have fulfilled themselves.... And more than anything we say to ourselves that after a horrible war we will not recognize the map of Europe.... Today, in an era of the most intensive national life, battles will not decide the fate of the nation. About the future of our nation we have no fear.... our future is in us, ourselves! If we do not bring about our own downfall, no one will destroy us![122]

The *Národní listy* also warned its readers, both explicitly and implicitly, to be wary of officially approved news. On August 3 it printed the following story:

German-language newspaper reportage has made clear to the entire world its tendentiousness and mendaciousness. In recent days even the highest commanders of our army have had very sad experiences with it.... According to a report from the "Leipziger Tageblatt" our high command announced...that *Budapest and Berlin reporters provided their papers with false reports from the southern front* [against Serbia]. The Prague German press is no better. Today's "Bohemia" reprinted from the "Neues W[iener] Tagblatt" *a refuted news report* about the breakout of revolution in Paris and the assassination of president Poincaré. There was not a word of truth in this rumor, and this was stated by "Bohemia" itself a few lines below, but...sensationalism simply burst forth into its columns. As is obvious, in this poison lies the spirit of the entire system.[123]

Similarly, just a week later, despite *Národní listy*'s location in Prague, it printed a report from the "Č.k. korespondenční kancelář" on patriotic demonstrations in the city. The entire story is a long direct quotation. *Národní listy*'s decision to run an official report rather than to cover the story themselves is an ambiguous statement. Were they leery of the censor? Or were they indicating to their readers that perhaps the official version might not be fully truthful?[124] Finally, in response to a story from the *Münchner Neueste Nachrichten* that alleged that German armaments could easily shoot from Calais to Dover or further, the *Národní listy* ran a long piece by a Professor Kučera of the Czech University of Prague, proving that the laws of physics prevented such a feat. It is easy to infer that the *Národní listy* is warning its readers about the overall veracity of German war claims or German newspapers.[125]

After mid-August, an increasing number of stories came from other newspapers: the *Wiener Allgemeine Zeitung*, the *Frankfurter Zeitung*, and the *Kölnische Zeitung*; the *Pester Lloyd*; the Wolff Agency; and various Polish and Ukrainian papers. This decision to avoid the censor's blue pen by opting for quotation allowed the *Národní listy* to broadcast its viewpoints in creative ways. For example, whereas the *Neue Freie Presse* and *Pester Lloyd* only ran excerpts from the German White Book and Austrian Red Book in explaining the war's onset for their readers, *Národní listy* also quoted the words of the monarchy's opponents: specifically, the British Blue Book, or at least those excerpts printed in the London *Times*.[126] *Národní listy* also ran smaller stories it picked up from the Western papers, such as a brief item titled "The English Army and Tobacco," which noted that the English generals had been forced to declare a ban on smoking unless at rest or off duty. At work, the British soldier could only smoke from a pipe, which had already become the symbol of the British soldier.[127] Why run this kind of human-interest story about the opposing side save as an attempt to awaken sympathy for the poor British soldier barred from his cigarettes—and, perhaps, to get anti-Austrian Czechs to take up the pipe?

THE EMPIRE WITHOUT QUALITIES

Very little of Austro-Hungarian newspaper coverage was unique to Austria-Hungary. Atrocity stories, claims to be the defender of Europe, and huzzahs for the might of the Allies rang from newspaper pages all across the European continent. Dr. Edgar Berillon, for example, lectured "all over France on the excessive defecation and distinctive body odor of Germans and on the fact that their large intestines were nine feet longer than normal."[128] Likewise, almost every belligerent nation used the "hoary semi-Orientalist mythos" of having once been Europe's bulwark against barbarism. The Russians pointed to their medieval defeat of the

Mongols. The Germans represented Slavdom as anti-European. And the French and Belgians also claimed to personify European civilization defending itself against savagery: that is, the Germans, now dubbed the "Huns."

Nevertheless, Austria-Hungary's presentation of its own war effort was distinctive, if perhaps mainly for its hollowness. The empire's own press coverage in the opening months of the war neglected to explain to its citizens exactly what they were fighting and sacrificing for—in fact, not until 1917 did the KPQ realize the depth of the need for "positive" propaganda. Despite press calls for greater Austro-Hungarian unity, and despite their attempts to link the monarchy with its historical position as *Kulturträger* (bearers of culture) to its peoples, the readers of the monarchy's press made few such connections. And even at the end of the war, the leaders of the empire were slow to understand the need to persuade the monarchy's subjects to remain loyal. Emperor Karl, who took the Austro-Hungarian throne in 1916, was famed for scorning propaganda: he noted that ideas "could not be recommended like laxatives, toothpaste and foodstuffs."[129]

Rather, it was censorship that tried to craft—if by exclusion and omission—a relatively unitary vision of the monarchy. Overall, though, it failed to do so. The Austria-Hungary described in the empire's metropolitan papers during the autumn and winter of 1914 was proudly united in martial struggle, strengthened in the crucible of war, and ready to prove its worth to Europe. Its nationalities were lining up to serve the colors bravely and sacrifice for the war effort. In the empire's provincial or "national" presses, things were different. Austria's nationalities were able to evade the censor to present opposing views and occasionally even to comment on the official line. Outright, flagrant subversion was close to impossible during the war's first two years.[130] Careful or encoded subversion, by contrast, was common.

But the overall effectiveness of a censorship-based strategy, of course, was doubtful. Newspapers, and especially censored newspapers, were inevitably a relatively limited source of actual news. As elsewhere in Europe, inhabitants of the Austro-Hungarian empire—and not just the rebel Czechs—read between the lines of their newspapers. By 1916, newspapers were typically regarded as one source of news among many, and far from the most reliable. Far more useful were stories brought home by soldiers about life at the front, or the tales of refugees fleeing battle zones for safer ground; these were passed from person to person. Russian propaganda in Austria-Hungary, which began operating almost immediately, spread myths of imminent Russian "liberation" of the Austro-Hungarian Slavs.[131] The more constructive and cheerful the reports printed in the officially censored newspapers, the more subjects of the monarchy turned to unofficial gossip and rumor, and the less they trusted anything with a government imprimatur. Personal contacts, especially in urban cafés, as well as underground newspapers circulated clandestinely, helped spread information corresponding more obviously to reality.[132]

Still, to contextualize the Habsburg wartime press as one source of information among many is not to dismiss its importance. Examining the Austro-Hungarian wartime press allows scholars to examine the empire's official presentation of the war and the way that presentation changed over time. We also more fully understand the closeness between the Habsburg and German presses during the war, and the way in which for most intents and purposes, the Central Powers comprised a single public sphere as early as 1914. It also sheds light on the distance from the metropolises to the peripheries, and the ways Habsburg nationalities found to communicate their unique perspectives as the war progressed. Finally, a study of the press highlights the shifting intensity of censorship and the difficulty of creating an effective censorship screen.

In the end, it is perhaps the Austro-Hungarian press's difficulty in effectively portraying its own state's war effort that is the most telling theme, with the collapse of the empire only four years away. I am not the only scholar to have noted this surprising emptiness: Steven Beller, in his study of Austro-Hungarian wartime culture, makes observations similar to mine here. He notes that Austro-Hungarian high culture during wartime was marked by instability and a lack of clarity. It proved impossible to create a unified Austro-Hungarian identity or patriotic culture, just as it was impossible to resolve the conflict between an Austro-German and supranational Austro-Hungarian identity.[133] Austria, compared to imperial Germany, was simply an empire without qualities. Or, to borrow the phrasing of a slightly later thinker: when Austrians wrote and thought about Austria, there was often no there there.

SELECTED READINGS FROM THE AUSTRIAN PRESS

The first three articles from the *Neue Freie Presse* highlight themes discussed in the chapter. Blame for the war is placed squarely on Russia, which is characterized as a non-European nation. A parallel is drawn between Russia's attack and the Turkish advances from previous centuries (with France helping to finance both), and Austria-Hungary is once again depicted as the bulwark against Eastern barbarism. Also worth noting is the praise of the German army above that of the Austrian army.

Neue Freie Presse, **August 1, 1914, p. 1**

"The Monarchy and its Ally, Germany, Take Up Arms" (lead editorial)

The events of recent days are too awesome for human comprehension. Thoughts swirl through the brain, hazy, uncertain; standards of previous experience break down; historical examples prove useless; and only the feeling speaks within us that the world now stands on the verge of incomparable experiences. In vain one broods over the possibilities that might come to pass once twenty million men are sent out against one another [on the fields of] Europe, intending with all their power to do one another harm, to bring pain to all of humanity, to spread chaos on the earth.

Should fate desire that we surrender, it would not be [merely] this Monarchy and our ally the German Empire but rather humanity itself that would suffer the worst blows. After the breakup of this ancient Empire, Russia would be the almost unconstrained ruler over Europe, and a world domination would be established, more terrifying than any preceding it. [Russia might extend its borders to Bohemia, Moravia, and Hungary, and the Balkans would fall under their rule: like the Turks' seventeenth-century siege of Vienna, this is an assault against the West and its culture.] European civilization was defended [once] at the walls of this city. This was, at the time, our historical destiny; it is still so today. We fight now, as then, for the unity of European culture, even if France, exactly as in the days of the Turks, [joined] the side of barbarism. The innermost law of [historical] development can not be [on the side of] the Russians. [French money might buy them military advantage or equipment,] but the core is unaltered. [...Austria and Germany will never be under Russian domination.]

[The war has not yet broken out.] Germany has posed, to the Russian cabinet, a question demanding a response within twenty-four hours: what goal their military mobilization had. When two such governments oppose one another this way, only a miracle can prevent their clashing. Kaiser Wilhelm has already ordered [that his staff research] the legal consequences of taking a belligerent position, which usually precedes a general mobilization. Europe is on the brink of war.

[But] Germany rises! Germany, with its sixty-five million inhabitants, with its stored power from decades of peaceful work, with its wisdom and with its ability, rises! Germany with the health of its people, with its honorable way of life, with its reliability and capability at all levels, rises! The finest, the most magnificent, the best-formed army that has ever before been equipped, will [fight] on the side of our soldiers.... [Our] Monarchy has an army capable of any task, allowing us to enter the battle with all earnestness but also with confidence. Russia has forced this war into being, because it hates the Monarchy and wants to force it into submission—and has, in the service of this overweening passion, mobilized its troops and made Serbia into the assistant for its cowardly, treacherous politics.

Neue Freie Presse, **August 2, 1914, p. 1**

Lead editorial

Five Great Powers have entered into war; [there will be] battles on land and sea, struggles under water and in the air, weapons of astounding thoroughness; and the millions that, on these lovely August days in which nature seems to be so pleased with itself, [will] abandon fields and meadows, workshops and writing tables, to hurl themselves at the enemy! All of this is so awe-inspiring, so [forces us to] wrestle for appropriate expression: the only sense which remains is that a Sophocles would be necessary to set into words this towering tragedy of the human race, to say what now moves our hearts.

...The Russian advance into Europe, subsidized by French billions, had to lead to a world war, and no one is shocked; each senses that what takes place was anticipated long ago.

...The exchange of correspondence, published today, between the Kaiser and Tsar Nicholas is a personal indictment. The German Kaiser felt himself deceived, and wished to inform his contemporaries of the attempt, so that they fully understand that a chasm separates Russian sensibilities from those of Europeans. Historical evidence of this kind of disloyalty has seldom been seen.

The Tsar asked the Kaiser to help him salvage the peace. Kaiser Wilhelm exerted himself in Vienna [in the creation of] a proposal, which might serve to transmit information [and thus avoid war]. The Russian Minister of War and Chief of Staff continually denied that military preparations were being made, and the diplomatic negotiations desired by the Tsar were [thus] advanced: and further days passed without Germany having mobilized to defend itself. Then, suddenly, the Russian army mobilized. These hoaxes—a reminder [of Russian treachery] such has never been seen before—have only contributed to the resolve of the German people to prove to the Russians that they are not permitted to spread murder and death through the world without atoning for it for generations to come.

Kaiser Wilhelm has ordered the mobilization of the entire German military force. Kaiser Franz Josef gave his order as of yesterday, and thus two armies of heroes approach combat, to carry the ideas of freedom and humanity towards Russia.... Beyond [our] borders, the Austrian and the German armies will be the messengers of [European] culture, justice and lawfulness.... We feel it as intimately as a bodily pain that France has allied itself with such depravity, and that perhaps at this very moment, on the boulevards of Paris, nerves are being whipped up by the singing of the Marsellaise and the tocsins sounding to announce the mobilization of the army of the [French] Republic as well. As if not even a slight shudder passed through their ranks at the memory of Sedan and the words of Count von Bismarck, who explained that in the next war, the loser will receive a blow so profound that [he] will bleed to death.

The world war is now here that will determine the fate of this ancient Monarchy.... The German army, [our] brothers, which unites today against the enemy at the behest of Kaiser Wilhelm, we greet in admiration and reverence. It has no equal and nothing can befall it, even should the gates of Hell [themselves] open.

Neue Freie Presse, **August 5, 1914, p. 1**

"To the Army" by Egon Zweig

There is no doubt left to lodge regarding the sense and goal of the monstrous struggle, which [will] expose us to one of the most fundamental experiences of world history. This [war] is about the begin and nothingness of human civilization [itself]. This [fact] stands before the gaze, sharpened by judgment and education, of thousands; it lives, unarticulated, in the dawning consciousness of millions; that now the fearful and terrible decision is called for between Occidental culture and Sarmatian servitude of spirit and body; that the world has been called upon to determine the orientation of [the next] centuries of its history. To those whose disposition and perception prohibit [understanding] the inner necessity of this titanic struggle, to them let it be said: that no decision or comparison exists between civilization and tsarism, between the ongoing self-determination of capable free peoples and their national energies, and the hollow dreamworld of Cossack theocracy, in which rigid cruelty...and a basic negation of human dignity persist. A third, middle [route] is inconceivable. Since Russia rose from the darkness of its [early] mob-based existence (*Hordenexistenz*) to its [current] greed for a universal theocratic monarchy, it has proven itself before all the peoples of the earth as a [pure] representation of force in the most actual, horrific meaning of those words: it has attested in hundredfold to the dreadful truth that blood is the mortar with which the fortresses of despotism are walled. Thus this world war will and must be a war of worldviews, a cultural struggle [*Kulturkampf*] in a higher and deeper sense than has ever taken place before.

To the Habsburg Empire, beset by all of these storms, is befallen the lot of protagonist in this tragedy of peoples, to tread the world stage as a pioneer, and in the face of the law of historical ingratitude and defiance, we hold fast to the confidence that history will praise us. The Danube Monarchy now must fight for its [continued] existence, law, and honor. Austria-Hungary—not Austria and Hungary as in wretched days now forgotten—has passed over the barriers of this ordeal with trust in a good thing, that which [guarantees] the law and justice, elation in our power, that which is both liege and champion [to the Emperor]: his army.... The holy name of Fatherland combines in itself past, present and future...the army is a truly altruistic organization, a model in breeding, duty, and loyalty, which has already aided [us] through its very existence.

The last two selections share a noteworthy quality. The first is a fairly ordinary poem that attempts to glorify the war as a divine mission. The second article, coming from a Czech nationalist paper, is quite interesting. In spite of its somber assessment of the situation and prescient insight into the consequences of the war on the map of Europe, the article still espouses the hope that the war can serve as a regenerating force that will purify the nation—although it is ambiguous as to whether it refers to Austria-Hungary or the Czech nation.

Neue Freie Presse, **August 5, 1914, p. 1**

"Das ist der Kampf..." (This is the struggle...) by Gräfin E. Salburg

Das ist der Kampf, den alle wir erträumt,	This is the struggle, of which we all have dreamed,
Der uns'rer Sehnsucht Wellen hoch getragen,	For which our longing has pulled the tides high,
Das ist der Kampf, dem die Begeist' rung schäumt,	This is the battle, for which our enthusiasm foams,
Der Manneskampf aus alten Heldentagen.	The manly war from the days/tales of ancient heroes.
Sieh! Alles schweigt, was Kleinheit war und Streit	See it! All falls silent, the dross, the divisive

Des Tags! Nur Öst'reich spricht aus
    seinen Söhnen,
	Of the everyday! Only Austria speaks
	    to her sons,

Ein Ziel macht alle uns're Herzen weit:	One goal [unites] all our hearts:

Lasst uns des Kaisers Stirn mit
    Lorbeer krönen!
	Let us crown the Kaiser's head with
	    laurel!

Den grünen, ew'gen Frühling
    seinem Haupt!
	[Let us prove] the green, eternal spring
	    of his majesty!

Und diese Glorie seinem Abendbrote!	Let these glories be his evening fare!

Es sag' ihm, eines grossen
    Öst'reichs Bote:
	He has been told, by one of Austria's
	    great messengers:

Nein, nicht umsonst hast du an
    uns geglaubt!
	No, not in vain have you believed in
	    us!

Umsonst gebt nicht über
    sechszig Jahre!
	Not in vain do you give [us] more than
	    sixty years!

Dein Friede, Herr, er gab uns uns're Kraft,	Your peace, Lord, gave us our power,
Wir ziehen aus mit heil'ger Leidenschaft,	We ready ourselves with holy passion,

Wir geh'n zur Schlacht wie Priester
    zum Altare.
	We go to the battlefield like priests to
	    the altar.

Denn all fühlen heute, was es gillt,	For we all feel today, what [this] means:

Franz Josef ruft! Und wenn der ruft,
    ihr Heere,
	Franz Josef calls! and that which he
	    calls—you, his army—

Dann steht die Zeit in grösster
    Zeichen Bild,
	[Will bring] our era into the annals of
	    history,

Franz Josef ruft: Für Völkerrecht
    und Ehre!
	Franz Josef calls: for nations' rights
	    and honor!

Národní Listy, August 4, 1914, p. 1

"World War" by Karel Kramář

The historic moment has arrived, that which so many feared and so many anticipated. The words of the German chancellor about the battle between Germandom
and Slavdom have come true. All Europe sends its health, its youth, to the field of
battle; and horrors will come to pass, horrors till now imagined only by soldiers in
fantasies out of novels.

No one can predict its end. We did predict that the Serbian conflict would
become a European conflict: that the question of murder, condemned by all, and
the question of its [appropriate] punishment would become a question of the
European balance of power, which would bring the whole world to arms. We were
criticized for a lack of Slavic feeling when we condemned the fact that twenty-
year-old boys were deciding the political fate of the nation, and now each can
judge for himself that we predicted correctly. But today ends all prophecy.

The states of Europe will [now] pay their last respects to their previous policies:
now every mistake in domestic politics will revenge itself. And we will say to ourselves as well that at the end of this horrible war, we will not recognize the map of
Europe. Bismarck once said, that the coming war must end in the total shattering
of the enemy, so that [that country] would be incapable of ever threatening the
peace again. "Saigner a blanc... "

In this moment, however, each of us thinks of the future of our nation. And perhaps many think to themselves how wise we would be were we not to squander our strength on internal arguments and, rather, to use it for internal strengthening, for the healthy, sturdy organization of all our national strength, so that we can await the dawning of our fate without fear. Those who called for such [wisdom] would call in vain!

[Yet] now nothing is left [to us] save to seek out our future manfully and without fear. Today, in the age of the most intensive national life, battles will not determine the fate of the nation. For the future of *our* nation we do not fear. Even if [fearful storms] and stress should come, we hope it will cleanse our public life, and from the difficult tests shall emerge only those who possess genuine moral strength. And these [few] can also lead us, the nation, away from the rockiest reefs.

Thus, let fate in the worst conflict history has ever seen—a conflict in which the entire world will be fighting about the future of European history, about the hegemony of one and the peace of the rest, however it should be decided: let these struggles result in severe tests and suffering, or the possibility of living in the fullness of our national life, to our advantage and to that of all others: our future is in us, ourselves! If we do not destroy ourselves, no one can destroy us!

NOTES

For kind assistance with this chapter I would like to thank Maureen Healy, Molly Molloy of the erstwhile Hoover Institution Library, and most importantly Iñigo García-Bryce.

1. Robert Musil, *The Man without Qualities*, trans. Sophie Wilkins and Burton Pike (New York: Alfred A. Knopf, 1995). The Parallel Campaign occupies much of the second half of the first volume. For commentary on this recent translation, see William H. Gass, "The Hovering Life," *New York Review of Books* 43:1 (11 January 1996), 56–63; as well as George Steiner, "The Unfinished," *New Yorker* 71:8, (17 April 1995), 101–106.

2. Even Austria-Hungary's ongoing difficulties in Galicia during the 1914 campaigns did not overshadow the achievements of the Germans in the pages of Austro-Hungarian papers.

3. I am adapting this phrase from Vladimir Lenin's term for Tsarist Russia. As best I can find out, this phrase was used first either in the 1899 work The Development of Capitalism in Russia or his 1916 essay "A Caricature of Marxism and Imperialist Economism."

4. Kurt Paupié, *Handbuch der Oesterreichischen Pressegeschichte 1848–1959*, vol. 2 (Vienna and Stuttgart: Wilhelm Braumuller Universitaets-Verlagsbuchhandlung, 1960), 145.

5. Maureen Healy, *Vienna and the Fall of the Habsburg Empire: Total War and Everyday Life in World War I* (Cambridge: Cambridge University Press, 2004), 187.

6. Arthur James May, *The Passing of the Habsburg Monarchy 1914–1918*, vol. 1 (Philadelphia: University of Pennsylvania Press, 1966), 303–6.

7. Ibid., 407.

8. John Ewart Wallace Sterling, *Diplomacy and the Newspaper Press in Austria-Hungary Midsummer 1914* (Ph.D. diss, Stanford University, 1937), 254, 312, 321.

9. Bruce Garver, *The Young Czech Party, 1874–1901, and the Emergence of a Multi-Party System* (New Haven, Conn.: Yale University Press, 1978), 105, 303, 313.

10. On *Národní listy* and the Young Czechs, see Garver, *Young Czech Party,* 102–9.

11. Ibid., 107.

12. See, for example, Robin Okey, *The Habsburg Monarchy, c. 1765–1918: From Enlightenment to Eclipse* (Basingstoke, England: Macmillan Press, 2001); Alan Sked, *The Decline and Fall of the Habsburg Empire 1815–1918,* 2nd ed. (New York: Longman, 2001); Zbynek Zeman, *The Break-Up of the Habsburg Empire, 1914–1918* (London and New York: Oxford University Press, 1961), 2–3.

13. Zeman, *Break-Up of the Habsburg Empire,* 1–4.

14. Krejci, in *Přehled,* 1 May 1914, cited in Zeman, *Break-Up of the Habsburg Empire,* 20.

15. These numbers are no more than suggestive. In Vienna, German-language titles were listed in H.O. Sperling, ed., *Sperlings Zeitschriften-Adressbuch,* vol. 2 (Stuttgart: Verlag von H.O. Sperling, 1915), 399–400. Slovene titles came from *Razstava slovenskega novinarstva* (Ljubljana: Jugoslov movimansko udruzenje, Ljubjanska sekcija, 1937), 16, 34–35, 64. For Czech titles, see František štedronsk, and Saša Mouchová, eds., *Zahraniční krajanské noviny, časopisy a kalendáře do roku 1938* (Prague: Národní knihovna v Praze, 1958), 29–55. For Budapest, information about the total number of Budapest papers comes from Mario D. Fenyo, *Literature and Political Change: Budapest, 1908–1918* (Philadelphia, Pa.: Transactions of the American Philosophical Society, 1987), 28. Non-Hungarian papers are to be found in Ungarischen Institut an der Universität Berlin, *Bibliographia Hungariae: Philologica, Periodica: Verzeichnis der 1861–1921 erschienenen, Ungarn betreffenden Schriften in nichtungarischer Sprache* (Berlin and Leipzig: Walter de Gruyter, 1928), 830–84. Slovak papers are detailed in Michal Potemra's *Bibliografia slovenských novín a časopisov do roku 1918* (Martin: Matica Slovenská, 1958), 63, 72, 77–78, 97–99, 101–2. I am profoundly grateful to Angela Cannon of the Slavic Reference Service at the University of Illinois Library, as well as to many members of H-Habsburg, for their assistance with this question.

16. See Derek Sayer, *The Coasts of Bohemia: A Czech History* (Princeton, N.J.: Princeton University Press, 1998), 93.

17. Mark Cornwall, "News, Rumour, and the Control of Information in Austria-Hungary, 1914–1918," *History* 77:249 (1992): 61.

18. Cited in Healy, *Vienna,* 187.

19. Sterling, *Diplomacy and the Newspaper Press,* 245. A similar statement of the government's position was made to the Hungarian press by Hungarian prime minister Count Tisza himself.

20. Sterling, *Diplomacy and the Newspaper Press,* 249.

21. Paupié, *Handbuch der Oesterreichischen Pressegeschichte,* 161.

22. Mark Cornwall, *The Undermining of Austria-Hungary: The Battle for Hearts and Minds* (New York: St. Martin's Press, 2000), 19. Paupié dates the KÜA to the 31st. See Paupié, *Handbuch der Oesterreichischen Pressegeschichte,* 142. But the organization had in fact been designed in 1912. See Cornwall, "News, Rumour," 52.

23. Cornwall, *Undermining of Austria-Hungary,* 19.

24. Ibid., 22–23.

25. Ibid., 24–25. Joseph Held argues that in Hungary, self-censorship tended to render actual censorship almost unnecessary between 1914 and 1916; but he also states that "most Austro-Hungarian newspapers outside Bohemia…decided to close up the white space left by the censor, [thus] only a very careful reading would indicate evidence of censorship." See Joseph Held, "Culture in Hungary During World War I," in *European Culture in the Great War: The Arts, Entertainment, and Propaganda, 1914–1918,* ed. Aviel Roshwald and Richard Stites (Cambridge: Cambridge University Press, 1999), 191.

26. Cornwall, *Undermining of Austria-Hungary,* 25. Cornwall notes that censorship became spotty from 1916 on, allowing Czech authors to publish nationalist manifestos, then forbidding demonstrations or banning newspapers. The military by 1918 was bitterly critical of its own censorship bodies, as well as of the domestic press. See Cornwall, "News, Rumour," 60–61, 63–64. But the censors had a Herculean task. Healy comments that the censors reading mail (including POW correspondence) had to contend with the following languages: German, Russian, Italian, Czech, Polish, Slovak, Ukrainian, Serbian, Croatian, Romanian and Bessarabian (Romanian in Cyrillic), Hungarian, French, English, Swedish, Hebrew, Sephardic, Spanish, Latvian and Estonian, Bulgarian, Greek, Albanian, Arabic, Turkish, Persian, and Tatar. See Healy, *Vienna,* 228 n. 51.

27. Healy, *Vienna,* 195–96.

28. Alfred Polgar, *Hinterland* (Berlin: Rowohlt, 1929), introduction. Cited in Healy, *Vienna,* 190.

29. Quoted in May, *Passing of the Habsburg Monarchy,* 302.

30. Jan Hajšman, *Česká mafie. Vzpomínky na odboj doma,* 2nd ed. (Prague: Sfmiy, 1934), 31, cited in Cornwall, *Undermining of Austria-Hungary,* 26.

31. Healy, *Vienna,* 192.

32. Although they were the most important, the AOK, KÜA, HFB, and KPQ were not the only Austro-Hungarian organizations or offices to deal with the press. The War Ministry had its own press section, as did the Foreign Ministry, the Prime Minister's office, the Hungarian Prime Minister's office, and district and regional governments. See Paupié, *Handbuch der Oesterreichischen Pressegeschichte,* 153–54.

33. Cornwall, "News, Rumour," 53.

34. Cornwall, *Undermining of Austria-Hungary,* 26.

35. Cornwall, "News, Rumour," 53.

36. Healy, *Vienna,* 190.

37. Steven Beller, "The Tragic Carnival: Austrian Culture in the First World War," in *European Culture in the Great War: The Arts, Entertainment, and Propaganda 1914–1918,* ed. Aviel Roshwald and Richard Stites (Cambridge: Cambridge University Press, 1999), 133–34.

38. Paupié, *Handbuch der Oesterreichischen Pressegeschichte,* 170–72.

39. Paupié, *Handbuch der Oesterreichischen Pressegeschichte,* 141, 153. As the war continued, the KPQ reached beyond its earlier role of liaison between the Austro-Hungarian military and its press. First, it took on the increasingly important tasks of boosting both military and civilian morale—for example, through cabaret shows for soldiers as well as commissioning patriotic and propaganda films and museum exhibitions of work by "war artists." Second, it became increasingly concerned with foreign opinion and propaganda about the Dual Monarchy.

40. *Neue Freie Presse,* 12 September 1914. I should note that this delay seems to have been universal, perhaps brought on by conditions of wartime censorship all over Europe. The article "Die Hoffnungen der Französen auf Russland: Die Träume des Herrn Maurice Barres" claims that not until 7 September was there a single word in the French press of Russia's catastrophic losses in East Prussia in late August. See *Neue Freie Presse,* 16 September 1914.

41. T. G. Masaryk, *The Making of a State: Memories and Observations 1914–1918* (New York: Howard Fertig, 1969), 30.

42. Cornwall, *Undermining of Austria-Hungary,* 25.

43. Cornwall, *Undermining of Austria-Hungary,* 26. Paupié writes that "die Presse, vor allem die *Neue Freie Presse, Zeit, Abend, Arbeiterzeitung,* und gelegentlich das *Fremdenblatt,* wehrte sich gegen die Zensur," but does not provide dates for this activity. See Paupié, *Handbuch der Oesterreichischen Pressegeschichte,* 145. In contrast, Cornwall notes that the *Neue Freie Presse* and other loyal papers such as the *Reichspost* were more tolerant, though the *Arbeiterzeitung* complained openly about the censor by 1916. See Cornwall, "News, Rumour," 54.

44. *Pravo Lidu,* 5 August 1914, cited in Zeman, *Break-Up of the Habsburg Empire,* 44.

45. Healy, *Vienna,* 181.

46. Holquist, "'Information is the Alpha and Omega of Our Work': Bolshevik Surveillance in its Pan-European Context," *Journal of Modern History* 69 (September 1997): 415–50. See also the *Journal of Modern History* issue on denunciation in European history: "Practices of Denunciation in Modern European History, 1789–1989," 68:4 (December 1996).

47. In the last week of July, the Viennese and Budapest press held out the hope that Russia would not intervene; then they placed their faith in the diplomatic efforts of British foreign minister Sir Edward Grey to localize the conflict. See Sterling, *Diplomacy and the Newspaper Press,* chapter 4.

48. *Neue Freie Presse,* 1 August 1914.

49. *Neue Freie Presse,* 2 August 1914.

50. *Pester Lloyd,* 30 July 1914. All editions of newspapers are the morning editions (*Morgenblätte*) unless otherwise noted. Sterling notes that even voices which had been oppositional, such as the *Arbeiter-Zeitung,* agreed in branding Russia the main disturber of Europe's peace. See Sterling, *Diplomacy and the Newspaper Press,* 301.

51. On the Ballhausplatz's decision to postpone an announcement about Russian mobilization, see Sterling, *Diplomacy and the Newspaper Press,* chapter 4, particularly 309.

52. "Russia Calls Forth the European War," *Neue Freie Presse,* 2 August 1914.

53. *Pester Lloyd,* 1 August 1914.

54. *Pester Lloyd,* 9 August 1914.

55. *Neue Freie Presse,* 15 August 1914.

56. *Neue Freie Presse,* 1 August 1914.

57. *Pester Lloyd,* 9 August 1914.

58. *Neue Freie Presse,* 5 August 1914.

59. *Neue Freie Presse,* 5 August 1914.

60. *Pester Lloyd,* 9 August 1914.

61. G. D. von Boroevic, *Neue Freie Presse,* 21 October 1914.

62. Between September 1914 and the summer of 1915, Austro-Hungarian forces were unable to advance, and at some points were unable even to successfully

defend their own territory. During this period Russian troops encroached on Krakow and entered Hungary, albeit briefly. Meanwhile, Serb forces successfully repelled three separate Austro-Hungarian attacks, and Austro-Hungarian losses in Serbia were one-third higher than those of the Serbs, despite great inequities of resources. By late 1914, according to American embassy reports, not just educated classes in Vienna, Budapest, and Prague, but even external observers like Winston Churchill, were predicting imminent defeat for the Habsburg empire. See May, *Passing of the Habsburg Monarchy*, 95–101.

63. *Neue Freie Presse*, 28 August 1914.

64. *Neue Freie Presse*, 16 September 1914.

65. *Pester Lloyd*, 9 August 1914.

66. *Neue Freie Presse*, 1 October 1914.

67. *Neue Freie Presse*, 1 October 1914.

68. *Neue Freie Presse*, 1 August 1914.

69. Quoted in May, *Passing of the Habsburg Monarchy*, 289.

70. *Neue Freie Presse*, 2 August 1914.

71. *Neue Freie Presse*, 8 August 1914.

72. *Pester Lloyd*, 28 August 1914.

73. *Neue Freie Presse*, 1 August 1914.

74. *Neue Freie Presse*, 20 November 1914.

75. *Pester Lloyd*, 31 July 1914.

76. Egon Zweig, *Neue Freie Presse*, 5 August 1914.

77. "Destruction as a Guiding Principle," *Neue Freie Presse*, 16 September 1914.

78. *Neue Freie Presse*, 10 October 1914.

79. *Neue Freie Presse*, 2 August 1914.

80. "Mobilmachung der gesamten Streitkraefte in Deutschland," *Neue Freie Presse*, 2 August 1914; "Der erste Tag des europaischen Krieges," *Neue Freie Presse*, 4 August 1914.

81. *Pester Lloyd*, 9 August 1914.

82. *Neue Freie Presse*, 6 August 1914, cited in Sterling, *Diplomacy and the Newspaper Press*, 304–5. *Arbeiter-Zeitung* interpreted the outbreak of war in nearly identical terms: see Sterling, *Diplomacy and the Newspaper Press*, 306.

83. *Neue Freie Presse*, 5 August 1914.

84. *Neue Freie Presse*, 16 and 19 October 1915, cited in May, *Passing of the Habsburg Monarchy*, 306.

85. "Alliance with England a Disappointment for France," *Neue Freie Presse*, 7 September 1914.

86. *Neue Freie Presse*, 20 October 1914.

87. *Pester Lloyd*, 1 October 1914.

88. On atrocity stories, see (among others) Arthur Ponsonby, *Falsehood in War-Time: Containing an Assortment of Lies Circulated throughout the Nations during the Great War* (New York: E. P. Dutton and Company, 1928); and James Morgan Read, *Atrocity Propaganda 1914–1919* (New York: Arno Press, 1972).

89. *Pester Lloyd*, 3 August 1914.

90. *Pester Lloyd*, 16 September 1914, Abendblatt. "Wie man in Frankreich die Gefangenen behandelt."

91. *Neue Freie Presse*, 21 October 1914.

92. *Neue Freie Presse*, 7 September 1914. I am grateful to Mark Milliorn for insight as well as references on this topic. The British had in fact used dumdums

("flat-nosed expanding bullets") during the late nineteenth century against their African and Indian colonial subjects, as well as against the Boers. However, by 1907 all European nations, along with the United States, had foresworn their use. Nevertheless, both sides accused one another of using dumdums during the Great War. See Read, *Atrocity Propaganda*, 68–71. See also Sven Lindquist, *Exterminate All the Brutes*, trans. Joan Tate (New York: New Press, 1992), 52.

93. *Neue Freie Presse*, 3 November 1914.

94. *Pester Lloyd*, 21 September 1914.

95. *Pester Lloyd*, 14 October 1914.

96. Cornwall, *Undermining of Austria-Hungary*, 19; Cornwall, "News, Rumour," 55. Jószef Galantai, *Hungary in the First World War* (Budapest: Akadémiai Kiadó, 1989), 95–96, offers the most detail.

97. Masaryk, *Making of a State*, 40–41. On the Družina, see Josef Kalvoda, *The Genesis of Czechoslovakia* (Boulder, Colo., and New York: East European Monographs, distributed by Columbia University Press, 1986), chapter 3; see also Todd Huebner, "The Multinational 'Nation-State': The Origins and the Paradox of Czechoslovakia, 1914–1920" (Ph.D. diss., Columbia University, 1993); and Karel Pichlík, Bohumír Klípa, and Jitka Zabloudilová, eds., *Českoslovenští legionáři* (Prague: Mlada fronta, 1996).

98. Cornwall, *Undermining of Austria-Hungary*, 19.

99. Cited in Cornwall, *Undermining of Austria-Hungary*, 21; see also Cornwall, "News, Rumour," 56.

100. Cornwall, *Undermining of Austria-Hungary*, 21.

101. Cornwall, *Undermining of Austria-Hungary*, 19; Cornwall, "News, Rumour," 55.

102. *Pester Lloyd*, 31 July 1914.

103. *Neue Freie Presse*, 15 August 1914.

104. *Neue Freie Presse*, 5 August 1914.

105. *Pester Lloyd*, 31 July 1914.

106. *Pester Lloyd*, 7 August 1914.

107. *Neue Freie Presse*, 14 August 1914.

108. *Neue Freie Presse*, 3 August 1914.

109. *Neue Freie Presse*, 8 August 1914.

110. *Neue Freie Presse*, 9 August 1914.

111. *Neue Freie Presse*, 10 August 1914.

112. On Austria-Hungary's commitment to a "binding political, military, and economic alliance" with Germany, see Holger Herwig, *The First World War: Germany and Austria-Hungary 1914–1918* (New York: St. Martin's Press, 1997), 369–70.

113. The Czech National Socialists were a moderate socialist party that espoused a fervent Czech nationalism. They had no connection to the German National Socialist German Worker's Party (Nazi Party).

114. May, *Passing of the Habsburg Monarchy*, 353.

115. May, *Passing of the Habsburg Monarchy*, 357.

116. "Valečnýstav," *Národní listy*, 27 July 1914; "Belgrade," *Národní listy*, 28 July 1914, evening edition; Dr. A.H., "Fejeton," *Národní listy*, 2 August 1914, příloha; *Národní listy*, 16 August 1914. On the official source of such stories, which also appeared in Viennese papers, see Sterling, *Diplomacy and the Newspaper Press*, 313.

117. *Národní listy*, 16 August 1914.

118.   "Feuilleton: Through Wartime Europe from London to Prague" ("Z Londyna do Prahy valčičí Evropou"), *Národní listy*, 25 August 1914, evening edition.

119.   Ibid.

120.   *Národní listy*, 9 September 1914.

121.   *Národní listy*, příloha k, 11 August 1914.

122.   Karel Kramář, *Národní listy*, 4 August 1914.

123.   *Národní listy*, 3 August 1914; italics in original.

124.   *Národní listy*, 10 August 1914.

125.   Professor Kučera, *Národní listy*, 25 October 1914.

126.   The *Times* quotations occurred frequently during the last two weeks of August 1914 and disappeared thereafter, although *Národní listy* still occasionally cited British papers, as on 12 October 1914, which reprinted two stories from the *Morning Post*.

127.   *Národní listy*, 5 September 1914, evening edition.

128.   Aviel Roshwald and Richard Stites, eds., *European Culture in the Great War: The Arts, Entertainment, and Propaganda, 1914–1918* (Cambridge: Cambridge University Press, 1999), 349.

129.   Ludwig Windischgrätz, *Helden und Halunken. Selbsterlebte Weltgeschichte* (Vienna-Munich-Zürich: W. Frick-Verlag, 1965), 134–35, cited in Cornwall, "News, Rumour," 64.

130.   Cornwall, "News, Rumour," 52.

131.   See Cornwall, "News, Rumour," 57.

132.   See, for example, Cornwall, "News, Rumour," as well as Healy, *Vienna*, in particular chapter 3.

133.   Beller, "Tragic Carnival," 130.

Closing Observations on Newspapers, Propaganda, and the Great War

Immediacy, one of the great assets of newspapers, may also be its greatest weakness. In a work on the American press in times of crisis, Lloyd Chiasson Jr. observed that the press was good at what Harold Lasswell had described as surveillance, but in order to meet the demand to provide readers with the latest information, newspapers focused on the present at the expense of the past and the future. Crises were well covered, but often in a superficial way that focused on individuals rather than the roots causes of problems.[1] This critique holds true for the European newspapers covered in this collection. The result is not quite the erasure of the past that Peter Fritzsche has suggested in *Reading Berlin 1900*, but depth is certainly sacrificed in the interest of expediency.

A striking common trait that arises after reading the contributions to this collection is the almost complete lack of reflection on the part of the participants considered in this study. It is not terribly surprising that the Entente powers were less focused on the events of July 1914 than the Central Powers. Not only due to the fact that it was the heir to the Habsburg throne that was assassinated, but also because Germany had been concerned about (some might argue obsessed with) the possibility of an impending war at least since 1912, when the publication of General Friedrich von Bernhardi's *Germany and the Next War* drew considerable public attention.[2] It is somewhat surprising to see that the general public in France and Great Britain did not realize that war was a possibility until less than a week before the outbreak of hostilities. This certainly can be partially attributed to the French and British public's lack of awareness of the exact nature of their respective governments' foreign commitments, the French to Russia and the British to France. Had the press and general public been more aware of the extent of their government's commitments, perhaps more attention would have been given to the events surrounding the assassination in Sarajevo.

The Central Powers are also guilty of a lack of reflection, and a certain degree of self-deception. The fact that Archduke Ferdinand was even scheduled to be in Sarajevo on June 28 reveals a degree of insensitivity or lack of awareness on the part of the Habsburg government. St. Vitus Day (Vidovdan) commemorates the fall of Kosovo in 1389 to the Turks, thus ending Serbian independence. The visit of the heir to the Habsburg throne on that day could only highlight the fact that 525 years later Serbia was still not completely free. Moreover, the Austro-Hungarian ultimatum to Serbia was intentionally unreasonable. No self-respecting sovereign nation, even a lesser power, could accept all of the terms imposed by the Habsburg monarchy. However, the Austrian government appeared to be more interested in crushing Serbian nationalism than in getting to the bottom of the assassination plot. This lack of reflection about the Habsburgs' role in events in the summer of 1914 is clearly illustrated in the press's reaction to the unfolding of the war. While the Austro-Hungarian military may have chafed at being considered an appendage to the German war effort, the German-language press in Vienna and Budapest praised the achievements of the German military more than their own.[3] The German government and press can be faulted for a lack of reflection, as well as a lack of candor. The decision to give the Habsburg monarchy a blank check to deal with Serbia meant that war was a distinct possibility. Claims of shock and disappointment aside, the German government could not honestly maintain that Britain's entrance to the war was a surprise. Certainly, a more forthright enunciation of Britain's position would have made matters clearer; however, German intelligence knew before the war that Britain and France had made plans for military cooperation in the event of war with Germany.[4]

Another common denominator in press discussions during the war is the absence of any reasonable analysis of the prehistory of the war. Not just the events of July 1914, which tended to be discussed in caricature—British duplicity, French lust for revenge, Russian or German aggressiveness, or Austrian unreasonableness—but also the longer prehistory of the war (i.e., since 1900) were either absent or one-sided. For example, the aggressive nature of Russian pan-Slavism or the deceptiveness of English diplomacy and the inherent anti-German nature of both were well-worn topics in the German press. However, German actions contributing to the heightened tensions in Europe, especially Wilhelm II's personal blunders such as the Daily Telegraph Affair or the Hale Interview, are ignored.[5] None of the belligerents were inclined to consider other points of view or attempted to understand different perspectives.

Adrian Gregory has shown nicely how these different perspectives could influence both views and conduct concerning naval warfare. The British followed an established code of naval warfare. The Germans tended to view war at sea in similar terms to land warfare. The result was indeed a culture clash over acceptable maritime behavior. This clash extended to the land war as well. The shelling of the cathedral at Reims could be considered a cultural war atrocity; however, if the tower was employed to monitor the movements of German troops, did German commanders have any other alternative? Arthur Ponsonby's blanket condemnation of the British press's reporting of war atrocities may need revisiting, not so much because he is wrong, although Gregory makes a good case for doing so on that basis alone. Rather, it needs revisiting because the problem is more complicated that Ponsonby realized. As Gregory contends, British journalists did try to report stories based on facts and did exercise some discretion in reporting more gruesome stories. Sometimes the sources of these facts, including the Belgian government, were erroneous. Also, quite simply, what constitutes a fact is not always clear. The extent of *Franc-tireur* activity in Belgium and elsewhere is an open question. Women and children firing weapons may not be members of a military unit, but they cannot be considered innocent civilians either. Perhaps these people were just defending their homes (and homeland). Nevertheless, one could not expect the German military to simply ignore such actions; but one can condemn the military for overreacting, and certainly evidence of such overreaction exists.[6] The problem of *Franc-tireur* activity made the question of who was an innocent civilian difficult at the time virtually insoluble now.

Another common factor was the rather high level of cooperation between the press and their respective governments. In Russia and Austria-Hungary, extreme opposition newspapers were shut down immediately, but for the most part newspapers, including the socialist press, supported their governments and the war effort. Once the war began, instances of newspapers being confiscated or shut down were the exception rather than the rule. Certainly the threat of both encouraged cooperation from opposition newspapers, but there appears to be a genuine level of commitment to the war effort, even in the socialist newspapers. This support did not translate into the *Burgfrieden, Union Sacrée*, or *vnutrennii mir* that conservatives extolled. In this regard, Jeffrey Verhey is correct in his debunking of the "Spirit of 1914."[7] Citizens from all five nations expressed reservations about the war, even as they sent their friends and relatives off to battle and hoped for a favorable outcome. Support for the war did not necessarily mean support for the government and its goals for the war. The press in Germany, Russia, and Austria-Hungary all supported the war but had reasons that often clashed with the goals of the government. As Eric Lohr noted, the liberal press in Russia supported the war and saw in Russia's alliance with Britain and France a step towards liberalizing the tsarist regime, whereas conservatives and pan-Slavs saw the war as a way to preserve the imperial throne and maintain the preeminence of ethnic Russians inside the multiethnic Russian empire. It is worth noting that the press in France and England emphasized the potential for reform in Russia as a way to rationalize their alliance with an autocratic state. Liberal and socialist newspapers in Germany harbored similar hopes that war would result in the liberalization of government; whereas their conservative counterparts thought of war as a way to return to "proven traditions." In Austria-Hungary, where censorship was particularly heavy (if inconsistent), newspapers employed more subtle strategies to get their message across to discerning readers. Andrea Orzoff aptly observes, where overt sympathy for the enemy would be tantamount to treason, the lack of vilification struck a resonant chord. The discussion of the repression of minorities in multiethnic Russia had clear implications inside the multiethnic Habsburg empire. And certainly large white spaces, representing what the censor has stricken, told even the least discerning readers that the whole story was not being told. The French and British press were the most supportive of the war, to the point of occasionally questioning whether the government was prosecuting the war as vigorously as was required.

The war itself was greeted by many on both sides as an opportunity for rebirth and renewal. With relative ease, a reader could find references to the war as an opportunity for the nation to purge itself of undesirable traits that were the results of decades of peace and relative prosperity. Although Russia did not experience the same level of either peace or prosperity the other nations had, the idea that the war would revitalize Russia was present in various circles. Of course, the shape of this revitalized Russia varied depending on the political views of the writer. The same held true for other nations, where any view that could remotely be construed as critical was tantamount to treason.

Still more tense was the relationship between the military and the press. Walter Nicolai's assurance that all of the information released to the German press would be truthful did not match the military's actions. The German military was not alone in misleading the press about the war through acts of omission or commission. Michael Nolan points out that the French press's almost complete collapse of confidence in the truthfulness of the French military illustrated the tensions between the press and military censors that existed within all the warring nations. While military officials did not invoke what Arthur Sylverster would latter claimed was the government's "right to lie" anytime it felt itself to be in a dangerous situation (Sylverster was openly admitting what had clearly been the practice of governments during times of war), the simple fact was that the military did not feel any obligation to report the truth to the press, a sentiment shared by many civilian government officials.[8]

In fairness to the military, complete disclosure of military information during a time of war would harm national security. However, the issue of who determines what is essential to national security is an important one. The examples of France, Austria-Hungary, and Germany all demonstrate that the military and government did not always act in a judicious fashion. That said, the military cannot be entirely faulted for in this situation. Eduard Bernstein's refusal to comment on military strategy because he was a layman was emblematic of the complexity of confronting military issues. Beyond the difficulty of access to information, there is the problem of training or ability to analyze the available information on the part of the journalist. The reliance on former or current military men to write about the war reveals the dearth of reporters capable of commentary and the need to have civilians who are informed enough about military matters to analyze information and ask the right questions.[9] Such civilians would also have to have the courage to stand up to accusations of disloyalty when questioning, however so slightly, the claims of the military.

Regardless of differences of the definition of French, Russian, or German patriotism, or loyalty to the Habsburg monarchy, newspapers were able to present a consistent, if not always united, front when describing the enemy and what was at stake in the war. For all the belligerents, the war was a clash of civilizations. Both Entente and Central powers were convinced that they were not only fighting for the higher ideals of humanity, but also that God was on their side. Germany and Austria-Hungary were alternately saving the world from Russia's Asiatic barbarism and decadent Western materialism. The use of Cossacks and troops from Africa and India were proof of the decadence of the Entente powers in the eyes of German press. Conversely, Russia, Great Britain, and France were saving the world from German militarism and the Hun-like Germanic *Kultur*. The invasion of Belgium and the bombing of cultural treasures in Louvain and Reims demonstrated German disregard for law and property. The world was painted in terms of black and white, good and evil. Whatever contributions to world culture that the enemy had produced were either anomalies or so far back in the past as to be irrelevant. In the British and French press, the land of Goethe, Schiller, Beethoven, and Kant had been replaced by that of Bismarck, Wagner, and the godless Nietzsche. Interestingly absent in almost all discussions was the role of Austria-Hungary. Just as the Austrian press seemed more intent on promoting their ally's victories (and virtues) in their pages, the French, British, and Russian press focused on Germany's vices. Perhaps this can be attributed to the fact that Germany was deemed the more formidable military threat, but it appears that Entente newspapers also considered the Dual Monarchy to be "an empire without qualities."

It is fair to say that the Entente powers had the upper hand in the propaganda battle to win the hearts and minds of neutral powers. The cutting of the transatlantic telegraph cable gave the British a decisive tactical advantage. But more important still was the fact that Germany did violate international law with the invasion of Belgium and that the German chancellor Theobald von Bethmann Hollweg admitted this to the Reichstag. This early admission put Germany at an initial disadvantage that it could not overcome. No attempts to defend its action or to prove that Belgium was not really neutral because of arrangements with France and Great Britain would be enough to overcome this early disadvantage.

Beyond the question of how the ideas and arguments presented in the opening phase of the war evolved over the course of the war, the chapters presented here point to a number of directions that merit future research. How ethnic minorities viewed the war is a question that both Andrea Orzoff and Eric Lohr explore in their respective chapters on Austria-Hungary and Russia. But it is a question that deserves more attention and research than this volume could allow. The same question could also apply to the study of the Polish minority in eastern Germany and the Irish in Great Britain. As noted in the introduction, some circles in Britain viewed the war as a way to turn attention away from the tensions in Ireland. Another important area that merits exploration is how newspapers in different regions, especially more rural areas, viewed the war. The overwhelming majority of the papers discussed here were either based in capital cities or in major cities. It is worth exploring how regional differences impacted the coverage or discussion of the war—for it certainly did. For example, the *Freiburger Tagespost* devoted much more space to the western front than the eastern front, for obvious reasons: it was a relatively short distance from the Alsatian front lines. But its moral outlook of the war was similar to that presented in the larger cities; themes such as Russian barbarism and English duplicity were staples of the editorial commentary, and it picked up on the government offensive, via the *Norddeutsche Allgemeine Zeitung*, to discredit England's claims about Belgian neutrality.

Another important question that merits further consideration is the origins of the depiction of the enemy combatants. The caricatures of Germans, French, British, Russians, and Austrians (when they were considered) were not an overnight creation by mighty propaganda machines. Not even the British were that effective. The ideas and images that aroused public support had to have preexisting roots. Examinations of the ideas of elites during the prewar years abound. But there is still relatively little about popular images of the foreign combatants that existed before the war and how war propaganda drew from these sources.

Explaining the origins of enemy stereotypes does not address the problem of superficiality or one-sidedness in the newspapers examined here. When reminded of the distinction between publicity and propaganda made in the introduction, one is forced to the conclusion that virtually all of what was presented to the reading public was propaganda, regardless of the intentions. Both the government's and military's reticence to release information and the press's reluctance to demand information or pursue lines of inquiry that could challenge official views meant that newspaper readers were not getting a complete view of events. If the role of the Fourth Estate is to serve as a watchdog on the government, then it is fair to say that it failed. Too little attention was paid to events leading up to the war and too little was questioned once the war began for the press to lay any claims to informing the public in an objective fashion.

Obtaining complete and correct information from the government is just as much a challenge for media in the early twenty-first century as it was in the early twentieth century. Governments acknowledge the power and potential influence of the press and attempt to cultivate good relations in order to receive favorable treatment in newspapers (and now the electronic media). However, governments and especially the military have traditionally kept the media at arm's length to prevent unwanted scrutiny.

With the demise of the political press in the twentieth century, the problem of getting information may have been exacerbated. In an effort to maintain good relations with government officials and to keep friendly sources open for possible exclusive revelations, most media outlets are reluctant to pursue lines of questioning that challenge the government's position.[10] Perhaps the most important lesson to be learned from the newspaper coverage of the Great War in Great Britain, France, Germany, Austria-Hungary, and Russia is the importance of openness, even in times of crisis, and the need for a critical and impartial press to inform the public.

NOTES

1. Lloyd Chiasson Jr., ed., *The Press in Times of Crisis* (Westport, Conn.: Greenwood Press, 1995), 219.

2. Friedrich von Bernhardi, *Deutschland und der nächste Krieg* (Stuttgart and Berlin: J. G. Cotta, 1912). The book would go through five printings in 1912 alone.

3. For examples of the occasionally strained relations between the two militaries, see Helmer Holwig, *The First World War: Germany and Austria-Hungary 1914–1918* (London: Arnold, 1997), especially chapters 2 and 3.

4. See Terence Zuber, *Inventing the Schlieffen Plan: German Military Planning 1871–1914* (Oxford: Oxford University Press, 2002).

5. For an excellent summary and analysis with documents of both the Daily Telegraph Affair and the Hale Interview, see Peter Winzen, *Das Kaiserreich im*

Abgrund. Die Daily-Telegraph Affäre und das Hale Interview von 1908 (Stuttgart: Franz Steiner Verlag, 2002).

6. See John Horne and Alan Kramer, *German Atrocities, 1914: A History of Denial* (New Haven, Conn.: Yale University Press, 2001); or their "German 'Atrocities' and Franco-German Opinion, 1914: The Evidence of German Soldiers' Diaries," *Journal of Modern History* 66:1 (March 1994), 1–33.

7. See Jeffrey T. Verhey, *The Spirit of 1914: Militarism, Myth, and Mobilization in Germany* (New York: Cambridge University Press, 2000).

8. Arthur Sylverster was an assistant secretary of defense for public relations in the John F. Kennedy administration. In 1962 he claimed that the government had the "right to lie." See William V. Kennedy, *The Military and the Media: Why the Press Cannot Be Trusted to Cover a War* (Westport, Conn.: Praeger, 1993), 129–42.

9. The inability of reporters to ask the right questions regarding the military is one of the key point in William Kennedy's provocative book *The Military and the Media.*

10. See William Kennedy's searing indictment of the American press in *The Military and the Media.*

Index

About the Contributors

DR. ADRIAN GREGORY is a fellow of Pembroke College, Oxford, and lecturer at the University of Oxford. His publications include *The Silence of Memory* (1994) and *A War to Unite Us All: Ireland and the First World War* (coedited with Senia Paseta; 2002) as well as several contributions to edited volumes.

ERIC LOHR received his Ph.D. in history from Harvard University in 1999, where he was an assistant professor of history until taking up a position as assistant professor of history at American University in fall 2003. He is the author of *Nationalizing the Russian Empire: The Campaign against Enemy Aliens during World War I* (2003) and coeditor with Marshall Poe of *Military and Society in Russian History, 1450–1917* (2002). He is currently working on a history of the theory and practice of citizenship in Russia from the 1860s through the Russian revolution, and on a history of Russia during World War I.

MICHAEL NOLAN received his B.A. from Columbia University, his M.A. from the University of Massachusetts at Amherst, and his Ph.D. from Brandeis University. He teaches at Western Connecticut State University in Danbury. He is the author of *The Inverted Mirror: Mythologizing the Enemy in France and Germany 1898–1914* (2004). He is currently researching images of the French colonial army in the visions of future warfare in France and Germany in the years before the First World War.

ANDREA ORZOFF is an assistant professor of history at New Mexico State University; she has also taught at Stanford University, where she completed her doctorate in 2000. Funded by the National Endowment for the Humanities and the American Council of Learned Societies, she is currently working on a book manuscript on intellectuals, propaganda, myth, and nationalism in interwar Czechoslovakia. Her publications include "Prague P.E.N. and Cultural Nationalism, 1924–1938," which appeared in *Nationalities Papers* in summer 2001, and "The President and the Press: Tomáı Masaryk and Journalistic Politics, 1925–1929," which ran in *Slavic Review* in summer 2004.

TROY R. E. PADDOCK is an associate professor of history at Southern Connecticut State University. He received his Ph. D. in History from Univ. of California at Berkeley. He has published articles in *German History, Internationale Schulbuchforschung,* and *Philosophy and Geography,* and has contributed to two edited volumes. He is currently finishing a manuscript about German perceptions of Russia before the First World War.

CPSIA information can be obtained
at www.ICGtesting.com
Printed in the USA
BVHW04*1459120918
527223BV00015B/194/P